D1625177

Why Firms Succeed

WHY FIRMS SUCCEED

John Kay

New York   Oxford
OXFORD UNIVERSITY PRESS
1995

Oxford University Press

Oxford   New York
Athens   Auckland   Bangkok   Bombay
Calcutta   Cape Town   Dar es Salaam   Delhi
Florence   Hong Kong   Istanbul   Karachi
Kuala Lumpur   Madras   Madrid   Melbourne
Mexico City   Nairobi   Paris   Singapore
Taipei   Tokyo   Toronto

and associated companies in
Berlin   Ibadan

Copyright © 1995 by Oxford University Press, Inc.

Published by Oxford University Press, Inc.,
198 Madison Avenue, New York, New York 10016

Oxford is a registered trademark of Oxford University Press

All rights reserved. No part of this publication may be reproduced,
stored in a retrieval system, or transmitted, in any form or by any means,
electronic, mechanical, photocopying, recording, or otherwise,
without the prior permission of Oxford University Press.

Library of Congress Cataloging-in-Publication Data
Kay, J. A. (John Anderson)
Why firms succeed / John Kay.
p.   cm.
An adaption of author's OUP/UK book Foundations of corporate success.
Includes bibliographical references and index.
ISBN 0-19-508767-4
1. Corporations.   2. Industrial management.
3. Competition.   4. Success in business.
I. Kay, J. A. (John Anderson).
Foundations of corporate success.
II. Title.
HD2731.K39   1995   658—dc20   94-29311

658
K23w
1995 .

1 2 3 4 5 6 7 8 9

Printed in the United States of America
on acid-free paper

Preface

In 1986 I was offered the opportunity, and substantial resources, to answer the question, What are the origins of industrial success? There are, perhaps, more important questions, but not many, and this was certainly the most important question that I felt in any way equipped to try to answer. So I accepted the challenge.

It was obvious that there was no shortage of data. Every corporation is required to file detailed returns of its activities. In all Western economies there are several journals that track the performance and activities of leading companies. Case studies, business histories, and business biographies describe how decisions were made and problems overcome. I began to understand that what was needed was not to collect new information but to establish a framework for understanding what was already known. The development of such a framework became my primary goal, and the purpose of this book is to describe that framework. I will have succeeded if the thoughtful senior executive thinks less often, "That is something new" than "That makes sense of my experience."

Some people told me that the task I had set myself could not be done or was not worth doing. Business problems were too complex to be susceptible to the use of analytic techniques. Every situation was unique, and so there could be no valid generalizations. Others (such as Abernathy and Utterback 1978) even argued that the attempt to apply analytic methods to business issues was at the heart of the Western economic decline.

It might be true that there can be no valid generalizations about business and that there can be no general theories of the origins of corporate success or failure. But it does not seem likely that that is true. It is not just that similar observations were made ahead of much greater leaps in scientific knowledge. How could we hope to understand something so complex, and so subject to change, as the motion of the planets or the makeup of genetic material? The issues considered in this book seem, on the face of it, to be ones that would respond to analytic tools. Indeed, I believe that the tools presented in this book do offer real help in han-

METHODIST COLLEGE LIBRARY
Fayetteville, N.C.

dling these questions. If they fail to do so, it is more likely that these are the wrong tools than that no tools will ever become available.

One paradox was immediately apparent: If I asked what was meant by corporate success, many different answers were proposed. Some people emphasized size and market share, and others stressed profitability and returns to shareholders. Some people looked to technical efficiency and innovative capability. Others stressed the reputation that companies enjoyed among their customers and employees and in the wider business community.

Yet this disagreement was not translated into disagreement about which companies were successful. Whatever their criteria of success, everyone seemed to point to the same companies—to Matsushita and Hewlett-Packard, to Merck and Procter & Gamble, to Wal-Mart and Coca-Cola. I formed the view that the achievement of any company is measured by its ability to add value—to create an output that is worth more than the cost of the inputs that it uses. These different opinions on how success should be measured were partly the result of the disagreement about how added value was created, but more the product of different views as to how, once created, added value should be used. Successful companies and successful economies vary in the relative emphasis to be given to returns to shareholders, the maximization of profits, and the development of the business. Different firms and different business cultures gave different weights to these purposes. But the underlying objective of adding value was common to all.

I began by asking the managers of successful companies to explain the sources of their success. They told me that success depended on producing the right product at the right price at the right time. It was essential to know the market, to motivate employees, to demand high standards of suppliers and distributors. I recognized that all these things were true but that those who emphasized them were describing their success, not explaining it.

I found that much had been written on strategic management. But stripped of rhetoric, most strategy texts offered only checklists of issues that senior executives needed to address in considering the future of their business. Although this literature posed questions, it yielded few answers.

Economists had studied the functioning of industry, but their concerns were mostly with public policy, not business policy, and I was sure that industrial success was founded on the behavior of firms, not on the decisions of governments. Even though sociologists had studied the functioning of organizations, only a few had matched the characteristics of the firm to the economic environment that determined its competitive performance.

I came to see that it was this match between the capabilities of the organization and the challenges it faced that was the most important issue in understanding corporate success and corporate failure. Accordingly, this perception led directly to the primary themes of this book. I see the firm as a set of relationships among its various stakeholders—employees, customers, managers, and shareholders. The successful firm is one that creates a distinctive character in these relationships and that operates in an environment maximizing the value of this distinctiveness. The rest of this book is concerned with the nature of these relationships, the ways in which they achieve distinctiveness, and the ways in which effective companies select and manage their environment in the light of these capabilities.

I am convinced that a description of that process can illuminate the origins of success in firms, in industries, and in national economies.

The book is divided into five parts. Parts I and II establish building blocks for the later analysis. Part I is concerned with what is meant by corporate success and corporate failure, and it presents a clear objective for the firm—adding value. A firm adds value through the distinctive character of the relationships it establishes with its stakeholders—its employees, customers, shareholders, and suppliers. These relationships and the variety of forms they take are the subject of Part II.

This unique set of relationships gives the successful firm a distinctive capability, something it can do that its potential competitors cannot. Part III is concerned with the forms that such distinctive capabilities might take. A distinctive capability becomes a competitive advantage only when it is applied to an appropriate market. The matching of markets to capabilities is the primary subject of Part IV. A distinctive capability becomes a true competitive advantage only when it can be sustained over time and appropriated for the benefit of the company that enjoys it and its principal stakeholders. In Part V, I sum up the lessons for both business and public policy of an approach based on maximizing the value of distinctive capabilities.

This book is based on *Foundations of Corporate Success*, published in England in 1993. But it is more than a translation of that book. It quickly became clear that it was not enough simply to convert £ to $ and to Americanize the spelling. Indeed, the very difficulties of illustrating some issues in an American context pointed to some important differences in the way that business is done internationally and itself provided some insights into the origins of corporate success. I return to that question in my conclusions.

This book also takes advantage of the opportunity, rarely available to an author, of writing the book that really should have been written in the first place. It is shorter and reflects both what I hope is greater wisdom and also (particularly in Chapter 14) my experience of applying the analysis. I have shortened this book also by focusing on the central issues of *corporate* strategy, the fundamental question, What business are we (should we be) in? In *Foundations of Corporate Success*, I described, in addition, some of the implications of my approach for *competitive* strategy: the relationships within the chosen markets—between the firm and its competitors, customers, and suppliers—and readers who wish to explore these questions further will find relevant material there.

A book such as this is synthetic in objective. That is, it seeks to draw ideas from a wide range of sources, and any claims to originality rest on the way in which it brings a variety of different approaches from business history, economics, law, and sociology to bear on a specific group of issues rather than on the novelty of these ideas themselves. Instead of attributing each of these strands of thinking fully as they arise, I have been sparing with references in the text but have provided relatively full bibliographical notes designed to serve the twin purposes of acknowledging my sources and suggesting further reading. In the Appendix, I describe the evolution of thinking in business strategy and relate my analysis in this book to the existing management literature, and so here a different and more conventional style is appropriate.

I should like to thank the many people who helped with this book. In particular, I am grateful to David Sainsbury, who proposed the challenge, and the Gatsby Foundation, which provided financial support. Evan Davis contributed greatly to developing the ideas that the book contains. Mark Fischetti provided invaluable assistance in adapting my approach to an American audience. The advice of Herb Addison, the American editor, was extremely helpful in suggesting how this should be done. Sharon Wu provided research support. I should also like to express my thanks to those who provided the information, ideas, or comments that went into this book and its predecessor: Charles Baden Fuller, Matthew Bishop, Richard Brealey, Michael Cronshaw, Andrew Dilnot, Simon Domberger, Romano Dyerson, Stephanie Flanders, Paul Geroski, Peter Grindley, Leslie Hannah, Robert Laslett, David Musson, Geoffrey Owen, Esther Perkins, George Richardson, Michael Roper, Laura Rovizzi, Nigel Savage, Andrew Schuller, Bettina von Stamm, Stefan Szymanski, David Thompson, and John Vickers. Barbara Lee managed the process of producing the manuscript for both this version and its European predecessor.

London   J. K.
January 1995

Contents

Part I   Corporate Success

1. Corporate Success and Corporate Failure, 3

2. Adding Value, 15

Part II   Business Relationships

3. Cooperation and Coordination, 27

4. Relationships and Contracts, 46

Part III   Distinctive Capabilities

5. Architecture, 63

6. Reputation, 81

7. Innovation, 96

8. Strategic Assets, 109

Part IV   From Distinctive Capabilities to Competitive Advantage

9. Markets, 125

10. Mergers, 142

11. Sustainability, 156

12. Appropriability, 174

13. The Value of Competitive Advantage, 190

Part V   The Strategic Audit

14. Strategies for Corporate Success, 213

15. Why National Economies Succeed, 227

16. Conclusions, 242

Appendix: General Electric, 246

Glossary, 274

Bibliography, 283

Index of Companies, 301

Index, 305

I

CORPORATE SUCCESS

1

Corporate Success and Corporate Failure

In this chapter, I describe three legendary stories of business success. The revival of the Disney Corporation was one of the most impressive business achievements of the 1980s. BMW—in 1959 a company on the edge of bankruptcy—recovered to become one of the world's most profitable automobile manufacturers. Honda's attack on the U.S. motorcycle industry is one of the most famous episodes in business history and became the prototype of Japanese success in Western markets.

But success is most illuminating when contrasted with failures. So I also describe how the Great Northern Corporation's aspiration to become the General Motors of the seas proved fruitless, how Saatchi & Saatchi's establishment of the world's first multinational, multidisciplinary consultancy business brought the company to the edge of financial collapse, and how Groupe Bull's attempt to become the European counterpart of IBM failed. And I explore the reasons for the very different outcomes of the personal computer revolution for IBM and Microsoft. The key lesson from these histories is that corporate success is based on an effective match between a firm's external relationships and its distinctive capabilities. Disney, BMW, Honda, and Microsoft all are firms that identified their distinctive capabilities, selected the markets best suited to these strengths, and built effective competitive strategies to exploit them. They did so sometimes belatedly and not always consciously, but it was this process that formed the basis of their subsequent success.

The other firms exemplify some of the most common causes of failure. Great Northern and Groupe Bull simply lacked capabilities sufficient for their aspirations. Saatchi & Saatchi misunderstood the nature of its own competitive strengths and entered, expensively, markets in which its capabilities had no value. IBM, with the most rewarding distinctive capabilities ever enjoyed by any corporation, saw its markets develop in a way that steadily diminished the value of the competitive advantages it derived from them. In a cruel twist of business history, IBM promoted these market developments but allowed most of its benefits to accrue to its much smaller collaborators.

The Keys to the Magic Kingdom

Walt Disney was not the first person to have had exceptional insight into the world of children. But Disney's good fortune was to enjoy that insight in an age of universal entertainment and mass marketing, and his particular achievement was to combine his gifts with a commercial acumen that enabled him to turn fairy tales into big business. That is why there is a Disney Corporation but the memory of Hans Christian Andersen is perpetuated only through the timelessness of his stories and the munificence of the Carlsberg brewery.

Disney not only invented characters as unforgettable as Donald Duck and Mickey Mouse and entertainments as enduring as *Fantasia* and *Mary Poppins*, but he also redefined the fairground. Disney invested his reputation and capital of a magnitude that itinerant entertainers had never contemplated. The theme parks he established have been imitated but never effectively challenged. Yet after Disney's death, the company drifted. There were no movie successes to rival *Mary Poppins*.

In 1984, corporate raiders were beginning to terrorize American business. After a family quarrel and the intervention of an arbitrageur, Saul Steinberg, Disney was one of the corporations to come "in play." A complex and acrimonious battle followed, and the result was the installation of a new executive team led by Michael Eisner. In his time at Paramount Pictures, Eisner had demonstrated some of the same combination of creative talent and commercial flair that had been the Disney hallmark. His supporters hoped that he would bring these qualities to Disney.

But this was not how things evolved. Touchstone Pictures, the appropriately named flagship for Disney's more adult image, performed adequately but was not distinguished from the other major studios. The real achievement of Eisner's team was to unlock the Disney assets. Visitors crossed continents and oceans to visit the Disney parks. This demonstrated they could pay more. Now they do. Disney owned much of the land surrounding its theme parks, and now it has realized its full commercial potential. Video was just becoming a major form of entertainment; the revitalized Disney Corporation made the most of this opportunity. And the repertoire of Disney movies once more fills the movie theaters whenever school lets out. By the end of the 1980s, Eisner was among the most respected, and best rewarded, of American corporate leaders.

The Blue and White Propeller

Even though Disney has had ups and downs, no American corporation has experienced such extreme twists and turns of fortune as BMW has.

The Bayerische Motoren Werke were established during World War I, specializing in the manufacture of engines. The company subsequently diversified into what are now its two principal product ranges: automobiles and motorcycles. Today BMW is one of Germany's largest and most successful companies.

BMW cars are not the most powerful or the most reliable or the most luxurious on the market, although they score well against all these criteria. No one has ever suggested that they are cheap, even for the high level of specification that most models offer. Although BMW rightly emphasizes the quality and advanced nature of its technology, its products are not exceptionally innovative. The design of its cars is conventional, and their model styling is decidedly traditional.

Rather, the achievements of BMW are built on two closely associated factors. The company achieves a higher quality of engineering than is usual in production cars. Whereas most car assembly has now been taken over by robots or workers from low-wage economies, BMW maintains a skilled German labor force. The company benefits, as many German firms do, from an educational system that teaches basic technical skills to an unusually high proportion of the population. Its reputation has followed from these substantial achievements. In this, BMW is representative of much of German manufacturing industry.

Yet BMW's success was neither easy nor certain. In 1945, the company was Germany's leading manufacturer of aircraft engines. Both its primary market and its capital equipment were in ruins. Its main factory at Eisenach was across the border in the Soviet occupation zone. And although Germany's recovery through the 1950s occurred at a pace that attracted the title of economic miracle, BMW did not prosper. Uncertain of its future, the company emphasized automobiles, but its products ranged from tiny bubble cars, manufactured under license, to limousines. By 1959, the firm faced bankruptcy, and a rescue by Mercedes-Benz seemed its only hope of survival.

Instead, BMW found a powerful shareholder—Herbert Quandt—who perceived the company's inherent strengths. The turning point came when the firm identified the market that most effectively exploited its capabilities—the market for high-performance sedans, which has since become almost synonymous with BMW. The BMW 1500, launched in 1961, established a reputation for engineering quality in the BMW automobile brand. The brand in turn acquired a distinctive identity as a symbol for young, affluent European professionals. That combination—a system of production that gives the company a particular advantage in its chosen market segment, a worldwide reputation for product quality, and a brand that immediately identifies the aims and aspirations of its customers—continues to make BMW one of the most profitable automobile manufacturers in the world.

Today, the BMW business is structured to maximize these advantages. Retail margins on BMW cars are relatively high. The company maintains tight control over its distribution network, a control that supports the brand image and also aids market segmentation. BMW cars are positioned differently and priced differently in the many national markets in which it competes. The same tight control is reflected in BMW's relationships with its suppliers, who mostly have continuing long associations with the company. BMW's activities are focused almost exclusively on two product ranges—high-performance sedans and motorcyles—which reflect its competitive strengths. The company also uses the brand to support a range of car accessories.

BMW is a company that recognized its distinctive capabilities, identified a market in which these distinctive capabilities gave it a competitive advantage, and focused its business on maximizing the value of that competitive advantage. These are the foundations of corporate success, and they are themes that will recur again and again throughout this book.

Honda

Sometimes this process—the identification of distinctive capabilities and the maximization of their value—is the result of conscious planning. Sometimes it creates corporate success by chance. Honda's penetration of the U.S. motorcycle market remains one of the classic, and controversial, cases in business strategy.

Motorcyles in the 1950s were associated with a subculture now best recalled through movies, leather jackets, the smell of oil, and teenage rebellion. In 1964, five years after its entry into the United States, one in three motorcycles sold in this country was a Honda. The best-selling product was a 50-cc supercub, marketed under the slogan "You meet the nicest people on a Honda."

There are two views of this achievement. In one, Honda's strategy was an archetype of Japan's penetration of Western markets. The aggressive pursuit of domestic volume established a low-cost base for expansion overseas. This was the conclusion of a Boston Consulting Group study for the British government (BCG 1975). A rather different account was given by Richard Pascale, who went to Tokyo to interview the elderly Japanese who had brought the first Honda machines to the United States. As they recalled it, Honda had aimed to secure a modest share of the established U.S. motorcyle market. "Mr Honda was especially confident of the 250 cc and 305 cc machines. The shape of the handlebar on these larger machines looked like the eyebrows of Buddha, which he felt was a strong selling point" (Pascale 1984, p. 54).

These hopes were not realized. The eyebrows of Buddha had little attraction for the leather-jacketed Marlon Brando. "We dropped in on motorcycle dealers who treated us discourteously and, in addition, gave the general impression of being motorcycle enthusiasts who, secondarily, were in business" (Pascale 1984, p. 54).

The first supercubs exported to the United States were used by Honda employees for their own personal transport around the concrete wastes of Los Angeles. It was only when these caught the attention of a Sears-Roebuck buyer and the larger machines started to show reliability problems that Honda put its efforts behind the 50-cc machines. The "nicest people" slogan was invented by a University of California undergraduate.

Neither of these accounts is convincing. The BCG account is an expression of the near paranoia created for many Westerners by Japan's achievement. Pascale's suggestion that Honda's success was simply the result of good fortune would be more persuasive if the company had not been blessed by such good fortune quite so often in the course of its spectacular rise. The "eyebrows of Buddha" are all too reminiscent of the South Sea island girls who teased Margaret Mead with ever more extravagant accounts of their sexual exploits.

Was Honda's success the result of chance or of rational calculation? We shall never know. Honda effected a brilliantly successful market entry. Like all successful strategies, it was based on a mixture of calculation and opportunism, of vision and experiment. Like all successful corporate strategies, it was centered on Honda's distinctive capability—an established capacity to produce an innovative but simple, low-cost product. In either case, the lessons of Honda's success for other companies—recognize your distinctive capabilities, identify the markets in which these distinctive capabilities create competitive advantage, and add value—are the same.[1]

---

[1] One outstanding recent strategy text poses for its readers the question, "Ask yourself while reading these accounts how the strategic behavior of the British motor-cycle manufacturers which received the BCG report might have differed if they had instead received Pascale's second story?" I do not know what answer Quinn, Minzberg, and James (1988, p. 81) expected. But I do know that the right answer is, "Not at all." Even if Honda's achievements were the result of pure chance, I know of no prescription for corporate success that advises waiting for similar good fortune to knock on the door. Nonetheless, this was the strategy that the British motorcycle manufacturers adopted, with a notable lack of success.

The General Motors of the Seas

When we watch a great athlete, what is for most of us impossible is made to seem effortless. Understanding corporate success through the achievements of the successful makes success seem too easy. Thus we must also study the origins of corporate success by analyzing the experience of the unsuccessful. Often we learn more. Great Northern's Prelude Corporation is an instructive example of why vision is only a very small component of corporate success.

The Prelude Corporation, briefly the largest lobster producer in North America, was designed around the vision of its founder, the Reverend W. D. Whipple, and his successor as president, Joseph S. Gaziano. The vision was established, as visions often are, by analogy with other companies and other industries. "We want to become the Procter & Gamble of the lobster business . . . the fishing industry now is just like the automobile industry was 60 years ago: 100 companies are going to come and go, but we'll be the General Motors." Sadly, however, it was the Prelude Corporation that came and went. The realization of that vision depended on the ability to use branding and scale economies—important in many other industries—in the lobster business. "We want people to ask for Prelude Lobster—not just lobster—similar to the Chiquita Banana strategy. . . . The technology and money required to fish offshore are so great that the little guy can't make out" (HBS 1972, pp. 1, 6). But the successful branding achieved by Procter & Gamble and United Brands depends on these companies' tight control of every stage of the production process, a control impossible in an industry in which the product is not created by the manufacturer but hunted down. And fishing, like other industries entirely dependent on the flair, skills, and initiative of people who cannot be supervised for days on end, does not lend itself well to large-scale organization. The vision bore no relationship to either the capabilities of the Prelude Corporation or the sources of competitive advantage in the markets in which it operated.

The Prelude Corporation is a parody of what I call *wish-driven strategy*, strategy that is motivated by a view of what the company would like to be, rather than what it is. Yet similar errors are made, even on a larger scale, by other companies. The Prelude Corporation's parent, Great Northern, eventually exhausted the patience of its bankers, whereas a firm that has a more accommodating banker, such as a government, can pursue its dreams longer.

A Would-be IBM

European politicians and businesspeople have long dreamed of creating a European IBM. The British government promoted ICL; the Germans, Nixdorf and Siemens; and the Italians, Olivetti. But these companies have succeeded only in subsectors of the computer market. The European government most determined to resist IBM's hegemony across the full range of computers has been the French, and the European company most determined to resist it has been Groupe Bull.

For thirty years, Groupe Bull—sometimes in various partnerships and sometimes on its own—has imposed losses on its indulgent shareholder, the French state. Throughout, it has been a company driven not by an assessment of what it is but by a vision of what it would like to be. Throughout it has lacked the distinctive capabilities that would enable it to realize that vision. Bull—and the other attempts at European clones of IBM—epitomize the wish-driven strategy, based on aspiration, not capability. An effective strategy, like that of BMW or Honda, starts from what the company is distinctively good at, not from what it would like to be good at, and it is adaptive and opportunistic in exploiting what is distinctive in these capabilities.

Margaret Thatcher's Advertising Agency

Sometimes achieving one's dream can be worse than failing to do so. Saatchi & Saatchi was, for a time, the best-known advertising agency in the world. An advertisement devised to promote birth control, which showed a picture of a pregnant man, created a mixture of controversy and envy that promoted a small agency controlled by Charles and Maurice Saatchi to national fame. Then the agency's contribution to Margaret Thatcher's first successful election campaign in 1979 turned that domestic reputation into an international one.

But international recognition was not enough. The Saatchis determined to create an international business. In 1983, it is reported (Fallon 1988, p. 203), Maurice Saatchi read a famous article in the *Harvard Business Review* on the development of global markets (Levitt 1983). Inspired by the vision it held out, he flew across the Atlantic to learn the full details of the new doctrine. These transatlantic flights were to become more frequent as the operating companies within Saatchi & Saatchi came to span not just Britain and the United States but other continents and other markets as well.

By the end of the decade, Saatchi & Saatchi was, as the brothers had intended, the world's first truly international, interdisciplinary marketing and consultancy organization. It was also in serious financial difficulty. Under pressure from bankers and stockholders, the Saatchis relinquished executive control, and a new management team set to work dismantling the empire that the brothers' vision had put together.

Saatchi & Saatchi began with a reputation that was unmatched in its business and a creative team that was almost equally admired. These are characteristic assets of the highly successful professional service firm. The firms it bought were firms that had precisely these assets themselves. Saatchi & Saatchi's largest acquisition, Ted Bates, was itself one of the largest and most respected advertising agencies in the United States and had no need of the Saatchi label. It already enjoyed an equivalent reputation in its own market, and there was never any suggestion that it would trade under the Saatchi name. International customers did not bring their business to the newly merged agency. Rather, they took it away, fearing conflicts of interest, as the enlarged concern was often already handling the accounts of its competitors. Consequently, Ted Bates was worth less to Saatchi & Saatchi than to almost any other purchaser, because Saatchi already had those things that made Bates valuable, and so they were worth less, not more, under Saatchi ownership.

But in the grip of the strategic objective of internationalization, Saatchi paid a large premium to gain control of that and other businesses. For a time, the inherent weaknesses of the strategy were concealed by the growth in the underlying earnings of the businesses and the capacity of the Saatchi share price to drift ever upward on a cushion of hot air. Eventually, the earnings faltered and the hot air escaped. The company was left with a mountain of debt and a collection of businesses that, while sound in themselves, were not worth the prices that had been paid for them.

The wish-driven strategy failed for Prelude and Groupe Bull because the goal was unattainable. The wish-driven strategy failed for Saatchi & Saatchi because the goal, although attainable and attained, was not a sensible one for this particular company to pursue. A wish-driven strategy emphasizes the importance of the corporate vision, frequently starts with an assertion of the mission statement, and creates a company driven by a view of what it would like to be. The Saatchi strategy was based on a dream rather than an analysis of the competitive strengths of the business, and the company adapted to market realities only when corporate collapse was staring it in the face.

IBM and Microsoft

If the two stories of Honda have been a business school classic of the last decade, today every beginning MBA student is confronted with the divergent fates of Microsoft and IBM. There is always a demand for David and Goliath stories, and the toppling of IBM is one of the best of them.

The cases focus on the differences in organizational style: IBM's corporate bureaucracy against Microsoft's campus informality. Whereas IBM's white-shirt dress code was strictly laid down by Thomas Watson, the creator of Microsoft imposes no such rules. "The jacket of Gates' rumpled, off-the-rack suit was fastened by the bottom button, making him bulge awkwardly," Fortune thought it necessary to observe (December 28, 1992, p. 36). If IBM was the corporation of the 1980s, Microsoft is the corporation of the future.

These differences in the nature of the two organizations are not irrelevant, but they are not the heart of the matter either. Today it is fashionable to decry IBM. But no analysis of corporate success should overlook the fact that from a long-term perspective, IBM is simply the most successful corporation in the history of the world. For thirty years, it dominated a large and growing market around the world and added more value to the inputs it used than did any other company. Indeed, the unprecedented scale of IBM's success is a more remarkable, and surprising, fact than its inability to maintain the scale of that success indefinitely.

Although IBM is in a high-tech industry, its strength was not founded primarily on its technology, in which it was often a follower rather than a leader. IBM's most famous advertising slogan—"No one ever got fired for choosing IBM"—was not devised or used by the company, but by its customers. It reflected the firm's true distinctive capability—its ability to deliver both hardware and solutions to its clients' problems, and its reputation expressed its customers' recognition of that capacity.

So what changed? IBM did not lose its distinctive capabilities. What happened was that the market evolved in a way that made these capabilities less valuable. There were few firms in the world that could manufacture and support mainframe computers, because their installation was configured to a customer's specific requirements. When they went wrong, the consequences could paralyze a whole organization. Diagnosis and rectification of the fault demanded skilled technicians and the assurance of successive layers of technical support. In that market, IBM was—and is—unparalleled, and its organization is structured to support these capabilities. The IBM uniform is designed to convey this sense of team structure to its employees and give corresponding assurance to its customers.

The personal computer market is very different. Today, a computer is a commodity, not a mystery, and can be found on every manager's desk. They are assembled largely from standard components. This means not only that many small firms can make them but also that they can be fixed by local repairers who, like those who fix television sets or washing machines, simply unscrew one part and install another. The competitive advantages in such a market are slight and short lived.There is one exception, and that is a competitive advantage based on a strategic asset: control of the operating system.

I describe in Chapter 7 those markets—which range from high-definition television to credit cards—in which compatibility standards are important. The PC market is one, and the extraordinary paradox of its evolution was that it was IBM's intervention and the use of its reputation to establish a compatibility standard and to make possible the market growth that in due course undermined its position so fundamentally. In a further twist to that paradox, a combination of antitrust concerns and strategic errors left Microsoft, not IBM, in control of the key element of the PC standard—the operating system. Microsoft capitalized fully on its strategic asset by realizing, as IBM failed to do, that the next round of competition in the standards market would be won and lost on ease of use, not on technological superiority. It was to be Windows, not OS/2.

So can IBM recover its previously impregnable position? Will Microsoft be the new IBM? The certain answer to both these questions is no. Although IBM's distinctive capabilities will continue to give it a competitive advantage in the market for mainframe computers, that market will never be as valuable in the future as it was in the past. For IBM to turn into some wholly different kind of organization would not be the route to restoring its fortunes but a means of destroying the distinctive capabilities that for so long made it great. And Microsoft's distinctive capability is entirely out of the ordinary in being at once so valuable and so transitory. It is a safe prediction that PC operating systems will have changed within a decade in ways we can yet only dimly imagine, and because Microsoft is only one of many firms with software development capabilities, the probability that the company will hold then the dominance it enjoys now cannot be rated very highly.

Visions and Missions

The dilemmas of American business are increasingly equated with the problems that face American businesspeople. When we read of the problems facing Kmart, it is through the eyes of Joseph Antonini, its chairman, chief executive, and president. When a Harvard class discusses Caterpillar's dilemmas, they stand in the shoes of Lee Morgan, its chairman and chief executive. Microsoft is Bill Gates; General Electric is Jack Welch.

There are other cultures in which this extraordinary personalization of business activity has only a small role. Senior executives of German or Japanese companies are not encouraged to take a high public profile. And when they do, they rarely enhance the respect in which they are held within the business community. It is notable that when Akio Morita— the founder of Sony and the best-known Japanese business leader— was considered as a candidate for a cabinet position, the post was at the Foreign Ministry, not Finance or International Trade and Industry.

Some of this personalization follows from the exigencies of business journalism. It is easier to interest readers in the personal life of Bill Gates than to explain to them the differences between MS-DOS and OS/2. Yet beneath these superficialities lies a fundamental difference in the views of the origins of business success. The contrast between the American perception (increasingly shared in Britain and France) of the senior executive as master of the organization and the Japanese perception (still held in most of Europe) of the executive as its servant can be translated into a difference of views about the origins of corporate success. In one view, business success is the result of *maximizing the value of an organization's distinctive capabilities*; in the other, of *effectively realizing the CEO's vision.*

Individual people did play a role in all the cases of corporate success described in this chapter. One stands out from all the others, and that is Walt Disney; without Disney, there would have been no Disney Corporation and few, if any, of the products with which that company is associated. But Disney was a genius, and the distinctive capability of this company at that time was his extraordinary talent. There are few business geniuses—Henry Ford, Thomas Edison—and genius by its nature is hard either to generalize from or to replicate. After Disney's death, it is said that the board often asked itself, "What would Walt have done?" It was a futile exercise. One might as well imagine the board of the Shakespeare Corporation, following the failure of its new play *Fortenbras of Denmark,* asking itself, "What would Will have done?" As both the Disney Corporation and the Royal Shakespeare Company found, a better strategy is to accept the historic repertoire and exploit it fully.

But Eisner, Quandt, and the (significantly) anonymous Japanese who enjoyed success with Honda were not men with unique talents. They made wise decisions—to unlock the Disney assets, to focus on the BMW 1500, to put the company's resources behind supercubs—but these were decisions that many others would have made if confronted with the same information at the same time. We learn from them not by studying their style or their personalities, or even by asking why they decided as they did, but by distilling the key characteristics of these correct decisions. The feature common to all is that they were based on an accurate identification of the firm's distinctive capabilities—what Disney, BMW, or Honda could do that competitors in the same marketplace could not expect to replicate. This process is the first step toward corporate success.

Many large companies have sponsored or encouraged histories of themselves. Often these are self-congratulatory panegyrics, but the best are substantial works of scholarship. BMW has one of the finest business histories (Mönnich 1989, 1991). There are probably more books about IBM than about any other company; some examples are De Lamarter (1986), Mercer (1987), Rodgers (1986), and Sobel (1981). The Disney story is recounted in Grover (1991) and Taylor (1987). Saatchi & Saatchi is the subject of a well-written journalistic account in Fallon (1988), which despite its unfortunate subtitle gives insight into the origins of the company's failures as well as its successes. One measure of true success—as it was for IBM—is that it attracts criticism as well as eulogy.

Business school cases, which are generally based on interviews with company management, provide both qualitative and quantitative information about company activities, especially for U.S. corporations. They vary considerably in quality. Few contain much analysis, which the instructor or student is expected to provide, and they often reproduce, in an uncritical fashion, the opinions and perceptions of the managers involved. Honda and Komatsu are classic business school case studies. For Honda, the original case is Harvard Business School (HBS) (1978), based on the 1975 Boston Consulting Group (BCG) report, and the revisionist version can be found in HBS (1983a, 1983b), based on Pascale (1984). The Prelude Corporation is discussed in HBS (1972, 1992).

Newspaper and magazine reports provide a constantly updated and replenished source of information and views of corporate performance. Text services now allow particularly easy access to these information sources. The accounts of the company operations given in Chapter 1 and elsewhere in this book drew on all these three sources of information: histories, cases, and reports.

A further account of the evolution of thinking in business strategy is given in the Appendix and the references listed there.

2

Adding Value

What is corporate success, and how is it measured? In this chapter I explore the strengths and weaknesses of common performance measures by comparing the performance of America's leading retailers—Wal-Mart, Kmart, and Sears-Roebuck. Some people judge success by size. They look at a firm's sales, its market share, and its stock exchange value. Sometimes performance is assessed by referring to the rate of return, which can be measured as the return on equity, on investment, or on sales. And sometimes success is measured by growth, reflected in an increase in output, movements in earnings per share, or, prospectively, the firm's price–earnings ratio.

All these are aspects of successful performance. But I argue in this chapter that the key measure of corporate success is added value, the difference between the (comprehensively accounted) value of a firm's output and the (comprehensively accounted) cost of its inputs. In this specific sense, adding value is both the proper motivation of corporate activity and the measure of its achievement.

This chapter defines and develops the objective of added value. It introduces the added-value statement and the analysis of the value chain as means of making a quantitative appraisal of a firm's operating activities. This contrasts with the usual financial statements that concentrate, appropriately for their purpose, on returns to investors. In Chapter 13, I explore these issues in greater detail and explain why added value is the basis of all the more familiar measures of corporate performance. Although this chapter identifies the various stakeholders in the business—employees, investors, customers, and suppliers—I postpone until Chapter 12 the issue of how added value is shared among these various stakeholders. In the final part of the chapter, I use the added-value criterion to identify the most successful companies of the last decade—in the United States and around the world.

*I*n Chapter 1, I contrasted IBM's perceived failure with Microsoft's acclaimed success. But what do we mean by corporate success? IBM's market value is still ahead of Microsoft's, and by any criterion except recent earnings, in which IBM's figures are distorted by write-offs, IBM is the larger company. Yet if size were the test, we might turn first to those firms with the biggest revenues (the two oil giants, Exxon and Shell) or the largest number of employees (the two German engineering conglomerates, Siemens and Daimler-Benz). If stock market value were the criterion used, then we might choose among Philip Morris, General Electric, Exxon, or even Wal-Mart. Among corporations that have added to this value in recent years, Philip Morris and Wal-Mart stand out. What about Japanese companies? There are few Japanese firms among the largest—Japanese firms are usually smaller than their Western counterparts. They do not earn especially high returns on capital either (although there are many problems in the international comparison of profit rates). Yet some Japanese companies do well on this criterion. On this basis, Nintendo would join Merck among the major companies with the highest rate of return on capital employed.

Adding Value

In sports it seems obvious what is meant by success. The successful baseball team is the one that wins the world series; the successful basketball team captures the National Basketball Association (NBA) championship. But there is more to it than that, and the difference between the two sports illustrates it well. The winning baseball team is, by and large, the club that puts the best players into the field. Teams bid up the salaries of the leading players to levels that match their abilities. Nine different clubs have won the world series in the last decade. But almost all the winners have come from the largest cities where the large number of people attending the games and the associated revenues have enabled the clubs to attract the most talented hitters and pitchers. What you pay is what you get.

In the recent past, basketball was dominated by the Boston Celtics and the Los Angeles Lakers. One or the other of these clubs won more than half the NBA championships since World War II. But whereas baseball success is associated with strong players, basketball success is associated with strong teams. The Celtics and the Lakers have had, on average, slightly stronger players than the league's average, but their outperformance has been far greater than the difference in their playing ability would suggest. Boston spends an average amount on its players, well below the most flagrant overspenders and the frugal franchisees. In both 1990 and 1991, only one Boston player had a salary ranking in the NBA's top twenty. Rather, the value of the Celtics has rested on their performance as a team in establishing an aggregate worth more than the sum of the parts. The written history of the Celtics, most of it not very scholarly, illustrates this. Red Auerbach, the longtime architect of the Celtic's success, is emphatic on this point: "The team is more important than any individual. If some guy couldn't live with that, my philosophy was to let him go and ruin the chemistry of some other team" (Auerbach 1991).

So when we talk of success or excellence in an organization, whether that organization is a sports team, an army, a state, or a business, we similarly need to distinguish between the attributes of the firm and the attributes of the persons in it. The people who made up the Roman army, ran British India, or staff Wal-Mart stores do not, in the main, have exceptional talent. Instead, the achievement of these organizations has been to make very ordinary people perform in extraordinary ways.

Contrast this with a professional service firm or a university. The achievements of Skadden, Arps rest principally on the talents of its partners, and those of Harvard University rest on its professors. Without the expertise of these partners or professors, neither institution would have much to offer its customers. The organization may add value to these talents through a reputation that attracts other talented partners and professors as well as clients, customers, and students. And it may be that further gains can be realized by pooling the skills and knowledge to be found in the institution. But no one doubts that the excellence of the institution is based primarily on the excellence of its individual members.

This distinction between the attributes of the corporation itself and the attributes of the persons in it has a commercial as well as a sociological significance. Only if the organization itself adds value is there an asset that belongs to the firm. When the organization's performance rests solely on the talents of the people in it, then the rewards of that performance accrue to these individual talents, rather than to the organization. We see this happening in professional or financial services firms in which the high fees charged to clients are largely translated into the high earnings of the firm's members.

The Added-Value Statement

What underpins the success of firms such as Disney, BMW, and Microsoft is their ability to add value to the inputs they use. Table 2.1 shows this for Microsoft. In 1992 the company bought materials worth $1.65 billion. Its wage and salary bill was around $400 million, and the cost of

**Table 2.1. How Microsoft
Corporation Added Value, 1992
(U.S.$ millions)**

Value of output	2,750
Wages and salaries	400
Cost of capital employed	50
Cost of materials	1,650
Total input	2,100
Added value	650

the capital that the company used—premises, factories, machinery, and equipment—was no more than $50 million. The resulting product was sold for $2.75 billion—$650 million more than it cost.

This figure of $650 million is a measure of the value that Microsoft added, the difference between the market value of its output and the cost of its inputs. It is also a measure of the loss that would result, to the national income and to the international economy, if Microsoft were to be broken up and the resources it uses deployed in other firms. Adding value, in this sense, is the central purpose of business activity. A commercial organization that adds no value—whose output is worth no more than the value of its inputs in alternative uses—has no long-term rationale for its existence.

This assessment of added value accounts comprehensively for the inputs that Microsoft used. It includes not only the depreciation of its capital assets but also a reasonable return on the capital invested in them.[1] Therefore, added value is less than the firm's *operating* profit— the difference between the value of the output and the value of the material and labor inputs (but not the capital inputs). It is also less than the firm's net output—the difference between the value of its sales and the cost of its inputs of materials (but not its inputs of labor or capital).

The strength of Microsoft's competitive advantage can be measured by looking at the ratio of added value to the firm's gross or net output. Each dollar of Microsoft's sales costs only 76 cents to produce. Microsoft's net output is the $1.1 billion difference between the cost of the materials it bought and the value of the output it sold. It achieved this with only $450 million of labor and capital, representing a cost of 41 cents per $1 of net output.

---

[1] The most appropriate means of charging for capital costs is a complex question that is discussed more fully in Chapter 13. The calculations in this chapter simply impose a rate of return of 10 percent on operating assets.

Not all firms succeed in adding value. Table 2.2 shows an added-value statement for United Airlines. Each $1 of United's output was obtained at a cost of $1.05. The case of the Dutch electrical giant, Philips, is also shown in Table 2.2.

Each $1.00 of Philips's output cost it $1.08 to produce, and it was unable to cover the full costs of its activities in the competitive markets it faced. Philips is a firm with enormous strengths and clear distinctive capabilities. Its record of innovation in consumer electronics is second to none—the company invented the compact cassette and pioneered the compact disc (CD) and the videocassette recorder (VCR). Yet it has repeatedly failed to translate these innovations into its own commercial success.

Would the world really be better off if United Airlines and Philips ceased to exist? If we resist this conclusion, it can only be because we feel that these firms have not succeeded in earning revenues that reflect the full value of their activities—that the services of United Airlines are worth more than the fares they charge, that the benefits of Philips's research accrue even to those who do not use their products. But it is a tenuous argument. In the long run, firms that fail to add value in a competitive market will not survive, nor do they deserve to.

U.S. Retailers

The relationship between added value and competitive market conditions emerges most clearly when we compare different firms in the same line of business. America's three biggest retail chains, each with annual sales between $30 billion and $40 billion, are Kmart, Sears-Roebuck, and Wal-Mart.

Sears is an American legend. Founded more than a century ago, its department stores spanned the continent; its catalogs took its merchan-

Table 2.2.   Added Value Statements: United Airlines and Philips, 1990 (U.S.$ millions)

	United Airlines	Philips
Revenues	11,037	32,491
Less materials	6,963	21,059
Value added	4,074	11,432
Wages and salaries	3,550	10,272
Capital costs	1,035	3,929
Added value	(511)	(2,769)

dise to every small town in the United States. With its reputation for uniform quality at a reasonable price, Sears helped establish a common identity for a nation of scattered communities and different ethnic origins. It diversified early into financial services, using its reputation to sell its Allstate Insurance as widely as the name suggests.

But Sears had become staid while the structure of American retailing was changing as demographic changes and widespread automobile ownership shifted the focus of shoppers' attention away from town centers. A small competing retail chain, S. S. Kresge, pioneered the formula of large out-of-town stores selling branded merchandise at discounted prices under the Kmart label.

But Kmart in turn failed to meet the changing tastes and growing sophistication of U.S. customers. Its increasingly tacky image became the butt of "attention Kmart shoppers" jokes. The company's response was to buy chains of speciality retailers, such as Waldenbooks and Pay Less Drug. At the same time, Wal-Mart, offering a friendlier store layout, replacing Kmart's aggressive promotions with "everyday low prices," and employing state-of-the art purchasing and inventory management systems, was opening stores directly positioned against Kmart. In the early 1990s, the Arkansas-based Wal-Mart, a company that had never earned a dollar of revenue outside the United States and that was still poorly represented in California and the eastern states, was the largest retailer in the world.

Size and market share are among the measures of corporate success. Table 2.3 shows them, and many others, for these three firms. Wal-Mart is the largest of the chains. It sells the most goods and makes the most profit, and its profit and its rating combine to give it by far the largest stock market capitalization of the three firms.

Wal-Mart had the lowest gross return on sales (those everyday low prices) but the highest net margin. It had the highest returns on investment, on equity, to shareholders, and the fastest growth. Sears's more recent stock market performance outshone Kmart's, because Sears was seen as addressing its problems, and the market was more skeptical about Kmart's position. Sears sold more per square foot (malls versus out-of-town stores), but Wal-Mart came out on top in its rate of stock turnover.

The added-value statement (Table 2.4) sums it up. Wal-Mart added $1.6 billion of value in 1992. Kmart added almost none. Sears subtracted it. Sears's position is unsustainable. Either the company must improve its competitive performance, or it must contract its activities; both are happening.

The difference to each firm in the cost of producing a unit of output

Table 2.3. U.S. Retailers, 1992 (U.S.$ billions)

	Wal-Mart	Kmart	Sears
Measure			
Size (U.S.$ billions)			
Revenue	44.3	37.7	25.4
Profit	1.61	0.94	−0.18
Market value	53.1	11.2	n.a.
Return (%)			
Net margin	20.7	24.5	28.7
Gross margin	5.8	3.8	−1.1
ROI	10.4	5.0	−1.7
ROE	23.0	12.5	n.a.
Shareholder 1 year	63.9	9.2	25.2
Return 5 years	224.6	61.1	33.1
Growth (%)			
Sales	34.8	9.1	2.7
EPS	22.8	2.0	neg.
P–E ratio	33.0	11.9	neg.
Efficiency			
Sales per square foot	279	184	328
Sales/inventory	44,289	37,724	25,418
	7,384	9,638	4,461

Note: Because of Sears's substantial financial services activities, market value and ROE are not comparable with that of Wal-Mart and Kmart.

measures the firm's competitive advantage. Wal-Mart's 82 cents per dollar gave it a competitive advantage over Kmart's 17 cents per dollar, and an even larger one over the value-subtracting Sears.

Winning Companies

Wal-Mart and Microsoft are successfully adding value; United Airlines and Philips are not. Table 2.5 shows the ten American firms that were most effective in adding value between 1988 and 1992.

What do these companies have in common? At first glance, not a lot. The list includes manufacturing companies (Abbott Labs and Kellogg) and service organizations (Disney and Marsh & McLellan). It includes corporate giants (Merck and Philip Morris) and relatively small companies (Nike and Wrigley). Some operate internationally (Coca-Cola); others are little known outside the United States (Liz Claiborne).

Paradoxically, what they have in common are their differences. What distinguishes each of these companies is that each has something that their rivals do not. Each has a distinctive capability that is readily

Table 2.4. Added Value for U.S. Retailers, 1992 (U.S.$ billions)

	Wal-Mart	Kmart	Sears
Revenues	44.3	38.1	25.4
Wages and salaries	6.1	5.2	3.6
Materials	35.3	31.1	22.0
Capital costs	1.3	1.7	1.0
Total input	42.7	38.0	26.6
Added value	1.6	0.1	−1.2
$\dfrac{\text{Input}}{\text{Output}}$	$\dfrac{7.4}{9.0}=0.82$	$\dfrac{6.9}{7.0}=0.99$	$\dfrac{4.6}{3.4}=1.37$

identifiable. But it is not easy for their rivals to emulate this distinctive capability even when they understand what it is. The list contains two companies—Coca-Cola and Philip Morris—that developed, in Coke and Marlboro, the most effective brands ever created. Merck has a strong pharmaceutical portfolio of which Vasotec, the world's best-selling drug for hypertension, is the most important component. Disney has a unique repertoire of characters and entertainments. Patent and copyright restrictions protect Merck and Disney to a degree that few other innovating companies can expect. Kellogg and Wrigley have strong brand names based on products that others have never quite successfully imitated. Abbott Labs demonstrates that the kind of reputation that can command a substantial price premium can be just as potent with a group of well-informed and sophisticated buyers as can resting on a consumer franchise with the strength of Coke or Marlboro. Nike is leader in a market whose explosive growth took almost everyone by surprise.

Nike is what *Business Week* once called a "hollow corporation." Most Nike shoes are made by subcontractors in East Asia and are sold

Table 2.5. American Winners, 1988–1992

Company	Principal Business	Cost per $ of Net Output
Merck	Pharmaceuticals	0.47
Coca-Cola	Soft drinks	0.49
Nike	Sports shoes	0.50
Abbott Labs	Hospital supplies	0.51
Liz Claiborne	Women's clothing	0.53
Kellogg	Breakfast cereals	0.56
Philip Morris	Cigarettes	0.57
Wrigley	Chewing gum	0.62
Marsh & McLellan	Insurance	0.68
Disney	Children's entertainment	0.68

by independent retailers. Nike is at the center of a web, orchestrating the process and providing branding and marketing. Much the same is true of Liz Claiborne and, in a different way, of Marsh & McLellan. Both companies stand as retailers' and manufacturers' interpreters of their clients' needs, and it is the structure of these relationships that is each company's distinctive capability. Something similar is true of Coke and Merck. Coke entrusts much of the bottling and distribution of its product to franchisees, and even though everyone would classify Merck as a manufacturing company, making things is a minor part of what it does. I prefer to think of a "hollow corporation" as an "added-value corporation." Its key characteristic is not that it is empty but that it is focused on the point in the chain of production at which value can be added most effectively.

It is not only American companies that succeed in adding value. Table 2.6 lists some other corporations with high ratios of added value to gross output.[2] (Microsoft is not in Table 2.5 because it is not quoted on the New York Stock Exchange.) The others include Nintendo, the Japanese leader in video games; LVMH, the French company that produces Louis Vuitton luggage, Moët et Chandon champagne, and Hennessy cognac; Glaxo, the British manufacturer of Zantac, an antiulcerant that is the world's best-selling drug; Reuters, which provides on-screen information to the financial markets in all time zones; and Elsevier, which publishes many of the world's leading scientific journals.

For these companies, too, success rests on distinctive capabilities, and what differentiates them is more striking than what they have in common. Yet it should be apparent that this must be so. If there were effective generic strategies—recipes for corporate success—then all companies would adopt them, and they would cease to yield returns for any company. Corporate success rests on distinctive capabilities—on those characteristics of an organization that others cannot easily replicate, even when they have seen what they are and have observed the added value that others create through them. This is a disappointing conclusion for many managers, who want to know how they can achieve equivalent success. But the lesson is that corporate success is not based on imitating the successful but on identifying the distinctive capabilities of each organization, nurturing them, and maximizing their value. That is the concern of the remainder of this book.

---

[2]The calculations in Table 2.5 measure added value relative to net output, or added value (the difference between sales and the cost of materials). Those in Table 2.6 measure added value relative to gross output, or sales.

Table 2.6. Other Successful Companies

Company	Country	Principal Business	Cost per $ of Gross Output
Glaxo	United Kingdom	Pharmaceuticals	0.76
Microsoft	United States	Computer software	0.76
Nintendo	Japan	Electronic games	0.77
Reuters	United Kingdom/ United States	Financial information	0.83
Astra	Sweden	Pharmaceuticals	0.84
Elsevier	Netherlands	Scientific publishing	0.84
LVMH	France	Luxury goods	0.86
Canal +	France	Television network	0.88

All jurisdictions require corporations to file annual financial statements. Their performance on the stock market is widely tracked, and the listing requirements of the principal stock exchanges impose further obligations to provide data. European company legislation generally requires firms to disclose overall employee remuneration and other information about their workforce and employment practices. American and Japanese firms do not have similar obligations, which makes it difficult to analyze the structure of their added value using published information. Several commercial databases provide standardized company analyses, mainly directed at potential investors.

Added value (called rent or supernormal profit by economists) is a concept with a long intellectual history. The original analysis is that of Ricardo (1819). The notion that rent seeking is the primary objective of industrial activity is Schumpeter's (1943, 1961), which was developed in a more recent tradition by authors such as Demsetz (1973, 1988) and Posner (1975). Explicit application to the field of business strategy can be found in the work of Stewart (1991), who uses the term economic value added. My approach in this book is developed more fully in Davis and Kay (1990) and is described further in Chapter 13 of this book. The calculations for Tables 2.5 and 2.6 are explained more fully in Davis, Flanders, and Star (1991).

II

BUSINESS RELATIONSHIPS

The added-value statement is not just a means of looking at the financial consequences of a firm's activities. It also describes the set of relationships that constitute the firm. These relationships are those with its suppliers, its customers, its employees, and its investors. In addition, the firm must have relationships with the governments of the countries in which it operates, and its performance is influenced by its relationship with its competitors. It is the totality of these relationships that defines the individual firm and creates its distinctive identity.

The first task of the management of any business organization is to ensure the consistency of its contractual relationships—to establish that the planned output can be achieved with the planned inputs of labor, capital, and materials. For each of these contractual relationships, there is a corresponding financial flow. The firm receives sales revenues from its customers, makes payments to its suppliers, meets its wage bill and its tax bill, and pays a return to its investors. Whereas these are totaled and summarized in the added-value statement, the competitive environment—the relationship between a firm and its rivals—determines the degree to which value can be added. The purpose of business activity is to put together a set of relationships that maximize this added value.

There are many kinds of commercial relationships. Some are contractual—specific and legally binding obligations that can be enforced in the courts. Others are informal, or implicit. Often, contractual relationships are supplemented, or effectively superseded, by implicit terms. Most formal agreements between firms and their competitors are illegal. Such relationships are defined by the rules of the competitive game, which may be disciplined—an understanding that everyone will lose in a price war—or may be unstable, aggressive, and undisciplined. Interactions with the government may be imposed through tax legislation, may be prescribed by regulation, or may involve the public sector as the provider of services or the user of output.

The simplest commercial relationship is a spot contract in which money is exchanged for goods, thereby both defining and settling the relationship. "Sharp in by clear agreement; sharp out by clear performance" (Macneil 1974, p. 738). That is how firms buy stationery or make telephone calls.

A spot contract is a simple bilateral exchange. Each party knows what it wants; there is a shared interest in meeting these requirements; and the transaction is of a type sufficiently common and sufficiently frequent to be made on standard terms. No extensive negotiation is required. Many business relationships meet these conditions. Many do not. Consider the following examples:

- Although the quality of a component is vital to a firm, it is impossible to monitor quality by means of inspection.

- Two firms with different standard specifications need to agree on which will be used.

- A market opportunity that is available to several firms will be profitable if one firm enters but not if more than one does.

In the first example, the buyer cannot determine immediately what he has bought. "Clear performance" cannot be established. In the second case, more than one agreement might be reached, and it is not apparent which is preferable. In the third, no agreement can be reached (and any formal agreement would probably be illegal).

There is a need for cooperation—to encourage individual persons to pursue a common goal against the contrary pressures of their own interests. There is also the problem of coordination. It often is important that everyone do the same thing, even though precisely what it is that everyone does is not important at all. But there also is a need for differentiation. Although all different aspects of an activity need to be covered by an organization, if all firms in a market adopt similar strategies, the outcome is unlikely to be profitable for any of them.

Chapter 3 defines and describes the problems of cooperation, coordination, and differentiation, and Chapter 4 explains how the various commercial contracts and relationships we observe have been developed in response to them. These two chapters are considerably more abstract than others in this book. If some readers find that difficult or uncongenial or are skeptical of the relevance of such an approach, I urge them to go on to Chapters 5 through 8; I hope they will find that the analysis there is relevant and comprehensible but that it is also more fully illuminated by the ideas put forward in Chapters 3 and 4.

3

Cooperation and Coordination

This chapter is a theoretical interlude that introduces tools, arguments, and concepts used extensively in my later analysis. The essence of a firm is the set of relationships among its stakeholders and between itself and other firms. This chapter describes the principal functions of these interactions. The most important objectives of commercial relationships are cooperation (the joint activity toward a shared goal), coordination (the need for mutually consistent responses), and differentiation (the avoidance of mutually incompatible activities).

I believe that game theory is a helpful way of describing these relationships. So although my discussion of cooperation begins from the familiar business problem of achieving success in a joint venture, I go on to explain how that issue can be described by the most famous of all games—the Prisoner's Dilemma. The objectives of coordination and differentiation are represented by the Battle of the Sexes and the game of Chicken, respectively. I also describe the paradox of commitment—how it is possible to gain by limiting one's own options.

One of the most important insights to be gained from this formal approach to these questions is an understanding of why recognition of these management problems is such a small step on the road to their solution. An explanation of the undoubted benefits of cooperation is rarely enough to bring about cooperative behavior. Rather, this response requires a more subtle reconciliation of the interests of the individual as an individual and those of the individual as a member of a group. Achieving coordination and differentiation also depends on the appropriate incentive structures. My discussion leads, in Chapter 4, to a discussion of how relationships can be structured to reduce or avoid problems of noncooperation, discoordination, and inadequate differentiation.

The Joint-Venture Problem

*I*n the last decade, many firms established joint ventures, believing that the transfer of skills and expertise between them would be to their mutual advantage. In entering such an arrangement, a firm can cooperate wholeheartedly, or it can hold back. Wholehearted cooperation imposes significant costs on each firm. The firm must educate its rival, and by doing so, it may strengthen a potential competitor. But the possible benefits from exchange make full mutual cooperation clearly, and strongly, preferable to an outcome in which each holds back.

There is an important and general distinction here between perfunctory and consummate cooperation—a distinction familiar to anyone who has dealt with children or difficult employees. Perfunctory cooperation is the degree of cooperation that can be imposed through legal agreement or the threat of sanctions. In consummate cooperation, both parties work together toward a mutual end, responding flexibly and sharing skills and information. The difference is the difference between a relationship with the local telephone company and a relationship with a marriage partner. Since consummate cooperation cannot be enforced by a legal contract, the question of how it is to be achieved is a fundamental management problems and one that will recur throughout this book.

Many joint ventures require consummate cooperation if they are to achieve their full potential. Yet each firm enters a joint venture uncertain about how the other will behave. If the other firm holds back, then it is clear that the best thing to do is also to hold back. But if the other firm cooperates wholeheartedly, then the best thing to do is, again, to hold back. Indeed, playing a cautious role oneself while receiving the full cooperation of one's partner is the most advantageous outcome. Holding back is a *dominant strategy*, which means that it is the best response whatever one expects the other party to do. But of course, it is a dominant strategy for the other party also. So both partners will choose to hold back. And that is the outcome despite the evident benefits of consummate cooperation.

This paradox is known as the *Prisoner's Dilemma*, after a story that I will relate shortly. It is particularly forceful because when most people are first exposed to it, they fail to grasp its full nature. It seems obvious that without effective communication and understanding of mutual benefits, the potential gains from cooperation cannot be realized. What is needed is better communication and understanding. Yet the essence of the paradox is that communication and understanding do not help. The partners may fully appreciate the mutual benefits of cooperation and recognize that the likely outcome is that they both will hold back. In discussion, they agree that wholehearted cooperation would be best and promise to provide it, but they nevertheless hold back.

There are two ways in which they can escape from this kind of difficulty. One is to change the structure of the payoffs. Suppose there were a penalty for holding back. If it were sufficiently large, it could turn consummate cooperation into a dominant strategy. If this were true for both parties, then the mutually advantageous outcome would be whole-hearted cooperation. Usually this is done by making legal contracts. The simplest transaction can have, in a trivial sense, a Prisoner's Dilemma structure—I would do better not to deliver the goods to you, and you would do better not to pay for them—but we can avoid that result by making a binding agreement.

This does not work for the joint venture, however, because a contract to cooperate fully is not one that the courts are able or willing to monitor. The alternative escape route is to establish a continuing relationship with the other party. These relational, or implicit, dimensions of business behavior—ones that cannot be enforced through legal agreements—are of great practical importance and will recur throughout this book. In some less developed countries, where managers and individual persons are unable to make binding commitments to each other, Prisoner's Dilemma outcomes are widespread and a serious obstacle to doing business.

The Prisoner's Dilemma: The Problem of Cooperation

Problems such as the joint venture can be analyzed in a more formal way using the language of game theory. This language is a means of specifying the intuitions that we all have about the outcomes of these situations. The games are best regarded as extended metaphors—never to be taken literally or implemented directly but capable of focusing attention on different aspects of why strategic interactions so often produce results that were never anyone's intention.

The metaphor that makes the Prisoner's Dilemma such a well-remembered game is based on the following story, told by Albert Tucker:

> Two prisoners are arrested and put in separate cells. The sheriff admits that he has no real evidence but presents the following alternatives: If one confesses, he or she will go free, and the other can expect a ten-year jail sentence. If both confess, each will be convicted, but they can expect a lighter sentence, seven years perhaps. If neither confesses, the likely outcome is a short one-year sentence for each one, based on a trumped-up charge.

Figure 3.1 shows the possible outcomes of this game. Each partner has the choice of confessing or not confessing, and the payoff to each strategy depends on what the other party chooses to do. A structure such as Figure 3.1—a *payoff matrix*—is a simple way of describing this kind of interdependence. Since the payoff is imprisonment, higher numbers

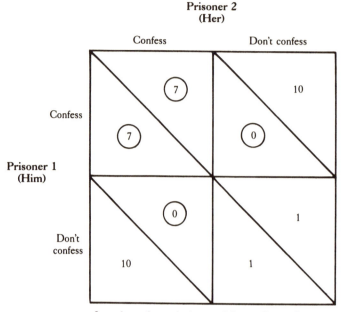

In each quadrant, the bottom left payoff is for Player 1
and the upper right for Player 2. Circles indicate that a
payoff is the best outcome for that player, given the
strategy of the other.

Figure 3.1.   The Prisoner's Dilemma

are worse. Prisoner 1 is uncertain what his collaborator in crime will do
but notes that if she confesses, he will get seven years for confessing and
ten for remaining silent; if she does not confess, he will go free on a
confession and otherwise serve a year in jail. So whatever his conjecture
about her actions, he will do better to confess, and so will she. Both go
to jail for seven years.

Despite the fanciful nature of this example, the Prisoner's Dilemma
is a real problem with application to daily business. Several instances
will be developed at greater length in later chapters of this book. One—
which is at the heart of the joint-venture problem—is the problem of
sharing information. This problem arises both within organizations and
between firms at different points of the supply chain. Typically, the best
overall outcome both collectively and individually is achieved by a free
and frank exchange of information; yet there almost always are strategic
gains to be made by withholding part of the picture. The problem of
signaling product quality when the buyers themselves cannot immedi-

ately judge the product being purchased is another Prisoner's Dilemma. The danger is that the purchasers expect low quality and the seller's incentive is to meet their expectations. Competitors' price behavior poses a Prisoner's Dilemma. All firms have a common interest in avoiding a price war, and each firm has an individual interest in undercutting its rivals.

We experience the Prisoner's Dilemma in our social and economic lives as well as in our business experience. For example, we drop litter in the street, although we know it would be better for all of us if no one did; we demand wage increases in excess of inflation, although we recognize that inflation will fall only if we show restraint. Those politicians who bemoan the irrationality of the outcome have failed to understand the issue. The problem—and the paradox of the Prisoner's Dilemma—is not that we fail to recognize where our best interests lie. The problem is that we do.

Repeating the Game

The Prisoner's Dilemma may be resolved if the game is repeated. This is not simply a question of learning by experience. Suppose we both have encountered the Prisoner's Dilemma, reached its inevitable outcome, and spent our seven years in jail. Released, we commit the same crime again and are faced with the same proposal. You might think that chastened by our previous experience, we might choose this time not to confess. But the same remorseless logic applies. If I believe that you are likely to listen to the lessons of experience and refrain from confessing, then I will confess. If I believe that you will confess, then the best strategy for me is to confess. Another seven years' imprisonment is in each of our futures.

So repetition does not, in itself, produce learning. But the prospect of repetition can modify behavior, by allowing strategies to be developed in which future behavior is conditioned on past performance. Suppose the two players know that they will play the game twice. One prisoner makes the following suggestion as they are taken to the police station: I will not confess this time. I suggest you do the same. Whatever you do on this occasion, I will do on the second. That is, if you squeal, I will too, and if you stay silent, I will as well. This proposal makes the prisoner's choice more complex. But the problem is that this offer is not credible. Instead, a credible strategy is one that is worth carrying out, and the strategy proposed here does not have this property. Although it pays to promise not to confess, once the promise is made, the rational action is to break it.

Theoretically, this would be true even if the game were to be played one thousand times. Both players are sure to confess on the thousandth game, so they might as well confess on the nine hundred and ninety-ninth, and so on. But actually, experimental evidence shows that people do not behave in this way, probably because a thousand times is so many that no one is certain how long the game will really last. In repeated trials of the Prisoner's Dilemma, the players usually reach cooperative solutions.

These experiments have identified some of the key features of successful cooperative strategies in repeated games: The players are nice—they begin by expecting that the other player will cooperate, not that he or she will cheat. Nevertheless, they respond to bad behavior and punish it. Yet they are forgiving. Noncooperative behavior should be punished, but not too severely. Tit for tat is a strategy with these properties—I do what you did last time; I respond to your deviant behavior but allow you to correct it.

A repeated game strategy establishes a relationship between the two players. Each behaves in a way that is conditioned by the other player's previous experience and by expectations as to how he or she will behave in the future. The existence of a past and a future implies that it makes sense to behave in ways that are not the best for either player in the short run. It always pays to confess, but not doing so is to everyone's long-term benefit. Only the creation of a long-term relationship can achieve that outcome.

This is how the joint-venture problem is generally resolved in practice. The decision must be turned into a reiterated game, and so you seek to break down the process into a sequence of small steps. You use the early meetings to explore each other's attitudes. You offer wholehearted cooperation and await a response. If the other side fails to reciprocate, the losses are not very great, and you can hold back in the future. If the other side does respond, you can continue to be wholehearted in your cooperation. In this piecemeal way, trust between the parties can develop, and you may succeed in establishing a cooperative relationship.

An important feature of this solution is that both parties expect the venture to continue. If it is likely to end, each party will begin to see the benefits of holding something back, of behaving strategically rather than maximizing the joint gains from the venture. The relationship starts to fray at the edges. Indeed, the possibility that such an outcome will eventually emerge may poison the atmosphere between the parties from the outset. Joint ventures are much more likely to succeed if they are perceived as a preliminary to more intimate cooperation than as finite activities.

Changing the Payoffs

There is another means of resolving the Prisoner's Dilemma and games like it, which is to change the structure of the payoffs. This is how criminals themselves deal with the issue. In Figure 3.1 the prisoner who confesses while the other does not escapes scot free. But suppose instead the likely consequence is a visit from the friends of the person who is serving ten years in jail, with consequences that could certainly be as bad as a five-year sentence. This new game is shown in Figure 3.2.

What is the outcome in this revised structure? Here the best strategy for each prisoner depends on what the other one chooses. If Prisoner 2 confesses, Prisoner 1 will do better to confess also—a seven-year sentence rather than a ten-year sentence. But if Prisoner 1 does not confess, Prisoner 2 will also be better off not confessing. A one-year jail term is preferable to a long period in the hospital. This interdependence—in which not only is the outcome for me dependent on what others do, but also the best strategy for me is dependent on what others do—is characteristic of most real business situations. The Prisoner's Dilemma is unusual in having a dominant strategy equilibrium—the best strategy is best regardless of the other prisoner's choice—and that is what lends force to the paradox.

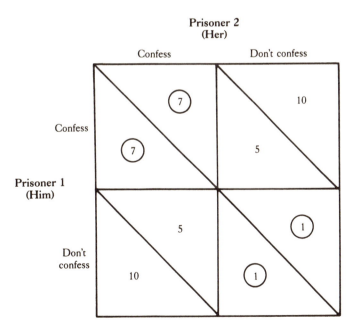

Figure 3.2.   **The Criminal's Revenge**

In the absence of a dominant strategy, each player must estimate the other's likely response. If espionage is ruled out, the best approach will be to put yourself in your rival's shoes. What would you choose if you were she? If she does have a dominant strategy, the choice is easy, and you can simply select the best outcome for yourself depending on her dominant strategy. But that is not true in this game or in most: Her action depends on her anticipation of your actions.

But of course, you know what you yourself plan to do, so you can find what her best response would be, given that knowledge. And then you test your own strategy: Is it a good one in the light of that response? If it is, then you have found what is known as a *Nash equilibrium*. The characteristic of a Nash equilibrium is that each player is making the best response given what the other player has chosen to do. And in the Criminal's Revenge, not confessing is a Nash equilibrium outcome. If Prisoner 1 does not confess, not confessing will be the best strategy for Prisoner 2, and vice versa. Both will go to jail for a year.

Types of Equilibrium

A manufacturer of a consumer product (Consco) had an excellent, long-standing relationship with a distributor (Distco) in one of its main territories. Then the founder, largest shareholder, and dominant figure in Distco decided to retire. He visited the CEO of the manufacturing company to suggest that his firm buy his business. "I've had an offer from Y corp," he said, mentioning the name of one of Consco's principal competitors. "But putting our two firms together would add more value. We could therefore do a deal that would be better for both of us." Consco's CEO acknowledged the truth of this. But he did not want to buy Distco (or, for that matter, any other distributor); he preferred to keep open his options regarding his company's choice of distributor, especially in the uncertain period that would follow the retirement of Distco's founder.

The payoff matrix for this game is displayed in Figure 3.3. When Consco's CEO thought the issue through, he quickly saw that his preferred option was not a viable one. Selling—to someone—is a dominant strategy for Distco. The game has one Nash equilibrium—Consco buys Distco—and that is what transpired. Each firm decided to choose the best course available given the anticipated actions of the other players, and the merger went ahead.

Although the Nash equilibrium was the outcome in this case, there is nothing guaranteeing that a game will have a Nash equilibrium, that it will have only one, or that if there is one the parties will reach it. A

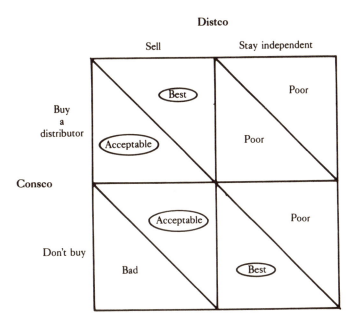

Figure 3.3.   Mergers and Alliances

Nash equilibrium is a much less certain outcome than is a dominant strategy equilibrium. What if I am not confident that we both see the game in the same way—something that is often true of almost all the business games we play in real life? Then I may be uncertain that my opponent will adopt what I perceive as her best strategy, and she may have the same concerns about me. If so, we may fail to achieve a Nash equilibrium.

The Problem of Coordination

The Criminal's Revenge has two Nash equilibria. Confess–confess is a Nash equilibrium also, because if Player 1 confesses, confessing will be the best strategy for Player 2, and vice versa. It is not certain that one Nash equilibrium will be reached rather than the other, even though it is obvious that one is better than the other, or even that any Nash equilibrium will be the solution. Perhaps the best that can be said is that games are less likely to reach outcomes that are not Nash equilibria, because players certainly have incentives to deviate from them. If Consco had opened merger discussions with another distributor, it would have provoked a merger approach from Distco, since the top left-hand outcome is better for both than the top right one is.

So communication does help here. If we discuss the problem beforehand, we both can agree that not confess–not confess would be a better outcome than confess–confess. And if we believe from our discussion that the other is likely to act sensibly, we will have no incentive to depart from the not confess–not confess outcome. There is a fundamental difference here between the Criminal's Revenge and the Prisoner's Dilemma. In the Prisoner's Dilemma we can agree that not confess–not confess is the best outcome, and yet it pays us, individually, to depart from it. In the Criminal's Revenge, the structure of individual self-interest now supports the outcome that is best for everyone.

But what if all the possible Nash equilibria are just about equally good? This is a common problem of coordination, and it is characterized as follows: There are several ways in which an activity that requires input from several persons or groups can be performed, all of them more or less equally satisfactory. Even though each group can make decisions independently, the achievement of any workable outcome still requires them to do much the same thing.

The metaphor used here is known as the Battle of the Sexes. A man and a woman are planning an evening out. He would prefer to go to the knitting demonstration, and she would rather go to sumo wrestling, but each would rather be with the other one than apart. The worst possible outcome, obviously, is that he end up at the wrestling and she at the knitting demonstration. The payoff matrix for this game is shown in Figure 3.4.

This game, like the Criminal's Revenge, has two Nash equilibria: Both end up at sumo wrestling, or both end up at the knitting demonstration. But unlike the Criminal's Revenge, there is no reason to think that one is better than the other. Which is the solution to the game? Take first the case in which the two partners are unable to communicate with each other and must decide for themselves, hoping to meet the other at the selected venue. Do you behave selfishly, hoping that the other will not? Or do you go to your second choice, knowing that there is a real risk that you both will end up with a wasted evening?

Suppose the two partners do have an opportunity to discuss the matter. Communication may help dispose of obviously bad outcomes— as with the Criminal's Revenge—but this is as far as it can go. It probably enables us to exclude the outcome in which he goes to sumo wrestling and she to the knitting, but that is as far as it can go. Everyone can remember, from both business life and social life, the ineffectual discussion in which each group states its preferences and each group offers to

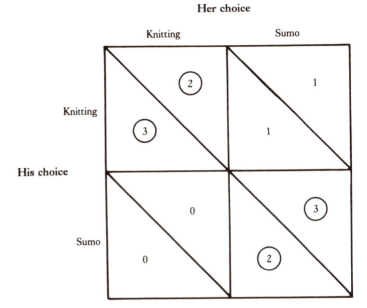

Figure 3.4.   The Battle of the Sexes

give way. The Battle of the Sexes is a game with no apparent solution, which is no doubt how it got its name.

And yet it is a game with almost too many business applications to list; from the choice of the corporate logo and the determination of normal working hours to the relationships between the firm and its suppliers and subcontractors. Each one of these demands a coordinated response, and yet each poses a question about which there will be different views of the appropriate coordinated response.

There are two ways of escaping from the Battle of the Sexes: *commitment* and *hierarchy*. Prior commitment is another means of resolving battles of the sexes. What is needed is simply something to break the symmetry—to distinguish one Nash equilibrium from the others. If we already have two tickets to the sumo wrestling, that will settle it. If we always go to the knitting, that will settle it, too.

Hierarchy breaks the essential symmetry of the problem by putting one of the two partners in charge. He decides where the couple goes, or perhaps she does. The main contractor determines the specification and timetable. The chief executive makes the decision on the logo, the personnel director on the hours of work. There is an issue of some subtlety here. One-way communication—an order—is preferable to two-way communication—a discussion. Hierarchy is necessary as a means of resolving the problem of coordination, not because of the superior wisdom of the decision maker or the greater significance of his or her preferences. Rather, the principal reason for giving authority to a chief executive is not to enable everyone in the organization to benefit from that person's unique insights but to fulfill the most important requirement, which is simply that somebody should decide. Seniority systems—in which high positions are achieved by length of service rather than by merit—have the advantage that they make this very clear, both to those who wield authority and to those who are subject to it. So do systems of hereditary authority, which once were as common in business as in politics. Business structures that emphasize seniority—as in Japan or Germany—often find problems of coordination easier to handle.

Commitment

Both the Prisoner's Dilemma and the Battle of the Sexes suggest that there are potential gains from commitment. Managers often emphasize the need for flexibility and the merits of keeping their options open. They often are right. But there also are advantages in being able to make commitments. There are gains from being able to close one's options as well as gains from keeping them open.

Look more carefully at how commitment resolves the Prisoner's Dilemma. At first sight, the best situation for me is one in which the other party commits herself but I do not. Suppose I know that she is perfectly truthful and reliable and that if she pledges herself not to confess, or to confess, I can rely on her word. For my part, I prefer to keep my freedom of maneuver.

In any preliminary discussion, we can quickly agree that we both would be better off if neither were to confess. I invite her to commit herself not to confess. She asks herself what I would be likely to do if she makes, and keeps, that commitment, and the answer is clear—I will confess. In that case, she will be better off confessing herself. So she chooses not to make the commitment in the first place. It is important to me not only that she should be able to commit herself but also that I should be able to commit myself.

The joint-venture game can be seen in the same terms. Suppose one party has a reputation for wholehearted cooperation, and the other prefers to remain flexible. The likely outcome is that although the first party could commit to the relationship, it will choose not to. The gains come from the ability to commit other people and also to commit oneself. Likewise, in the Prisoner's Dilemma game, if you can offer a commitment not to confess, you and the other party both will reach the not confess–not confess outcome. If the commitment is available from one side but not the other, then the outcome will be that both confess. The gains from flexibility are illusory. And the same is true in the joint venture. If you wait and see, the unavoidable outcome is that you will not like what you see.

The opportunity to make binding commitments is the central function of a system of contract law, and there do not seem to be any examples of industrial societies that have flourished without such a system. Yet the courts are not the only—or often the most important—means of enforcing commitments. In frontier societies or even in parts of modern Italy, respect for central authority is weak. There, local codes, supported by social rather than legal sanctions, enable people to make effective commitments. And these mechanisms are important everywhere because there are many things that the courts cannot enforce. The law can force you to deliver goods or try to make you deliver goods, but it cannot elicit your wholehearted cooperation or insist that you respond flexibly to changes in conditions of demand and supply. As modern economies evolve, the features of relationships that cannot be legally enforced come to matter more than the ones that can.

Ulysses S. Grant was the most admired, and successful, of the Union generals in the Civil War. Grant was famed for both the commitment he displayed himself and what he aroused in his soldiers. When he was heavily criticized after the bloody battle of Pittsburg Landing, Lincoln was reported to have said of him, "I can't spare this man; he fights."

Grant's strategy at Vicksburg was his most effective demonstration of commitment. He took his forces downriver past the Confederate stronghold in order to make his attack from behind enemy lines. Figure 3.5 shows the sequence of decisions by the Union and the Confederacy. Grant's tactic effectively made a Union retreat impossible and, by restricting his own options in this way, reduced the range of opportunities for a Confederate victory. In this way, Grant strengthened the resolve of his own troops (by increasing the costs of defeat) and undermined that of the defenders (by reducing the probability of victory). Grant's success at Vicksburg was one of the decisive battles of the war, and it was also decisive for Grant himself: He went on to become the leader of all the Union forces and ultimately president of the United States.

Grant was, in effect, an entrant in a new market—the western states of the Confederacy—and the lessons of his success stand for anyone who would now consider entering. Grant won in part because of the strength of his credible commitment; the Confederates lost in part because the

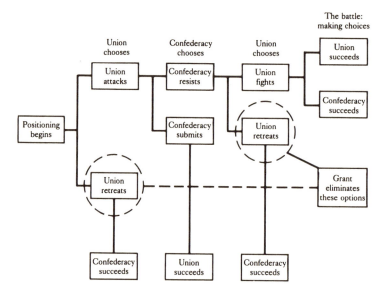

Figure 3.5.   The Vicksburg Campaign

strength of their commitment to continue that segment of the struggle was less clear than Grant's.

If commitment is a valuable tool, the inability to make commitments may prove costly. The Prisoner's Dilemma arises from the prisoners' inability to make credible promises not to confess. Governments have often pledged not to negotiate with terrorists who take hostages. The extensive-form game of Figure 3.6 makes clear why. If we rule out the option of negotiation, the terrorists will be worse off if they take a hostage than if they do not. So they do not take a hostage; the government has no choice to make; and it achieves its desired outcome. Unfortunately, the government's commitment is not *credible*. Although it makes sense for it to say that it will not negotiate, once the hostage is actually taken, the government usually prefers to negotiate than to stand firm. That is what governments have usually done, and unfortunately, terrorists know this.

Voluntary commitment in business takes many forms. Firms often make a public commitment to a market. They incur expenditures that are of value only in relation to that particular market, in order to persuade potential customers of their quality or their ability to provide service in the long run. Firms make gratuitous commitments to customers or to suppliers when they invest in a relationship, in order to induce the customer or the supplier to make a tangible commitment, perhaps by

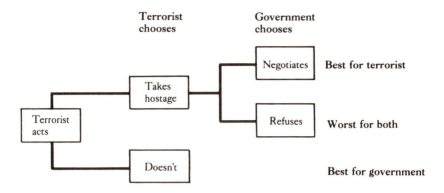

Figure 3.6.   Taking a Hostage

investing in training or assets. There may also be opportunities to make commitments to competitors. Subsequent chapters describe all these types of commitments.

Chicken: The Problem of Differentiation

In 1986, the deregulation of London's financial markets allowed any firm to offer its services as a market maker in government bonds. Twenty-eight firms—representing most of the major banks of the world—decided to do so. Taken as a whole, the London bond market is the world's largest financial center, and the market in British government securities is a key part of it. It was obvious to every participant that the market could not conceivably be profitable with twenty-eight firms in it. But not to enter would have been to cede an important and potentially lucrative market to rivals. Five years later, eighteen firms are still in business, and their cumulative losses have been put at more than $1 billion. The banks that participated—and those banks that decided not to or subsequently quit—were engaged in a war of attrition, which is one example of a class of games that I shall call *Chicken games*. The essence of these games is that a strategy is rewarding if used by one player but disastrous if employed by all. If the Battle of the Sexes is the archetypal game of coordination, Chicken is the archetypal game of differentiation.

Because of their dramatic structure, Chicken games have a fascination for movie makers, and the classic war of attrition is found in the James Dean film of the 1950s, *Rebel Without a Cause*. The Dean version is particularly difficult to analyze, and the game considered here can be found in a more recent movie, *Stand by Me*. The rules are the following: Two vehicles drive toward each other, waiting for one to swerve. The winner is the player who perseveres while the other swerves. If both swerve, they are poor players of Chicken. If neither does, they may not have an opportunity to play Chicken again. The payoffs are shown in Figure 3.7.

Chicken is another game with two Nash equilibria. In each, one player swerves and the other does not. But this is not much help, because it does not identify which player is which. Nor does communication help, because what each player should do is proclaim absolute determination not to swerve. Here too, commitment may help; one suggestion is that one player should tear off the steering wheel and throw it out the window. If the other driver sees the commitment, the result will be clear. So might reputation, though it did not do enough for Dean's opponent.

But if this is not an available option (and it often is not—the list of firms announcing that they are committed to staying in a particular market is materially longer than the list of firms that have actually done so), what is the solution? A feature of Chicken is that it is a game with a solution in *mixed strategies*, meaning that you should sometimes swerve and sometimes persevere.

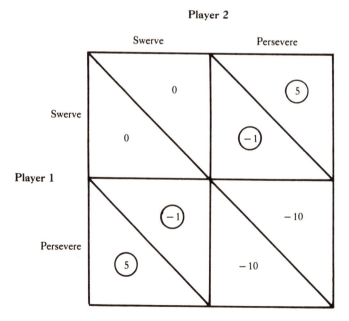

Figure 3.7. **Chicken**

The idea that it may make sense to randomize behavior is quite difficult to accept. Yet it seems to be central to the differentiation problem. One way to understand why differentiation benefits from randomization is to think of games in which the only solutions are in mixed strategies. The childhood game of stone–scissors–paper (in which both players choose an object simultaneously and paper covers stone, stone sharpens scissors, and scissors cut paper) is a good example. There, random behavior is the only possible way to play, and any systematic strategy is a loser. The game of Chicken described in Figure 3.7 has a specific equilibrium in mixed strategies, with each player swerving nine times and persevering five times in fourteen tries. If they do this, the two players will crash around one time in ten and win nearly one time in three and—most surprising of all—it actually pays to enter the game. If they were to repeat the game many times, the overall outcome would be positive. Yet this should not dispel the strong feeling that we all have on encountering a game of Chicken—that we should not be playing this game at all. Instead, we should be looking to change the payoff structure, to improve the odds, or to transform the game into one that is repeated or has an extensive form.

Some Lessons of Game Theory

The games just described all are, in an obvious sense, pathological. Although they describe social and business situations that we all encounter, they also require interactions leading to perverse results. In the Prisoner's Dilemma, the players are driven to select an outcome that everyone recognizes as inferior. In the Battle of the Sexes, it is not clear that there can be any outcome at all unless we change the structure of the game. And Chicken seems to have a solution, but one in which no one can feel in control, and the outcome is clearly unsatisfactory. Yet these issues of cooperation, coordination, and differentiation are fundamental to business life.

The precision of the game theory approach makes clear some basic problems in the strategic interactions among individual persons, groups, and firms. The problems that arise in these games are not the result of any lack of goodwill or understanding on the part of the players or of any failure to perceive the benefits of cooperative or coordinated action. Individual persons can fully appreciate the benefits of coordinated action or cooperative behavior and yet fail to realize them. Firms can recognize the dangers of differentiation and still fall victim. One of the tasks of management is to structure, and restructure, situations so that these problems are less likely to arise. Later chapters of this book describe practical applications of the various mechanisms—long-term relationships, reputation, and commitment—that have been developed to overcome the problems inherent in these pathological games.

Talk of relationships, reputations, and commitment has a slightly old-fashioned ring. It dates from an older business tradition that has been supplanted by a more aggressive individualism; a world in which, it is suggested, we can no longer afford these kinds of self-imposed restraints. The truth is that these are mechanisms that have evolved over centuries as means of dealing with problems in social and commercial relationships that have always been recognized and that these games do no more than formalize them. They are mechanisms we discard at our peril.

Chapters 3, 4, and 5 are concerned, respectively, with game theory, with the analysis of contracts, and with the value of a structure of relational contracts as a system of business organization. Each of these subjects has a major literature of its own, which is discussed under the appropriate headings. But the common theme throughout is that contract structure, and therefore organizational form, must be adapted to the characteristics that the transactions in this structure and form handle.

This general argument derives from transaction-cost economics, a subject whose major proponent is Oliver Williamson; see particularly Williamson (1975, 1985, 1986). Williamson is the most important recent contributor to an organizational tradition in economics that, slightly apart from the mainstream of economic thought, can be traced through writers such as Arrow (1974), Coase (1937), Hirschman (1982), and Milgrom and Roberts (1992). Williamson and Winter (1991) survey this tradition, and Perrow (1986) offers a standard critique of this approach.

The concept of the firm as a collection of contracts originated with Alchian and Demsetz (1972) and was extended by Klein (1983). This perspective is often contrasted with the transaction-cost approach, as, for example, by Johanson and Mattson (1987), but the presentation here illustrates the essential complementarity of the two approaches.

The theory of games originated with von Neumann and Morgenstern (1944). There are many good nontechnical accounts of game theory. A recent and outstanding one is by Dixit and Nalebuff (1991). As I have tried to do here, they use games to motivate structured thinking about general problems of interaction and interrelationship. Other textbooks (in ascending order of difficulty) are those by Luce and Raiffa

(1957), Rasmusen (1989), and Tirole (1988). Vickers (1985) has a help-ful introduction to business applications of game theory. Fudenberg and Tirole (1987) and Fisher (1989) offer divergent views of the value of game theory in these contexts. The Nash equilibrium was defined in Nash (1950, 1953). A discussion of the variety of alternative solution concepts that have been proposed can be found in Harsanyi and Selten (1988). Each of the principal games described here has a literature of its own. Axelrod (1984) explores experiments in the Prisoner's Di-lemma and its applications across a wide range of disciplines. Cooper et al. (1989) describe experiments in the Battle of the Sexes. Commit-ment and its business applications are emphasized by Ghemawat (1991).

4

Relationships and Contracts

As it was in Chapter 3, my purpose here is to develop concepts that are applied in later chapters. Firms establish many different kinds of commercial relationships, the most common of which is the spot contract, an agreement for an immediate exchange. But many important relationships are made as classical contracts—long-term legal agreements containing provisions specifying how dealings between the parties will evolve as events unfold. A relational contract also is a long-term relationship. But its provisions are often only partly specified, and it is enforced not by legal process but by the parties' need to continue doing business with each other.

Sometimes one of these contract forms is appropriate, sometimes another. Long-term contracts are necessary when both parties must make specific commitments to the relationship. Frequently, however, even though such commitments may be necessary, the critical terms of an agreement cannot be enforced by the courts. This is most often true when timely flows of honest information between the parties are essential or when a flexible response is required in circumstances that cannot be fully anticipated. Here relational contracts come into their own. For example, although marriage is a long-term contract, it is best conducted as a relational one, and the same is often true in business dealings. Some business environments are conducive to relational contracting. Others allow or encourage opportunistic behavior. These differences among firms and among commercial cultures are important to the nature of competitive advantage in firms and nations.

Most business relationships are made on the basis of spot contracts. I sell, you buy, and that is that. We might or might not engage in a similar transaction next week or next year. Spot contracts are easy to make and cheap to transact. They do not need lengthy negotiation, nor are expensive lawyers called to draft their provisions. Spot contracts are based on standard terms and take place at market prices.

We make so many spot contracts that we often hardly think of them as contracts at all, and the law infers a contractual intention from our behavior. When I buy lettuce at a supermarket, it is as if I say to the

produce manager's assistant, "I offer to buy this lettuce at the price displayed," and he or she replies, "As an authorized representative of the
supermarket, I accept your offer." Even lawyers do not actually conduct
such conversations. But later, if there is any dispute, the courts will act
as though such an exchange did take place. It is most unlikely, however,

Illustration 4.1.   Three Spot Contracts

that there would be such a dispute. The transaction is complete, and there is not much left to have a dispute about. And the unit value of a lettuce is so low that it is not worth either party's time to engage in litigation. If I buy meat that turns out to be spoiled from my local market, then next time I will shop elsewhere. If I buy a disappointing peach from a street vendor when I am on my vacation, then I will write off my losses to experience.

But although spot contracts form a majority—by number—of business relationships, the most important commercial relationships are rarely spot contracts. Managers do not raise money, rent property, hire senior employees, or deal with their principal suppliers through spot contracts. Although spot contracts predominate in number in business portfolios, they rarely predominate in value. Spot contracts are effective when individually selfish behavior works to the best joint interest of the parties. I have, you want, we exchange. We may need to haggle a little over terms, but that is all. But many relationships require cooperation, coordination, and differentiation, or they benefit from commitment. Both parties will do better if they pursue a recognized joint interest or if they need to agree to do the same thing, or different things. Such relationships risk falling victim to the Prisoner's Dilemma, the Battle of the Sexes, or Chicken.

Chapter 3 showed how these problems can often be resolved by changing the payoff structure or by engaging in a repeated game. In either case, the behavior of each party is conditional on the earlier behavior of the other. This means that the contract becomes *contingent*—it contains statements of the form "if x then y"—and it acquires a time dimension and so becomes a long-term contract. These interrelated features distinguish *classical* and *relational* contracts from spot contracts. Classical contracts are *explicit*—they correspond to changes in the payoff structure—and relational contracts are *implicit*—they are expressions of strategies for playing a repeated game.

The Weakness of Spot Contracts

Why do firms make long-term classical contracts for their building or location but buy paper clips through a spot contract? Buildings (properties) are individual commodities. Most people buy a house because it suits their own particular needs. The same is often true of business premises. If the firm were evicted tomorrow, it could find a substitute, but an imperfect one. And a property is a large purchase. The rent bill is often the largest single payment that firms make to any supplier. The contract therefore is important, and if you have made a shrewd deal, you would like to be sure you can get an equally good one tomorrow. The same is true for a landlord, as a vacant property may lead to a significant loss of income. Both sides to the bargain thus value the certainty provided by a long-term relationship.

There is another reason for entering a long-term relationship. If a company moves into an office, it will print stationery with its address. It may buy furniture to fit. It will install a telephone and computer system. In all these ways, it incurs substantial expenditures specific to that office and that address. Before a firm moves in, it probably has the choice of many equally good properties. But after it moves in, the property selected will be much preferred to any likely alternative, and this gives the landlord a strong bargaining position. Under a system of spot contracts, the landlord could promise a low rent and then attempt to increase it after the tenant had made a commitment to the property. Knowing that this might happen, however, the tenant would be reluctant to move in at all. Whenever there are expenditures specific to an individual buyer or seller, there is scope for such opportunistic behavior. A long-term relationship protects the tenant against opportunism by the landlord.

The landlord may have similar feelings. He will incur costs if the tenant moves out abruptly. He will have to pay an agent to find a new tenant and will lose rent in the interim. By threatening to move out and impose these costs, the tenant might hope to renegotiate a lower rent. A long-term relationship protects the landlord against such opportunism by the tenant.

These business relationships require an investment specific to the relationship. Sometimes such an investment is tangible. Subcontractors manufacturing automobile components may need to dedicate their tooling to producing an item designed according to the requirements of an

Illustration 4.2.   A Classical Contract

The property lease provides for

Period of tenure
Rent
Repair and maintenance obligations
Use of premises
Rights of assignment
Basis of adjustment to rent
Rights to regain occupancy
Basis of resolution of dispute

individual assembler. A gasoline retailer must identify his pumps in the Texaco or Chevron style. Often the investment is intangible—the firm needs to learn its customers' systems or their special requirements. A McDonald's franchisee must study the McDonald's manuals; a solicitor or accountant can advise effectively only when she understands her client. The sharing of information may be important to making the best of a relationship, yet frankness may leave the parties to a spot contract exposed and in a weak position to negotiate good terms. It is obvious that banking and insurance will work to the best advantage of everyone in the long run if banks and insurance companies are well informed about the risks they assume. Yet in every spot contract with a bank or insurance company, the borrower or the insured has an incentive to represent his or her position in the best possible light.

Asset specificity—the need to dedicate an investment to a particular transaction or business relationship—is an important reason for making long-term contracts, but not the only one. If there are few buyers or sellers of a particular commodity, it is risky to rely on spot contracts. You cannot be sure—as you can be sure in a wider market—that there will be a continuing stream of sellers or buyers ready to supply or to purchase your output at a fair price. So standard commodities are bought on spot contracts, but managers look for longer-term arrangements for specialized components.

It is often supposed that long-term assets require the support of long-term contracts. In reality, the scope of spot contracts is much wider. A firm may buy business stationery every month and a shopper may visit the local supermarket every week, but it is likely that they will make a separate spot contract with the stationer and the supermarket on each occasion. The stationery supplier will set up a distribution system, and retailers will build their supermarket without any long-term contracts whatever for selling their output. Both parties are willing to make sub-

Illustration 4.3.   Spot and Long-Term Contracts

Common spot contracts	Common long-term contracts
Standard components	Customized components
Capital goods purchase	Capital goods finance
Variable-rate finance	Fixed-rate finance

stantial capital expenditures that rely entirely on a succession of spot contracts for their viability. Although a good taxicab will last ten years, all cab drivers make spot contracts with their passengers. Indeed, spot contracts are intrinsic to the service that taxicabs provide. Much business is conducted using long-lived assets financed by revenues earned from spot contracts.

Long-term relationships are necessary to secure cooperative, or coordinated, behavior. Mutual commitments are essential, or information flows are important, or a flexible response is necessary, and the parties cannot achieve what they need by means of a simple bilateral exchange. Long-term relationships with competitors are needed if Chicken games are to be avoided or disastrous outcomes to them are to be averted. Sometimes these long-term relationships are best established through classical contracts—formal, binding, legal arrangements. Sometimes they are better accomplished by means of relational contracts—tacit agreements between the parties that are enforced not through legal processes but through the parties' shared needs to continue doing business with each other.

Relational Contracts

What legal theorists call a *relational contract* is termed an *implicit contract* by economists and a *trust relationship* by sociologists. All these terms denote important aspects of these arrangements. The enforcement mechanism is between the parties themselves, not through the courts, and the lawyer's formulation stresses this. The terms of the relationship are not written down and often cannot be precisely articulated; hence the term *implicit contract*. The relationship depends on trust between the parties and is not—in the terms in which the word is commonly used—a contract at all.

The most familiar relational contract is the marriage contract. It is intended to be long term and generally is. Most of its rights and duties are implicit, with the remainder determined by agreement between the parties. The courts provide a means by which the parties to the contract can escape from it, but as long as it remains in force, they will generally not be interested in enforcing its terms.

To see why a relational contract is used here, it is necessary only to look at attempts to define marriage according to a classical contract. Although the Canadian contract is, no doubt, an effective contract, it does not cover any important aspects of the relationship. The American con-

Illustration 4.4.   Marriage Contracts

Extracts from a Canadian marriage contract

In consideration of the mutual love and affection of the husband and wife, they agree as follows:

1. The spouses acknowledge that, except as set out in the Marriage Contract, Part I of the Family Law Act, 1986, SO 1986, Chapter 4, as amended from time to time will apply to them. . . .
2. The spouses acknowledge that this Marriage Contract is not to be construed as a bar now or at any time in the future to the spouses entering into other Marriage Contracts or other domestic contracts. . . .
6. If there is any dispute as to the ownership of Property, title to any Property shall be conclusive proof of the separate ownership of the Property. . . .

Extracts from an American marriage contract

Relationships with others, jealousy, and trust

The parties agree to discuss plans for activities that involve persons of the opposite sex when the other party is not involved, and where such activities are not directly a part of one's work.

They also agree to allow each other the power to veto such activities for a six month period. . . .

Realising that trust is built by practical arrangements as well as by good intentions, the parties also agree to set aside one evening during the week and one evening each weekend to spend alone together. . . . A calendar will be posted two months in advance.

Care and use of the home

The household work schedule now in effect, which assigns household tasks . . . will be attached as a modifiable amendment to this agreement. . . .

The parties agree to continue their current practice of assigning one person the task of inspecting household work for cleanliness and neatness. Once a month, when Robert is inspector, we will conform to his standards. He will conform to the standards set by the other three inspectors in their weeks.

Source: Law Society (1991).

---

tract does seek to do that, but most people who read it know that such an agreement will not work. Indeed, the attempt to define the arrangement in these terms denies its essence. It sacrifices the responsiveness and frankness that are at the heart of a successful personal relationship. In such a contract, the parties trust each other not to abuse the opportunities that such openness creates and acknowledge that the disadvantages of a detailed specification of rights and mutual obligations would far outweigh the benefits of clarifying what these rights and obligations are. Most people enter marriage on the basis that it is far more important—even from their own selfish perspective—to maximize their joint welfare than to maximize their share of it through hard negotiation with their partner. They look for a larger cake rather than a larger slice.

An employment contract is usually a relational contract. As do all business arrangements, it contains a formal legal contract. But this is not the substantive agreement, and usually its provisions become relevant only when the relational contract is terminated by one or the other party. Indeed, so important are the relational elements of an employment contract that "working to rule"—strict observance of the terms of the legal contract—is sometimes used as a form of industrial action and can be seriously disruptive. Relational contracts usually have a legal heart, but they also are used when the commercial reality is different. In a relational contract, the parties have expectations of each other that go beyond—perhaps far beyond—the terms of the contract.

Employment contracts are best made as relational contracts because they suffer rather than benefit from too precise a specification of their obligations. Each party must be encouraged to respond to events. Both parties must invest in teaching and learning that is specific to the particular business environment. Actions may often have consequences that emerge only much later. Each of these factors—response, information, and learning—tends to become more important at higher levels of seniority in the organization. A firm may hire a cleaner through a spot con-

Illustration 4.5. An Employment Contract

Normally mentioned

Job title
Sickness and pension arrangements
Hours of work
Holiday entitlement
Initial pay
Termination arrangements

Normally not mentioned

Specific responsibilities
Basis on which pay adusted
Promotion procedures
Expected performance

Sometimes mentioned

Managers to whom responsible

tract—the job is well defined, the performance is easily monitored—but it needs a relational contract with its management. The range of jobs for which spot contracting is suitable is steadily diminishing.

Relational or Classical Contracts?

Relational contracts work best when all parties recognize that they are bound to a repeated game. Lifetime employment, seniority-based promotion, generous pension schemes, and other forms of deferred remuneration all serve this purpose. Although many managers have come to see these as outmoded ways of doing business, this is often a serious error.

Relational contracts generally are advantageous when the returns to the parties to the contract are more sensitive to the size of the cake than to its division. This is true also when the advantages of flexibility in the relationship between the parties, or a rapid flow of information between them, are important to the joint outcome. A classical contract is designed to eliminate flexibility: What each party must do is, as far as possible, precisely defined by the terms of the contract. Conversely, a relational contract allows flexibility and often encourages it. A classical contract inhibits the free flow of information, as such information might be used against one of the parties. In a relational contract, however, information flows are the most natural thing in the world. This is why fashion businesses are generally characterized by relational contracts. Designers, manufacturers, and retailers have established associations. Legally, these take the form of a series of spot contracts, but in practice, both sides assume that they are continuing affiliations. They expect to be provided with the latest designs and also to be willing to stock them.

If the advantages of relational contracts are so obvious, why is not all business done in that way? The reason is that relational contracts also have disadvantages. There is an inevitable conflict between the desire to

Illustration 4.6. Classical Versus Relational Contracts

Common classical contracts	Common relational contracts
Finance	Employment contracts with skilled workers
Property leases	Professional services
Long-term energy contracts	Relationships among fashion designers, manufacturers, and retailers

get the best deal and the development of a relational contract. It is intrinsic to the relational contract that the parties to it do not obtain the best spot contract that they could achieve on all, or perhaps any, occasions. The Prisoner's Dilemma framework clearly illustrates this. A good relational contract here leads to a "nice–nice" outcome being achieved in each repetition of the game. Yet in every single trial, both parties know that they could do better by being nasty. In business contexts, there is never any shortage of tough bargainers who will point that out. The primary advantage of a relational contract is that it allows an easy flow of information. Yet every textbook on negotiation emphasizes the importance of maximizing information advantages. In the fashion business, all parties benefit from a speedy flow of accurate data concerning the popularity of individual items. But the way to get the best price is to manage that flow of information strategically. As a manufacturer, I want to ensure that retailers accept my slow-selling lines as well as my hot properties. As a retailer, I want to get adequate stocks of winners before they are generally recognized as winners. So both parties lie. The sales force tells retailers how well the dud lines are doing elsewhere; retailers express reluctance to stock goods for which they know customers are clamoring.

If I believe that I am a good bargainer or that I enjoy the stronger bargaining position, I may be reluctant to enter a relational contract. Relational contracts often rest on an even division of the gains from contracting between the parties to the contract. It is not impossible to have a relational contract between unequal parties, but it is harder. It is harder still if the relative strength of the two parties varies over time and either or both wish to see this reflected in the terms of the exchange. In such a context, the tension between maximizing the value of the contract through freely sharing information and maximizing the firm's own share of it is evident. We have to care more about what we get than about who gets it, and often this is impossible (or wrong).

The Problem of Opportunism

Strategies for reiterated games, such as relational contracts, work as long as the game continues indefinitely. But they will break down if one or the other party believes that the game is likely to end. Both prisoners will confess on the last trial of the Prisoner's Dilemma, and worse still, if they believe the last occasion may be approaching, they will start to confess right away. Opportunistic behavior occurs in relational contracts when one or the other party believes—perhaps rightly, perhaps wrongly—that it pays to exploit the relationship even if that will lead to its termination.

One purpose of a long-term contract—whether relational or classical—is to induce the parties to invest in the relationship. McDonald's franchisees have to learn the McDonald system. They must then buy equipment and fittings that are specialized not only for hamburgers but also for that particular hamburger franchise. A car component supplier must tool up for an individual manufacturer. Professional advisers must expect to spend time getting to know their clients.

A relational contract allows scope for opportunism once these investments have been made. If McDonald's wishes to impose new and onerous demands on its franchisees, their ability to resist will be much weaker after they have assumed the franchise than before. If the franchisees had known what would be proposed, they might have preferred to join a different chain or stay out of the hamburger business altogether. They might therefore prefer the security of a classical contract. An automobile component supplier risks the possibility that the car manufacturer will seek to drive a harder bargain once the car is in production than it might have before the supplier was committed to the manufacturer. Again, a classical contract, or an arrangement in which the manufacturers fund the capital investment, might be better. A professional firm will be reluctant to invest in a client relationship unless it either is paid for that investment or has a clear expectation of a continuing flow of business.

How do the parties to a relational contract protect themselves against such opportunism? They will be in a stronger position if the other party also has had to make contract-specific expenditures. Insisting on this may even be part of the contract—a process known as *taking hostages*. Many franchise contracts are designed for this purpose—the franchisor imposes particular requirements on the franchisee in order to increase the franchisee's commitment to the relationship. But better insurance against opportunism is for the parties to be truly convinced that they are playing a repeated game.

Relational Contracts and the Business Environment

Short-term gains generally can be made from breaking relational contracts. This follows from the very nature of the relational contract itself. The contractor's freedom of action is not restricted by any legal requirement, but by concern about his or her subsequent reputation. But since these short-term gains are available, breaking a relational contract is a common way of generating immediate profits after acquisitions or buy-outs. Thus, relational contracts are more difficult to make in business environments in which such changes of control are customary. The parties are less certain that the terms of the relational contract will be honored.

In an environment in which relational contracts are unusual or unimportant, opportunism is not necessarily damaging to reputation. This may be cultural. The strongly individualistic values of the United States mean that the penalties for opportunism are often low. Taking maximum advantage of a strong bargaining position may be seen as good business rather than questionable practice. In countries like Switzerland, Italy, or Japan, however, social attitudes are different, and opportunistic behavior may prove personally and professionally damaging. Industries vary also in their capacity to develop relational contracts. Most of us deal with a particular real estate broker only once. We expect real estate brokers to behave opportunistically, so they do little damage to their reputation when they do behave opportunistically. Most of all, it is easier to develop relational contracts if you already have many relational contracts. The value of a reputation for fair dealing is apparent to all, and it creates networks and clusters of relational contracts. Some firms and industries trade extensively in this way; others hardly at all. Some economies are characterized by the widespread use of relational contracts; others seldom use them. The next chapter describes how architecture, a firm's network of relational contracts, can be used by firms to establish a competitive advantage.

This chapter draws on largely separate but parallel thinking in law, economics, and sociology. The concept of relational contracts in legal theory originated principally with Macneil (1974, 1978, 1980). Economists use the term implicit, or incomplete, contracts to refer to the same phenomenon. Olson (1965) has an early account. Grossman and Hart (1983, 1986) made major contributions to this theory, and Hart (1988) provides a survey. In a sociological framework, MacAulay (1963) offers a seminal discussion of the same issues. The concept of trust relationships belongs to Fox (1974). The interaction between trust and social structures is spelled out by Granovetter (1985) and Zucker (1986). A valuable synthesis is provided by Bradach and Eccles (1989) and abridged in Thompson et al. (1991). Schleifer and Summers (1988) analyze the takeover phenomenon in terms of opportunism.

The idea that a firm's economic role is defined by its contracts originated with Coase (1937, 1988) but emerged more clearly from Alchian
and Demsetz (1972). Williamson used the phrase "a nexus of treaties"
to describe this approach. I believe the term treaties also has many inappropriate connotations and so preferred to couch the discussion in
this book in terms of contracts and relationships. Aoki, Gustaffson, and
Williamson (1990) contains a number of contributions in this vein.
Reve (1990) is a specific attempt to base a discussion of corporate strategy on a transaction-cost view of the firm. The analysis of organization
structure in terms of contract design is often called the principal–agent
problem. For this, see Fama (1980), Fama and Jensen (1983), Hart and
Moore (1990), Jensen and Meckling (1976), and Pratt and Zeckhauser
(1985). Eisenhardt (1989) is a business-oriented survey.

III

DISTINCTIVE CAPABILITIES

A firm is defined by its contracts and relationships. It adds value by successfully putting these contracts and relationships together; that is, it is the quality and distinctiveness of these contracts that add value. This distinctiveness is at least as important as the quality, because in an efficient market there are few opportunities to make good contracts.

The term *efficient market* is most frequently used in financial markets.[1] An efficient market is simply one in which there are no bargains, because what can be known about the item being sold is already reflected in its price. The advice "Buy Wal-Mart shares because Wal-Mart is a well-managed company with an outstanding business franchise" is worthless, even if it is a type of advice that is often given, because these facts about Wal-Mart are well known and already fully incorporated in the value of its securities.

In broader business terms, the more general implications of market efficiency are much the same. Opportunities that are available to everyone will not be profitable for everyone or perhaps anyone; what other people can equally see and do is unlikely to be a sustained source of added value. So the question that every firm must ask of an apparently profitable opportunity is, "Why will we be better at doing that than other people will?" This is not a justification for the conservative executive we all have met who disparages every new proposal on the grounds that anything worth doing has already been done. Often the question, "Why will we be better at doing that than other people will?" has a clear and affirmative answer, and it is typically those firms that can give that answer and act on it that are successful.

The efficient-market hypothesis denies that there is such a thing as an objectively attractive or unattractive industry or, more precisely, denies that it will remain fundamentally attractive or

---

[1] Fama (1970) is the principal survey of evidence on the efficient market hypothesis, which is described in any good finance text, for example, Brealey and Myers (1991, chap. 13). The June 1977 *Journal of Financial Economics* is a survey of anomalies in market behavior.

unattractive for long. This means that it directly conflicts with the portfolio-planning approach to strategy, one of the most influential styles of thinking of the last two decades. I consider this issue more extensively in Chapter 11.

The implication of the efficient-market hypothesis is that value cannot be added on a sustained basis simply by making better contracts than other people do, since these opportunities are unlikely to remain. Instead, value is added by creating a set of relationships that others are unable to create. A firm can add value only on the basis of some distinctive capability—some feature of its relationships that other firms lack and cannot readily reproduce.

The firm may make a new contract or arrangement of contracts, perhaps for a new type of good or service, such as ordinary product or process innovations. Or the innovation might lie in the form of the contract itself, as is often the case for financial services. The difficulty in establishing a competitive advantage from this source is soon apparent: Most innovation can be quickly replicated. Sustained competitive advantage depends on the ability to protect the innovation, through legal restriction (Merck's patents, Microsoft's copyrights) or through strategy.

Value can be added if customers or suppliers are systematically willing to undertake relationships on terms that they would not make available to other people. Usually this is the result of the supplier's reputation. For example, international car rental firms offer the same models of cars on the same terms as local firms do, but at higher prices. They attract customers not because the quality and reliability of their service is necessarily any better but because these customers believe that the reputation of the franchisor ensures that quality and reliability. Reputation is often—as in this case—associated with a brand name.

The distinctiveness of a firm's relationships may rest in the group of contracts taken as a whole. Although any part of it can be reproduced, the complexity of the set defies imitation. Typically, this requires that many contracts have implicit, or relational, terms. If you can write down a contract, others can also implement it.

A firm with no distinctive capability may still achieve a competitive advantage if it holds a strategic asset. A concession to exploit a resource or an exclusive right to supply is a strategic asset. In other markets, being first or being the incumbent firm may in itself confer an advantage over any potential entrant. Some

Table III.1.   Sources of Competitive Advantage

Company	Distinctive Capability or Strategic Asset
Abbott Laboratories	Reputation with customers
Astra	Innovation (particularly Losec)
Canal +	Strategic asset (licensing)
Coca-Cola	Brand
Disney	Historic repertoire
Elsevier	Reputation (established scientific journal titles)
Glaxo	Innovation (particularly Zantac)
Kellogg	Brand
Liz Claiborne	Architecture (supplier and distribution relationships, brand)
LVMH	Brand
Marsh & McLellan	Architecture (market networking)
Merck	Innovation
Microsoft	Standard (MS-DOS, Windows)
Nike	Architecture (subcontracting and marketing relationships)
Nintendo	Standard
Philip Morris	Brand
Reuters	Strategic asset (incumbency), reputation
Wrigley	Brand

companies are no better—and perhaps are worse—than other firms would be at the activities they perform—but they enjoy the strategic asset that they alone perform them.

The firms described in Chapter 2 illustrate all these sources of competitive advantage—architecture, reputation, innovation, and strategic assets (Table III.1). Marsh & McLellan and, to a degree, Liz Claiborne and Nike have competitive advantages based on the structure of their relationships. Coke, Philip Morris, and Wrigley have powerful brands; Abbott Labs and Marsh & McLellan demonstrate that reputation can be a competitive advantage without necessarily being derived from consumer advertising. Merck, Microsoft, and Astra have competitive advantages based on innovation; Reuters and Microsoft enjoy strategic assets.

METHODIST COLLEGE LIBRARY
Fayetteville, N.C.

5

Architecture

Architecture is the first of the three principal sources of distinctive capability. It is the network of relational contracts within or around a firm. Firms may establish these relationships with and among their employees (internal architecture), with their suppliers or customers (external architecture), or among a group of firms engaged in related activities (networks).

The value of architecture rests in the capacity of organizations that use it to create organizational knowledge and routines, to respond flexibly to changing circumstances, and to achieve easy and open exchanges of information. Each of these is capable of creating an asset for the firm—organizational knowledge that is more valuable than the sum of individual knowledge, flexibility, and responsiveness that extends to the institution as well as to its members.

Accordingly, I introduce architecture through the experience of the Boston Celtics, who have both consistently performed well and consistently performed better than the individual talents of their players would seem to allow. This distinction between the attributes of the firm and the attributes of its members is important to appreciating both the social and the commercial implications of architecture. But such structures can be created and protected from imitation only in a framework of relational contracts. What can be written down can be reproduced. Architecture therefore depends on the ability of the firm to build and sustain long-term relationships and to establish an environment that penalizes opportunistic behavior. As with other distinctive capabilities, it is easier to sustain architecture than to set out to create it.

Some companies—like Procter & Gamble or Hewlett-Packard—have a powerful and identifiable corporate culture. The term *culture* has been widely used, and abused, in business over the last few years, often to refer to rather superficial aspects of corporate organization. But in regard to these firms, everyone knows what is meant. Although admiration for their products and their achievements in the marketplace is virtually universal, these firms' culture is not to everyone's taste. Employees are,

in the main, fiercely loyal, and those who find the organization uncongenial leave.

Both companies have a rich history that relates the modern company
to its founders. Harvey Procter devised the marketing strategy for Ivory
soap in church; Dave Packard invented management by walking around.
But the myths that surround these figures draw attention away from central current reality: how little either organization depends on any one
person or group of persons. Each company has established a structure, a
style, a set of routines, that operates to get the best out of relatively ordinary employees, and these routines have continued to produce exceptional corporate results for many years and through many changes in the
economic environment.

Other styles of management also are distinctive and also are successful. In the last twenty years, Japanese firms have dominated the consumer electronics industry and have become market leaders in automobiles. Initially, their output was exported from Japan, but in the face of
the rising value of the yen and protectionist reactions in both Europe
and the United States, they have shifted production to the West. Honda
now builds cars in Ohio, and Akai makes video equipment in Nor-
mandy. In Western environments, these firms have pursued Japanese
styles of relationships with subcontractors and employees and have
achieved impressive levels of quality and productivity. They have succeeded in avoiding the alienation and abrasive labor relations seen in
large-scale assembly activities in most Western countries and have built
demanding but productive associations with their suppliers.

These facts are well known, especially to the Western competitors
of these Japanese firms. The successful implementation of these Japanese
models in the West, however, has been undertaken by Japanese companies. Those competitors that have responded most forcefully, such as
Ford and Caterpillar, did so through the more effective implementation
of a traditional Western management style. At the same time, an important part of the Western automobile and consumer electronics industries is now based in newly established plants in rural areas, with new
workers and new management systems, under Japanese ownership and
control, while much of the indigenous industry has closed down.
Change has been effected, not incrementally, but by starting again. The
structure of commercial relationships has been fundamentally and per-
manently influenced by the past experience of these relationships.

The power of shared knowledge and established routines benefits
more than just large companies. The Lumezzane valley in Brescia in
northern Italy is not on many tourist itineraries. Although its natural
scenery is attractive, its calm is shattered by the noise from hundreds of

small metalworking establishments, which often continues late into the night. In some parts of the valley it seems as though almost every house has a small factory attached. Casual tourists would probably be surprised that this style of economic organization has lasted so long. Indeed, they might plan to revisit Lumezzane in a few years' time when these industries have finally been swept away by the forces of international competition, reinforced by global marketing and the research and development and quality control resources that only large firms can command.

That assumption could hardly be more wrong. Far from threatening Lumezzane, the opening of international markets has brought unparalleled prosperity. Most of the valley's output is exported, and the region is one of the richest in Italy. Nor does it rely simply on traditional craft skills. Lumezzane is a market leader in a range of sophisticated metal-manufacturing products, including valves, taps, and the customized machine tools used in their production. The structure of the relationships among the small firms of the Lumezzane valley, often specializing in a single component of the final product—which gives each access to the knowledge, abilities, and resources of the whole—has given Lumezzane a competitive advantage in its markets that has endured and grown.

There are strong common elements in these very different stories of organizational design and evolution—the corporate cultures of Procter & Gamble and Hewlett-Packard, the style of Japanese management, the networks of Lumezzane. In each, there is a pattern of relationships variously within firms, around firms, and among firms that is complex, subtle, and hard to define precisely or to replicate. This pattern is the product of history, and it is almost impossible to reproduce in the absence of that history. It is also a pattern of relationships that can bring a substantial competitive advantage to those firms or groups of firms. Their com-

Illustration 5.1.   Architecture

- -

Types of architecture

Internal	Between the firm and its employees and among employees
External	Between the firm and its suppliers or customers
Networks	Between a group of collaborating firms

How architecture adds value to individual contributions

Through the creation of organizational knowledge
Through the establishment of a cooperative ethic
By the implementation of organizational routines

- -

petitive advantage typically arises through the acquisition of organizational knowledge, the establishment of organizational routines, and the development of a cooperative ethic. This allows a flexible response, the sharing of information, and a process in which the monitoring of quality is such a natural characteristic of the organization that it is often barely necessary to make it explicit.

These patterns of relationships are the distinctive capability that I call *architecture*. They rest on relational contracts; they rely on a strong sense that the participants are players in a repeated game; and by doing so, they offer answers to the problems of cooperation, coordination, and commitment. Their distinctiveness comes partly from the implicit terms characteristic of the relational contract—what cannot easily be written down cannot easily be reproduced—and partly from the overall complexity of the structure, of which no one person sees, knows, or understands more than a small segment. In Chapter 2, I explained why corporate success depended on establishing a capability within the organization that was greater than the sum of the capabilities of the people within it. Thus architecture is distinct from "excellence," which often derives from the excellence of the raw material. The remainder of this chapter elucidates these themes.

An organization with a distinctive architecture, like Procter & Gamble or Hewlett-Packard, often emphasizes its dependence on its people. But this dependence should be interpreted in a particular way. That is, the organization is dependent on its people taken as a whole, because the product of the organization is the product of this collectivity. It is not dependent on any single person; everyone in the organization is readily replaceable. It is only in these circumstances that added value can be appropriated for the organization itself.

The Boston Celtics

In Chapter 2, I described the outstanding basketball league performance of the Boston Celtics. The essence of this club's achievement is not just that it has done well; it has added value by attaining a performance for the team that is better than would have been predicted from the quality of its players. What are the origins of the Celtic's achievements (or the almost comparable performance of the Los Angeles Lakers)? If we were to build a model of the game of basketball, it would show that every time a player has the ball, he faces the alternative of shooting for a goal or passing it to a better-placed player. If he passes the ball to a player of a caliber similar to his own, he will score fewer goals, but the team will score more. If everyone in the team plays a passing game, every member of it can expect to score more goals than they could if their normal instinct was to shoot. That choice is repeated every minute in every match the team plays. The choice that each player makes is influenced by his expectations about the behavior of the other players to whom he passes. One is more inclined to pass to players who are themselves inclined to pass.

This is, of course, a Prisoner's Dilemma, and an understanding of the Prisoner's Dilemma makes clear why simply pointing out the benefits of cooperative behavior—the passing game—is insufficient to bring it about. Even when these benefits are understood, selfishness is still the rational response. Nor is it enough to make rewards collective rather than individual, as this only substitutes one Prisoner's Dilemma for another. If there are no direct returns for individual effort, everyone's best course of action will be to ease off.

The Celtics illustrate the principal ways in which architecture can form the basis of a distinctive capability. The club has created an intangible asset—its organizational knowledge—which, although it is derived from the contributions of individual members, belongs to the firm and not to the individual members and cannot be appropriated by them. In some organizational routines, such as complex maneuvers perfected through practice, each player fulfills his own role without needing, or necessarily having, a picture of the whole. And in the cooperative ethic of the "passing game," the player's instinct is to maximize the number

Illustration 5.2.   The Cooperative Ethic

The military contract demands the total and almost unconditional subordination of the interests of the individual if the interests of the group should require it.

The military leader who views his oath of office as merely a contractual arrangement with his government sets the stage for a style of leadership critically different from the leader who views that oath as his pledge to contribute to the common good of his society. For the former, "duty, honour, country" is a slogan adopted temporarily until the contract is completed; for the latter, "duty, honour, country" is a way of life adopted for the good of all and accepted as a moral commitment not subject to contractual negotiations.

Source: van Fleet (1984).

of goals the club scores rather than the number of goals he himself scores. Each of these sources of sporting success has its precise business analogies.

Most firms hope to establish a cooperative ethic. But the essential question here is how to create consummate, rather than perfunctory, cooperation. Although consummate cooperation is often achieved in small groups, it is rarely attainable across large organizations, in which strategic bargaining among units is generally inevitable. Still less often is it accomplished among firms or within groups of firms. Perfunctory cooperation marks the limit of what can be prescribed in a spot or classical contract. Consummate cooperation demands a deeper relationship.

The sporting metaphor illustrates the distinction well. If basketball were a more predictable game than it is, the team manager could define a set of instructions that would specify when players should hold the ball, when they should pass, and when they should shoot. He could monitor the players' adherence to his instructions and reward or punish them accordingly. This would be the analogue of running a business according to a comprehensive system of classical contracts. It is how some coaches—rarely the best—try to run their teams, and it is also how some managers—rarely the best—try to run their businesses.

The reasons that such a structure would not work in basketball are clear enough. The game moves too fast and unpredictably for the instructions to be able to deal with the almost infinite variety of situations that might arise. This might not matter if the coach were always in a position to shout orders from the line—another common characteristic of bad coaches—but no coach is in a position to obtain, or to assimilate sufficiently quickly, the range of information that the players must process every minute. The need for a rapid response and for the quick absorption and exchange of information means that the passing game can be implemented only by the players themselves. It cannot be imposed. The maintenance of a cooperative ethic relies on the underlying structure of relational contracts—the unwritten rules, the tacit understandings, the common purpose that is sustained by the expectation of all parties that these will be part of the continuing relationships.

These structures are of particular value—and here the basketball analogy is again helpful—when the nature of the business requires flexible responses and a ready exchange of information. Fashion businesses or film and television production are good examples. Sometimes the architecture is internal—the key cooperative ethic is within the firm itself, as it is for the Celtics. Sometimes it is external—the passing game is played between the firm and its customers or suppliers or among a group of cooperating firms in the same industry. Often both characteristics are found in combination.

Organizational Knowledge

All firms possess organizational knowledge in the sense that an insurance company knows about insurance and an automobile manufacturer knows about automobiles. But what an insurance company knows about insurance is, as a rule, what its employees know about insurance and is much the same as what other insurance companies know about insurance. Organizational knowledge, as I define it here, is distinctive to the firm, is more than the sum of the expertise of those who work in the firm, and is not available to other firms. If an insurance company builds up data and skills in the assessment of a particular category of risk, and if those data and these skills are truly those of the company and not those of a small group of employees, then it has created organizational knowledge. And this organizational knowledge gives it a distinctive capability and may yield a competitive advantage in the market for that risk category. In the purest form of organizational knowledge, each employee knows one digit of the code that opens the safe; such information is of value only when combined with the information held by all the others. The analogy makes clear, too, why the issue is important: Any person who knows the whole code has access to the safe.

For some firms—professional service firms and many small companies in high-tech industries—technical knowledge is the business. But if the company is to add value, it needs to create organizational knowledge from the skills of its members, which can be achieved when the combined skills of two experts increases the value of each. The problems that the organization faces are, first, those of securing this exchange of knowledge and, second, those of preventing that knowledge and the rewards associated with it from being captured by one or both of the people concerned. Both issues have been evident in major accounting firms in which the supposed synergies between auditing and consulting have increasingly turned into tension for precisely these reasons.

Organizational knowledge is more easily captured by the firm when it results from the specific application of generally available technology. For instance, most of an automobile company's knowledge base is derived from technical skills that are general to the industry, but the now very large investment in the development of individual models leads to the creation of organizational knowledge specific to that design. The

Illustration 5.3.   Internal Architecture

While firms all around it split up, merge, or oust partners, Cravath[a] continues to employ a pie-division system that approximates our price sharing model, does no lateral hiring, has no written partnership agreement, and apparently suffers no defections. And the explanation for so stable a sharing model[b] seems clear. If the earnings figures are correct, it seems unlikely that very many of the Cravath partners could make more money elsewhere. In other words, there is plenty of firm-specific capital to "glue" the partnership together.

Contrast a Washington firm that split up:

Partners believed that rainmaking was credited so much and with such rigidity that partners' individual interests were put ahead of the firm's overall interests. The system allowed certain partners to establish their own fiefdoms without any regard to the firm as a whole.

But not all law firms succeed in this way:

Of the two firms widely considered to be the nation's most profitable, one—Cravath, Swaine and Moore—uses a sharing model and the other—Skadden, Arps, Slate, Meagher and Flom—follows a marginal product approach.

[a]Cravath, Swaine and Moore, perhaps the most prestigious Wall Street law firm.

[b]The remuneration of partners is determined entirely by seniority and does not depend on individual performance.

Source: Gilson and Mnookin (1985), 351, 355–56, 392.

application of information systems in a bank raises similar issues. The requirement here is to turn individual expertise into business know-how. The problem of reappropriation hardly arises in such a case. Rather, the difficulty is capturing the expertise in the first place. By passing on their expertise, experts give up precisely what makes them valuable to the organization, and this can be a rational strategy only in the context of a relational contract and a repeated game. This is especially true of consultants for whom the buildup of skills within the client organization is a threat to their continued role.

Organizational knowledge is often distinctive only at the cost of being applicable to a narrowly defined market. Large competitive advantages come when the organizational knowledge is unique, appropriable to the firm, and relevant to a market that is large or to a range of markets that is wide. This does not happen often. It was, perhaps, achieved for a time by IBM but eroded even there as the knowledge base became diffused and the market more fragmented.

In other cases, organizational knowledge may take the form of organizational systems and routines. This is very much a key part of the effectiveness of strong retailers, and indeed, it is the power of routines that lies behind the capacity of military organizations to turn inexperienced youths into a disciplined force. The transcription of individual expertise into organizational routine is a means by which some professional service firms—particularly management consultants such as McKinsey or Bain—seek to add value that arises from, and adheres to, the organization and not just to the able persons within it.

The Sources of Architecture

Boston's achievements are the product of a structure of relational contracts. The relationships among the players are rich and complex but implicit, resting on repetition and reciprocation. There is no room for team spirit in a world of spot or classical contracts. Instead, distinctive capabilities in organizational design must rest on relational contracting, for two reasons. One is the essential Prisoner's Dilemma characteristic of the "passing game," of the sharing of information, of flexibility in response. It is in everyone's collective interest to do these things, but in no one's individual interest. One can benefit from a cooperative ethic, or the knowledge and expertise of others, only in a context of reiteration and reciprocation.

This is apparent in organizations that have established a strong architecture. There is an expectation of long-term relationships both within the firm and among its members, a commitment to sharing the rewards of collective achievement, and a high but structured degree of informality. This informality is sometimes mistaken for disorganization—in popular discussions of chaos, entrepreneurship, or adhocracy as conditions for innovation—but truly chaotic organizations rarely perform well, and a system of relational contracts substitutes an extensive set of unwritten rules and expectations of behavior for the formal obligations of the classical contract.

If we look at historic examples of immensely powerful organiza-

Illustration 5.4.   Relational Contracting with Dealers

Cat [Caterpillar] tied the dealers close to it by enhancing the dealers' position as entrepreneurs. . . . The company conducted regular training programs for dealers and product demonstrations for their customers. It even offered a course in Peoria for dealers' children, encouraging them to remain in the family business. Cat's chairman summed up his company's attitude, "We approach our dealers as partners in the enterprise, not as agents or middlemen. We worry as much about their performance as they do themselves."

Source: Harvard Business School (HBS) (1985), p. 7.

tional architectures—those of ancient Greece and Rome, medieval Italy, and British India—we see that all of them were characterized by unwritten codes of behavior, of great strength and considerable complexity. Indeed, many of the tragic heroes of literature are people who, for apparently good reasons, broke these codes and were destroyed by them.

But there is a closely related issue of imitability. If the structure of relationships underpinning corporate architecture can be formalized, it also can be imitated and so will at that point cease to be a source of competitive advantage. Much as been written about Procter & Gamble and Hewlett-Packard. Many employees have left these companies and are available for other firms to hire. Yet attempts to replicate the architecture of these organizations has not been comparably successful. Clearly, there is more to the architecture than this literature contains—more to the architecture than any individual employee, or group of employees, knows. Neither reading the book nor recruiting the employee is sufficient to reproduce the Procter & Gamble or Hewlett-Packard architecture.

Internal Architecture

Internal architecture is the structure of relational contracts between a firm and its employees and among the members themselves. Some features of a firm's formal structure follow immediately from that definition: Jobs are secure if the labor contract is a spot contract; it cannot be a relational one. This stability of employment must be mutual; it is not just that the firm rarely terminates the contract but, rather, that the employee rarely chooses to leave. There is a flat remuneration structure, or at least one in which differentials reflect seniority as well as merit, and performance is measured by reference to intangible as well as tangible criteria. If the labor contract is a classical contract, it cannot be a relational one.

Relational contracting offers scope for opportunistic behavior. In the main, the firm is concerned about its reputation in future relational contracts, and this is a sufficient deterrent to its own opportunistic behavior. But it needs to protect itself against such behavior in its employees. Remuneration may be deferred, through seniority-related payment structures or generous pension arrangements. Opportunism among employees is inhibited by linking social and business life. Geographical concentration, or domination of a town by a single company, often helps, and so does the recruitment of employees of a similar background or personality type.

The objective is to stimulate collective rather than individualistic behavior. Indeed, the suppression of individuality is a serious objective of army training, for very necessary reasons. If soldiers thought of themselves as individuals rather than as part of a collectivity, the irrationality of sacrificing the individual for the collectivity would immediately become apparent.

All of this produces disadvantages as well as benefits. For most people, working for the company never has as powerful a motivation as does working for oneself. Since firms with a strong internal architecture tend to restrict individuality and to recruit employees of a characteristic and familiar type, inflexibility is a potential weakness of such a structure. It is easier to keep a supertanker on course than it is a flotilla of small ships. And the supertanker is more effective at plowing through choppy seas. But changing the course of the supertanker may be more demanding, and organizations with a distinctive architecture, including successful ones like IBM, have often proved to be monothematic or rigid.

Competitive advantages may accrue from structures that are so distinctive that others find them hard to reproduce—or, conceivably, may not wish to reproduce. Such cultures are powerful weapons, as the continued success of Procter & Gamble or Hewlett-Packard or a number of Japanese corporations demonstrates, but like many powerful weapons, they also are dangerous ones. That is, they are dangerous to themselves: Many of the most potent corporate cultures of the past are associated with organizations—such as railroads and shipyards—that no longer exist or, like the Ford Motor Company, have been forced to abandon these cultures in order to survive. Sometimes, furthermore, such strong cultures have appeared more widely threatening.

Although most organizations with a strong internal architecture—whether the Boston Celtics or Procter & Gamble—would be described as firms with a strong corporate culture, architecture and corporate culture are not the same. Drexel Burnham Lambert had a strong, if deeply unattractive, corporate culture built around highly individualistic behavior. The elaborate rituals surrounding the marketing activities of life insurance companies may be classed as corporate culture, if culture is defined as patterns of collective behavior, but they are in no sense internal architecture. In these companies, strengthening individual motivation is everything. Cooperative behavior is not necessary or expected; organizational knowledge is minimal; and organizational routines are purely administrative.

If the passing game creates problems as well as solving them, then the same is true of organizational knowledge. We all are familiar with companies whose organizational knowledge is of the kind, "We don't do things that way here" or "We tried that in 1970 and it didn't work." Organizational routines may be pursued for their own sake long after their purpose has vanished. Such structures can have negative value:

Illustration 5.5.   Contracts Without Architecture

Milken expounded on this point, saying, "I would say there is no second in command. You could say on some days there's one hundred seventy people that are second in command, and other days, you know, there's ten. It depends on what's happening, what the situation is. People have responsibilities, rather than a formal organization chart."

Indeed, someone once tried to draw an organization chart of Milken's group and it became a joke, a maze of crisscrossing lines, which was then screened onto T-shirts. Thenceforth, Milken's group was dubbed the "T-shirt organization."

If the absence of clearly defined responsibilities caused some pushing and shoving among a highly aggressive and incentivized group of people, Milken probably did not mind. According to one former member of this group, Milken preferred that there be a certain amount of friction among his people, so that they would not develop alliances—and he could better maintain control.

Source: Bruck (1989).

The whole is less than the sum of the parts; the organization produces less than the sum of the talents of its individual members.

External Architecture and Networks

External architecture is found in firms that share knowledge or establish fast response times on the basis of a series of relational contracts between or among them. Marks & Spencer, now Britain's leading retailer, pioneered a system, first for clothing and later for a wider range of commodities, particularly food. The retailer comes up with a detailed product design, and then these products are manufactured by a few suppliers whose activities are closely monitored. These suppliers often commit a major portion of their output to Marks & Spencer, and many of them have been suppliers to the company for decades, although there are no formal long-term agreements between them. These are very clear and very potent examples of relational contracts.

The merit of such relational contracts is that they facilitate the sharing of product knowledge and encourage a flexibility of response. These advantages are important to businesses such as fashion retailing, in which the customers' requirements may change rapidly and there is strategic posturing by both parties. These arrangements again expose both sides to the risks of opportunistic behavior. Typically, this is inhibited by the reputation of the parties to the relational contract and by the investment of both sides in the relationship.

Networks are groups of firms that make relational contracts with one another. The metalworkers of Lumezzane were described earlier, but

Illustration 5.6. Contracts with Suppliers

It was to Sears' advantage to have its suppliers sell their own national brand because it forced the manufacturer to keep up new product development. Though Sears could design its own products, it did not have the engineering capability necessary for continued development of new features or imitation of competitors. . . .

Sears' response was to develop strong ties with Whirlpool (home laundry and refrigeration/freezers), Design and Manufacturing (distributors), and Roper (rangers), but to avoid ownership. Of these three companies, Sears had a controlling interest only in Roper and this position was reduced from 76% to 59% by the sale of 300,000 shares of Roper stock in 1965. One observer commented that, "The mutual dependency between these suppliers and Sears allows Sears to buy at a low price while allowing the suppliers a fair profit, especially when the cost savings on their other sales are considered. And then," he said, "the Sears organization takes over."

Source: Christensen, Andrews, and Bower (1978).

many other Italian products, from tiles to ties, are manufactured by geographically concentrated groupings of small firms. Typically, these firms share, draw on, and contribute to a common knowledge and skill base; make spare capacity available to one another; and implicitly and explicitly monitor one another's quality while retaining a speed of response and a degree of motivation that large firms find difficult to emulate. Although Italy has developed this form of organization particularly far, an analogous network can be found in Silicon Valley, California. Such networks are particularly important to financial services and explain the continued preeminence of New York as a financial center, even though its economic power seems to have moved elsewhere. These networks create distinctive capabilities for both firms and groups of firms.

The "pulling power" of J. P. Morgan is based on the strength of its list of corporate and institutional clients. Competitive advantage in brokering generally rests on similar factors. The competitive strength of Lloyd's of London in the world insurance market is due to the ability of many underwriters gathered in a single room to exchange information relevant to risk assessment.

Some firms have obtained a competitive advantage by developing distinctive supply networks, often in areas of the world that others have found difficult to penetrate. United Brands achieved this in Central and South America, and Japan's *sōgo shōsha*, trading companies at the center of the *zaibatsu*, were for a long time at the core of Japanese economic development. As with all other types of competitive advantage, the profitability of this type of architecture rests on the inability of others to replicate it. In advanced economies, no company can expect to achieve the sort of position that a firm like United Brands enjoys in the

Illustration 5.7.   Architecture in Networks

- -

[A] nation's competitive industries are not spread evenly through the economy but are connected in what I term *clusters* consisting of industries related by links of various kinds.

Source: Porter (1990).

When an industry has thus chosen a locality for itself, it is likely to stay there long; so great are the advantages which people following the same skilled trade get from near neighbourhood to one another. The mysteries of the trade become no mysteries; but are as it were in the air, and children learn many of them unconsciously. Good work is rightly appreciated, inventions and improvements in machinery, in processes and the general organization of the business have their merits promptly discussed; if one man starts a new idea, it is taken up by others and combined with suggestions of their own; and thus it becomes the source of further new ideas.

Source: Marshall (1890).

- -

countries in which it operates. Even so, in small countries, a dominant local firm may develop a unique network of contacts and interrelationships. In Belgium, Société générale has achieved that position, with interests across much of Belgian industry and finance. When the Italian Carlo de Benedetti saw a takeover of the somewhat sleepy Société as a means of enhancing his Pan-European ambitions, the political strength of the company, on top of its economic interests, enabled it to survive his attack.

Architecture in Japan

Japanese industry has been the most successful in creating distinctive capabilities through architecture. In Japan we can identify the power of internal architecture, external architecture, and networks.

The "three pillars" of the internal labor market in Japanese firms are lifetime employment, the seniority system, and enterprise unionism. The lifetime employment system emphasizes the long-term relationship between the employee and the company. But even Japanese companies, particularly small ones, cannot completely predict their labor requirements, and so fluctuations are dealt with by employing part-time or irregular workers on spot contracts without damaging the basic lifetime employment system. Although lifetime employment is associated mainly with Japanese companies, employment relationships in large continental European firms are similar. Labor practices in the United States, however, are very different.

The seniority system in wage determination and in promotion, heavy investment in on-the-job training that is specific to the company, and an emphasis on enterprise unionism are similarly designed to support relational contracting. The industrially based structure of Western unionism is designed to increase the union's negotiating power by diluting the common interests of firm and worker. The Japanese system is intended to reinforce the identity of that interest. As in any relational contract, these concerns are reciprocated in the emphasis that Japanese managers place on their employees' interests over those of the shareholders.

Continuity and stability in supplier/assembler relationships are well-known features of Japanese business, and firms such as Toyota and NEC are surrounded by their *keiretsu*, or supplier group. Just-in-time inventory management, as developed by Toyota, is a striking example of a structure possible only under relational contracting. The urgent demand requires the urgent willing response of the partner in a long-term relationship, not the hard-nosed spot contract that can be used when the opposing party is most vulnerable. In the United States, customized components are generally manufactured in-house or by wholly owned subsidiaries of the assembler (Monteverde and Teece 1982). In Japan, such items are produced by independent members of the *keiretsu* who are willing to take the risk of establishing dedicated production facilities and installing transaction-specific assets. The same supply processes are achieved through classical contracting in one country and through relational contracting in the other.

Japan has a long tradition of cooperative groupings of companies, originating in the *zaibatsu* which were dissolved by the Allies after World War II. Today's networks are looser associations of companies. Some of these *kigyō shūdan*, such as the Mitsui group, are descendants of the *zaibatsu*, and others, such as Daiichi Kangyō, are new formations. These groups typically include one company in each main industrial sector, including a bank and a trading company, commonly with reciprocal shareholdings among members of the group.

Although there is some presumption in favor of intergroup trading among these networks, members of them also trade extensively with Japanese companies outside the group. The power of the network seems to rest partly on the exchange of information through it (hence the emphasis on "one-set-ism," the requirement that the group contain precisely one company in each sector) and on the group's ready ability to support transactions that benefit from relational contracting, such as financing, overseas distribution, and joint venture.

The Social Context of Architecture

The Japanese experience and the contrast between Japan and the United States illustrate the degree to which relational contracting and architecture are the product of the broader commercial and social environment. Geographical proximity is important to networking, although the role it plays is not entirely obvious. Since transporting ties is neither slow nor expensive, why are most Italian ties produced in a single small region? At first sight, it seems absurd that at a time when capital markets have become international and when the worldwide communication of data, funds, and information has become instantaneous, the financial institutions of the world should be concentrated in tiny and fabulously expensive areas of lower Manhattan and eastern London.

What lies behind this is the need to establish trust and penalize opportunism in a network of relational contracts, which is facilitated if business relationships are supported by a corresponding network of social relationships. We all are more inclined to trust people we know, a view partly based on instinct and emotion, partly on our capacity to make our own judgments (we also are inclined to mistrust some people we know), and partly on a rational calculation that people are less likely to cheat us if by doing so they will sacrifice a social reputation as well as a commercial one.

The country club plays an important, if imprecisely defined, role in the business life of many American towns. The City of London's preeminence rested on the homogeneity of background and values created by the English class system and the English school system. In this way, architecture is rooted in a particular historical and social context, and so conscious attempts to emulate the competitive advantages of networking through replication are rarely successful. The extensive entertainment that is integral to Japanese business similarly serves to reinforce relational contracts.

It follows that some social environments are more conducive than others are to the development of competitive advantage through architecture. Since the essence of architecture is that organizations or groups of organizations have values—social and economic—different from those of their members, there is a direct conflict between individualism and the creation of architecture. This conflict is reinforced by the absence of powerful sanctions against opportunistic behavior in an individualistic environment. Competitive strengths based on these architectures are therefore relatively rare in those environments where the prevailing ethos is strongly individualistic. Where they do exist—such as in the financial sector, in networking activities in less developed countries, and in the performance of companies with a very distinctive corporate ethos—the activities concerned are commonly viewed by outsiders with a degree of hostility and suspicion. Nepotism is a term of abuse; contact networks are corrupt; and the organization man is regarded with uneasy laughter.

Our reaction is the same when we hear about Japanese workers gathering to sing the company song. But our incomprehension of this cultural divide applies also to countries where the difference is less apparent. Networking in Italian communities has resurfaced in the United States in the form of criminal conspiracies and political corruption (as it has in Italy also), and we feel relieved when it is stamped out, but we also observe it in Italy itself as a potent form of commercial organization. It would be wrong to make too much of the cultural origins of competitive advantage through architecture. Many relational contracts are made in the United States, and many classical contracts are made in Japan. But it would be equally wrong to ignore them.

The relationship between organizational structure and firm performance is a subject pursued in sociology, in economics, and in popular management literature. The most substantive tradition is in organizational behavior—indeed, Weber's (1925) principal concern was with precisely these issues—but the more recent literature begins with Burns and Stalker (1966) and Child and the Aston group (Child 1974, 1975, 1984). Mintzberg (1979) is a managerially oriented synthesis. In economics, see, for example, Arrow (1974), Cyert and March (1963), Simon (1961), and Williamson (1975, 1985) and, for an empirical analysis, Steer and Cable (1978). Among management books, Peters and Waterman (1982) is the originator of "excellence"; Morgan (1986) describes the style of organizations in terms of metaphors. Hampden-Turner (1990a, 1990b), Kono (1990), and O'Reilly (1989) review "corporate culture." Camerer and Vepsalainen (1991) assess culture in a manner closer in spirit to the arguments here. Although the style is very different, there are many similarities between my approach and that of Lloyd (1990).

On the more specific concerns of this chapter, the intermediate ground between markets and hierarchies has been delineated by writers from a variety of different perspectives. Thompson et al. (1991) is a valuable collection of articles drawing on these different disciplines. Richardson (1972) is an early contribution in economics; Pfeffer and Nowak (1976) (interorganizational behavior), and Miles and Snow (1986) (networks) in sociological terms; whereas Johnston and Lawrence (1988) dis-

cuss "the value-adding partnership." Other contributions on networks include Blois (1990), Jarillo (1988, 1990), and Thorelli (1986). Joint ventures and strategic alliances are currently in fashion, and discussions of them include Hamel et al. (1989), Norburn and Schoenberg (1990), and Ohmae (1989).

The distribution of the product whose whole exceeds the sum of its individual contributions is described by the economic theory of teams (Akerlof 1976, Marschak and Radner 1972, and Radner 1985). Organizational routines are identified by Nelson and Winter (1982) as a source of competitive advantage. Organizational knowledge is developed as "core competence" by Prahalad and Hamel (1990). The role of trust in exchange is emphasized in different ways by Arrow (1974), Hirschman (1982), and Ouchi (1981). Zucker (1986) provides a historical analysis of the way in which trust relationships are supported by organizational form and the social and cultural environment. Gambetta (1990) is a collection of related essays.

Italian networks have been widely studied. See Lorenzoni (1979), Piore and Sabel (1984), and Porter (1990). Lorenz (1991) describes analogous relationships in French industry. Gerlach (1987) and Odagiri (1991) emphasize the role of networks in Japanese management. The operations of Japanese companies in the West are described in Dunning (1986) and Gordon (1988).

6

Reputation

The second principal distinctive capability is reputation. Reputation is the most important commercial mechanism for conveying information to consumers. But reputation is not equally important in all markets because customers find out about product characteristics and product quality in many ways. Sometimes they learn from searching. Other attributes become apparent as soon as a product is used. The importance of reputation can be seen in those markets—from car rental to accounting—to which product quality is important but can be identified only through long-term experience. In these markets, reputations are difficult and costly to create but, once established, can yield substantial added value.

Most of this chapter is concerned with how reputations are built, maintained, and lost. The process of building up a reputation can be accelerated by staking a reputation that has been established in a related market or by making a clear public demonstration of a commitment to a market. But it does not always pay to maintain a reputation. Indeed, the best strategy may be to milk it. In some markets this is so often true that few worthwhile reputations survive.

Reputation has been important to successful traders since preindustrial society. Merchants were concerned with demonstrating the purity of their assays or the fullness of their measure. Craftsmen stressed the quality of their workmanship. But how were their ignorant customers to judge purity, fullness, or quality?

Sometimes they looked to the state to regulate the market for them. In other cases, traders banded together in guilds to monitor one another's work and, in that way, established an honest reputation for the whole group. Some craftsmen relied on their own name or that of their family. All these mechanisms are still important today.

Reputation is the market's method of dealing with those attributes of product quality that customers cannot easily monitor for themselves. The composition of an apparently precious metal is such a characteristic. It is more costly to offer an assay of the declared specification. It is less profitable, in the short run, to provide a full measure or good workmanship. The quality trader can thus recover the higher costs of good quality only if consumers know that the quality is good. If customers do not know this, then the firm will incur higher costs but not obtain a higher price. This is both a problem and an opportunity.

In a market in which consumers can easily ascertain the characteristics of the goods they buy, there is no reason that in the long run, the price of any characteristic—including better quality—should exceed the cost of providing it. But if a product's quality cannot easily be established, then the firm that can give its customers not only higher quality but also the assurance of higher quality may be able to command a price premium far exceeding the difference in costs.

Firms convey information about their products to their customers through advertising and branding. But firms also tell customers about their products in other ways—most notably through the product itself. Nor is providing information about product quality the only function that branding and advertising serve.

Reputation also needs to have a name attached to it, whether it is the name of a person, a profession, or a company. In some markets in which quality standards are variable, names like Hertz or Avis, Price Waterhouse or Peat Marwick command large price premiums (Table 6.1). Both car rental and international accounting firms offer goods whose quality their customers have difficulty assessing in advance, and major firms with strong brand names have come to dominate these markets. Yet in other markets—used cars or real estate —the sales agents generally are held in low regard. Car manufacturers have tried to remedy this by offering quality certification, but these efforts have not proved very successful. This chapter defines the narrow class of markets in which building reputations can be a powerful source of competitive advantage, and it explains how firms have achieved it.

Table 6.1. The Cost of a Car, an Accountant, and a Reputation

Renting an Economy Car in New York, per Week (1994, U.S.$)		Hiring an Accountant in Dublin, per Hour (1990, £1R)	
Hertz	450	Partner, international firm	90
Alamo	356	Manager, international firm	60
Avis	289		
ABC	269	Partner, local firm	40
NY Rent-a-Car	249	Manager, local firm	30
Arrow	239		

Source: Quotations by firms; Davis, Hanlon, and Kay (1992).

Search and Experience Goods

Consumers find out in many ways about the quality of the goods they buy. They may learn by searching—inspecting the good or service and comparing it and its specific features with alternatives. When a customer takes a train journey or buys oranges or a camera, he or she establishes most of what needs to be known about the commodity before purchasing it.

You cannot learn much about the taste of the soup in a can or the flavor of the beer in a bottle before you buy it. But you do discover these things almost as soon as you consume them. Knowledge of the quality of other commodities is acquired only slowly. For example, it takes time to tell whether a cure for baldness is actually promoting the regrowth of your hair. Perhaps experience is difficult to interpret. If you recover from an illness, you do not know whether the reason was that you consulted a good doctor or whether you would have gotten better anyway. Often reliability is the key attribute. Reliability may be represented by the consistent flavor of a McDonald's hamburger, the frequency with which a machine breaks down, or the soundness of a professional adviser's opinions. In each case it is only time and extensive experience that will tell.

Some goods are consumed on behalf of other people, and they may be slow to convey their experience of them to you. Few people will tell you whether your underarm deodorant or breath freshener is working or what they really think of the wine or whisky you serve them. You have to infer your cat's opinion of its food. Learning about the quality of these products is a slow process. Experience is even less useful if commodities are purchased infrequently, but it is a surer guide to a brand of beer or shampoo than to a vacation destination or a real estate broker.

There is a small category of goods to which neither search nor experience is of much value. Some goods cannot be inspected and are consumed only once, like pension plans and funeral services. But there are less extreme instances. Search yields little information about the efficiency and reliability of a consumer durable such as a washing machine or a car. Experience does offer such information, but by the time the consumer is ready to purchase again, the range of models available may well be quite different. One seldom buys exactly the same dishwasher twice even if it is an excellent one. For such goods, neither search nor experience helps much, and so consumers use other criteria in making their choices. They rely on their knowledge of the manufacturer (as distinct from their experience of the product), on the advice of the retailer, or on the recommendations of consumer magazines or trusted friends.

Most goods have many different characteristics. Some properties are revealed by search; others emerge immediately upon consumption; and yet others are discovered through long-term experience. There almost always are some attributes that are never ascertained at all. But although no hard and fast distinctions can, or should, be made, the ways in which customers acquire information have important influences on market structure. Table 6.2 categorizes some goods by reference to the principal ways in which consumers learn about their salient characteristics. This classification largely determines the ways in which these goods are sold and influences the nature of the competitive advantage in different markets and industries.

How Producers Convey Information About Products' Characteristics

All producers need to convey to prospective purchasers information about their goods and services. It may relate to the *availability* of the product. Indeed, the simple fact of availability is often the essential content of the advertisement. This is what the classified ad "Bicycle, $100, call 123–4567" is saying. It is aimed at consumers who already know they want a bicycle and are well informed about the properties of a bicycle. The advertisement also indicates the means of availability. Often it is unnecessary to explain how you buy the product—consumers already know that branded food is on sale in supermarkets. But advertising may be necessary to bring about that availability in the first place. Supermarkets have limited shelf space and therefore will stock a new product only if they believe that advertising will generate sufficient initial demand.

Manufacturers also need to convey information about the product's *features*. Marlboro cigarettes are made from fine Virginia tobaccos. A Golf GTi has a top speed of 120 MPH. Some Minolta cameras have an autofocus facility. Full specifications of cars or cameras may often be

Table 6.2. How Buyers Learn About Products' Characteristics

Search	Immediate Experience	Long-Term Experience	In Other Ways
Office furniture	Beer	Medicines	Computers
Clothes	Canned food	Detergents	Shares
Fresh fruit	Newspapers	Accountants	Pension plans
Electricity	Caterers	Managers	Dishwashers
Term loans	Production workers	Security services	

Illustration 6.1.   What Consumers Need to Know About Products

Subject	What the Producer tells them
Product availability	
Where and how you buy it.	The truth.
Product specification	
What it is, what it does, and what it costs. Who is likely to buy it.	A generous interpretation of the truth.
Product quality	The producer's claims are not credible.

lengthy, and so an efficient method of briefly describing a product's features often is to offer information about the characteristics of *potential* buyers. It is possible to say, "These trousers are made from heavy-gauge denim with a pleated front," but it may be easier and more effective to say, "Jeans for the fashion-conscious generation." More concisely still, you can simply show a picture of the wearer. Producers also wish to convey information about the *quality* of their goods, and they will be more anxious to do so if the quality of their goods is high than if it is not.

All attempts to convey such information are governed by a fundamental principle: *Information is credible only if the provider has an incentive to tell the truth.* In general, producers want to be as accurate as possible about the availability of their product. It is not sensible to announce that a product is available if it is not (preemptive product announcements are an exception), and producers want to be as specific as possible about where it is available.

It is generally futile and frequently illegal to specify inaccurately the verifiable aspects of a product. There is no point in saying that a camera has autofocus if it does not. The publishers of this book have a difficult task to perform in describing its potential readership. If they assert that "everyone should read this book," they run the risk that those for whom the book is truly intended will not be able to distinguish it from the many other volumes in the bookstore. On the other hand, if they define the category of potential readers too precisely, they may deter some potential purchasers. They therefore should err on the generous side of accuracy. A real estate broker gains nothing by describing a small bungalow as a mansion, since the purchaser will discover that this description is false. But some exaggeration may induce prospective purchasers to inspect the property. Other aspects of it may then appeal to them and lead them to buy it. So descriptions may be flattering but not absurd.

We typically buy high-value items by assembling, from a variety of sources, a short list of possible products and examining it more carefully. An important function of advertising is to encourage you to put the advertiser's product on your short list. But it is simply a waste of time to be short-listed for jobs to which you will never be appointed. When we apply for a job, we describe our skills and experience generously, but we are foolish if we claim skills we do not have. The descriptions of features and of potential buyers given in advertisements may contain some exaggeration, but not too much. We all recognize this and discount accordingly.

The Product-Quality Game

What about those performance characteristics that consumers cannot readily verify? In particular, how do producers communicate information about the quality of their product? Manufacturers have an incentive to exaggerate, and they do. Consumers have an incentive to view these claims skeptically, and they do. The product-quality game is shown in Figure 6.1. We would usually be better off if producers told the truth and were believed, but this does not happen because a low-level Prisoner's Dilemma equilibrium prevails.

Its presence leads directly to a second problem: If the producer is unable to communicate a product's quality effectively, what should he do? Consider the following problem:

> A commodity can be made to a high- or low-quality specification. Goods of known low quality command much lower prices, which reflect the trouble they will cause and the expenditure necessary for repair, maintenance, and replacement. These costs far exceed the additional cost to the manufacturer of ensuring a high-quality specification. What if customers cannot tell, by inspection or immediate experience, whether the good is of high or low quality? They can offer to pay the high price or the low one; they might receive a high-quality item or a poor-quality one.

This is another Prisoner's Dilemma (Figure 6.2). The consumer offers a low price and receives a low-quality product. Both consumer and producer would be better off in the high-price–high-quality position. But even if both recognize that, they cannot bring it about, either unilaterally or by agreement. Chapter 3 described the two ways of escaping from a Prisoner's Dilemma.

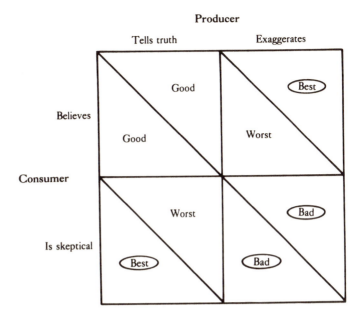

Figure 6.1.   The Product-Quality Game: Stage 1

One way is to change the payoff structure, and the second is to play the game repeatedly. There are no others. If buyers and sellers are engaged in one-shot transactions in which the buyers cannot monitor the quality of the product, then it is almost inevitable that their expectations will be low and that the sellers will fulfill these expectations. This is what goes wrong in the used car and real estate markets.

These means of escaping the two Prisoner's Dilemmas correspond to the two ways in which companies play the product-quality game— commitment (a way of changing the payoffs) and reputation (a readiness to play the game repeatedly). Frequently, these two strategies are combined. Indeed, commitment is the most common means of imitating the creation of a reputation. The most common strategies involve

- Introductory offers, warranties, and money-back guarantees
- Substantial advertising and launching expenditures
- Staking a reputation derived from elsewhere

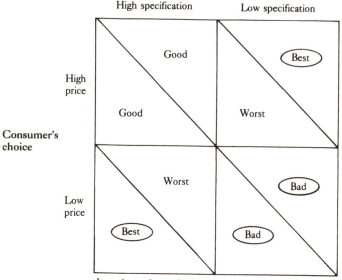

In each quadrant, the bottom left payoff is for Player 1 and the upper right for Player 2. Circles indicate that a payoff is the best outcome for that player, given the strategy of the other.

Figure 6.2.   The Product-Quality Game: Stage 2

Building a Reputation

Japanese producers of automobiles and hi-fi equipment chose to change the payoff structure of Figure 6.2 when they entered the market. Although the manufacturers knew that their products were of high quality, their potential customers did not. In fact, many of them believed that Japanese goods were shoddy imitations of Western products. Accordingly, Japanese manufacturers offered more extensive warranties than had been usual in the car and hi-fi markets. The effect of an extended warranty is twofold. It will save you money if the product breaks. But the purchaser is typically looking not so much for insurance against fault when it occurs as assurance that fault will not occur. An extended warranty is expensive to offer if your product is likely to go wrong. Offering it, therefore, gives you an incentive to keep the quality high and is a credible demonstration of your faith in the product. A producer who offers an extended warranty is making a commitment that will prove expensive if—but only if—the product is unreliable.

Advertising is a similar statement of *commitment*. We have just spent millions of dollars drawing your attention to our product, says the advertiser (implicitly). If we intended to disappoint your expectations, to withdraw from the market, or to produce a poor-quality product, that would be a foolish thing for us to have done. The advertisement assures the reader that the product is good, but not because it says that the product is good. Indeed, it does not say the product is good, and if it did, the claim would be viewed with appropriate skepticism. Rather, the assurance that the product is good comes from the mere fact that the advertiser advertises. And the strength of this assurance is directly related to the amount that the advertiser spends. Otherwise it would be difficult to explain the prevalence of advertising. It is inconceivable that many people are unaware that Marlboro is a cigarette or Coca-Cola is a soft drink. The very ubiquity of their advertisements is a measure of the manufacturer's commitment to the marketplace.

This chain of consumer reasoning is, of course, implicit rather than explicit. Consumer experience has confirmed that heavily advertised products tend to be of relatively good quality, and so consumers react accordingly. Observing this reaction, producers have found that advertising is an effective means of signaling quality to the marketplace.

This historical evolution can be seen in Figure 6.3. The 1905 advertisement emphasizes the qualities of Coca-Cola—delightful, palatable, healthful, indispensable, the favorite drink of ladies. But why should the customer believe these assertions? Would not the Coca-Cola Corporation make them even if Coca-Cola were unpalatable, not healthful, and entirely dispensable? The 1990 advertisement gives no information whatsoever about the product. "Coke is it." "It's the real thing." It is difficult to think of valid grammatical constructions with less content. Over a shorter period, Philip Morris abandoned any reference to the "clean fresh taste" or "all-day smoking enjoyment." One of the most successful marketing campaigns in history invites you only to "come to Marlboro country. Where the flavor is." And cigarette advertising has continued despite restrictions in most countries precluding advertisers from making any claims at all about the product. Advertising began from the belief that customers could be persuaded that quality was high by repeated assertion that it was high. But it no longer tries to do that; instead, the medium itself has now become the message. The persuasive quality arises from the fact, not the content, of advertising.

The advertising we see and read falls into two broad categories. Some advertising is designed to convey information about a product's availability or features. Such advertising can apply equally to all the categories of commodities defined in Table 6.2—to search goods, like cam-

"Coca-Cola" and the Countour Bottle design are registered trademarks of The Coca-Cola Company.

Figure 6.3. How Advertising Has Evolved

eras; to short-term experience goods, like beer; to long-term experience goods, like pet food; and to consumer durables to which experience is of little value. And then there is advertising that supports a brand; it is conspicuously expensive and generally uninformative. Such expenditures make sense only if the brand that is established through this activity is correspondingly valuable.

Spreading a Reputation

Brand extension—taking a reputation established in one market to another—is a third means of establishing one's commitment and staking one's reputation. Endorsement by famous personalities is a curious, but very clear, example of how a reputation can be spread. Everyone knows that the celebrities give their endorsement not because they have scoured the market for the best product but because they have canvased their potential sponsors for the highest fee. So why are consumers influenced by such an endorsement?

Purchasers of the endorsed product are not behaving entirely irrationally. The sportsman is, to some degree, putting his reputation at risk. If the product is of low quality, he will damage his sporting reputation and his value to other sponsors, and he therefore should have some incentive to ensure that the product meets its avowed standards. For the manufacturer, payment of the endorsement fee is a demonstration of its commitment to the market. Willingness to pay the endorsement fee is therefore actually a measure of the product's quality. All parties are concerned about demonstrating their intention to participate in a reiterated game.

Endorsement is, of course, simply the most explicit example of the most common mechanism for developing a reputation in a new market quickly: staking a reputation that has been acquired in another market. BMW's reputation in cars reinforces its reputation in motorbikes, and vice versa. BMW also endorses a range of "Active Line" sportswear. There is little reason to believe that the capabilities distinguishing BMW cars are applicable to the manufacture of sportswear. But since the revenue from the sale of sportswear is very small relative to the revenue from the sale of BMW cars, it would clearly be foolish for BMW to attach its name to poor-quality sportswear. The company is, however, pushing it a bit. If it were to endorse, say, garden furniture, it is not clear that its reputation would genuinely be at stake. If the garden furniture is disappointing, why should this lead me to think worse of BMW cars? The likely consequence is that the BMW logo is less likely to be effective in selling garden furniture, and indeed the attempt to do so may actually damage BMW's reputation as a whole, by suggesting that the owner is careless of its value.

Maintaining or Devaluing a Reputation

Since reputations are difficult and costly to establish, traders with good reputations might be expected to work hard to sustain them. Usually they do. But a reputation for good quality is valuable to those who provide poor quality as well as those who provide good quality. Sometimes, in fact, it may be more valuable to those whose quality is poor. Swindlers have been aware of this for millennia. On a more modest scale, spreading a reputation may ultimately stretch to milking it. Hilton began as a brand name for a premium hotel. But the Hilton hotel group devalued the product. It first sold its hotels outside the United States to an airline, TWA, which had limited skills in hotel management and a public reputation that, although not bad, did not compare with the original Hilton image. Within the United States, the Hilton Hotel Corporation expanded through franchising. In 1970, it owned three-quarters of the hotel rooms that bore its name, but by the mid-1980s, this proportion was little more than one-third. Then the company moved into casinos and suffered the humiliation of being refused a license to operate in Atlantic City, New Jersey. Toward the end of the decade, the U.S. group began to trade under a new brand name, Conrad Hotels, and joined with the new owners of the international hotels in a marketing campaign to restore the name's jaded image.

Maintaining a reputation is most worthwhile if two conditions are met. The first is that the premium available for providing high quality—or, more precisely, the premium for being known to provide high quality—is large relative to the cost of providing high quality. It is not much more costly to be a good doctor than a bad doctor, and so this makes a good reputation particularly valuable to a medical practitioner. It is cheaper for Toyota to ensure high standards in its cars than it is for some other producers, and so this makes Toyota's reputation for reliability especially important to it.

The value of a reputation also depends on the likelihood of a repeat purchase. If you are unlikely to provide the service again, there is little reason to maintain a good reputation. This is another recognizable characteristic of the Prisoner's Dilemma. If you are playing the game only once or for the last time, then the right strategy always is to cheat. In markets in which quality is not easy to determine and in which buyers and sellers generally meet only once, quality is likely to be generally low unless consumers are willing to share their experiences with one another. Risqué nightclubs in unfamiliar cities are generally disappointing.

A reputation is valuable, or worth maintaining, only in a continuing market, and its value disappears with that market. It is difficult to transfer such a reputation to a different product group, and it is likely to be apparent to all that the reputation is of diminishing value in its existing market and consequently a less powerful asset to stake in a new one. The names of the great shipping and railroad companies have, in the main, simply fallen into decline. Where the market continues, however, their reputation may be transferred even if those who provide the service change. Why should lawyers continue to turn with confidence to *Halsbury's Laws of England* when they know that Lord Halsbury has been dead since 1921? The answer is that the current owners of that title (the publishers, Butterworths), perceiving that its reputation for reliability is an asset of considerable value and that the demand for legal reference books is an enduring one, have a powerful incentive to ensure that the current editors maintain high standards.

The Profitability of a Reputation

All firms want to have a good reputation with their customers and the community at large, and it is difficult to imagine any situation in which a good reputation would not be of commercial benefit. But the class of markets in which a good reputation is a source of substantial and sustained competitive advantage is limited.

A reputation is seldom of critical importance when consumers learn about product quality by searching. True, the search is costly, and customers generally proceed by short-listing only a few of the available products. A good reputation helps put you on that list, and a bad reputation can take you off it. But so will other mechanisms, such as advertising, widespread availability, or a retailer's recommendation. A reputation is rarely a major competitive advantage in selling search goods, and branding is the least significant in markets in which consumers learn about products through search (Chapter 16). Nor is a reputation important to immediate-experience goods. If consumers can quickly learn about product quality for themselves, they need not rely much on reputation.

If customers cannot easily determine a product's quality through searching or their own experience, they will be swayed by reputation. If a product's quality does emerge eventually, through long-term experience, then a reputation will be hard to maintain unless its quality is indeed high. It is these reputations that may command high prices.

International car rental firms such as Hertz and Avis are predominantly franchise operations. They provide certification for local traders who would otherwise find it difficult to demonstrate the quality of their product to what—by the very nature of the product—is a transient clientele. Without this certification, these traders would gain nothing by providing quality, since they would not expect to recover the above-average costs of doing so by charging above-average prices. In this market, the price advantage accruing to reputation is very large, as Table 6.1 shows. It is especially large in the business rental market, where reliability is of particular importance. The overall cost of a business trip is such that the greater confidence that one will not spend time at the side of the road waiting for a tow truck is worth buying, even at a high price.

The accounting market is increasingly segmented. The major international firms bring an international reputation to their services. They cater particularly to multinational clients who are often ignorant of the abilities of local practitioners. The reputations of local firms—if they exist at all—are valid only in a local market, and in many countries the best local practitioners now trade under the brand names of the international firms. To what extent are these returns for being the best, and to what extent are they for being perceived (or supposed) to be the best? There is a distinction here in principle, and although in practice it becomes blurred, the answer is critical to the distribution of the added value that a reputation creates. In most markets it is not too difficult for a potential franchisee to meet Hertz's standards, and the returns from the franchise accrue in large measure to the franchisor. In accounting, several international firms often chase only a few outstanding local practitioners. This, together with the partnership structure characteristic of the accounting industry, has ensured that the value added through reputation largely remains in the country in which the service is provided.

In the long run, reputation can be based only on the provision of high quality in repeated trials. Such a record takes longest to establish in precisely those markets for long-term experience goods in which it is most valuable. There is no paradox here—it is precisely what market efficiency would predict. Only after much experience will consumers come to recognize that quality is high, and only after further experience will they recognize that it is consistently high. The process of spreading a reputation is more rapid in markets in which consumers are likely to share their experiences than those in which they are not. We talk to one another about movies we have seen, restaurants we have visited, and stores we have patronized. Reputations are created and destroyed relatively quickly in these markets. We are less inclined to discuss underarm deodorants, and so established reputations in these markets tend to be both profitable and enduring.

Reputations frequently originate from another source of competitive advantage, which may be transformed into a reputation over time or may be supplemented by it. Microsoft's competitive advantage today rests on its innovation and standards in MS-DOS and Windows, and they have given the company a reputation that guarantees the widespread trial of any new product it brings to market. Merck's leading drug, the antihypertensive Vasotec, faces increasing competition from similar products and ultimately, as the patents expire, from generic substitutes. The challenge the company faces, as do other pharmaceutical firms, is to transform its initial innovation advantage into a more sustainable advantage based on reputation.

The same process can be seen at work in many other cases. BMW's initial competitive advantage was based on its architecture, but this has been enhanced—and perhaps overshadowed—by the competitive strength of its reputation. Those firms with another source of competitive advantage are the best placed to develop a reputation. The existence of another competitive advantage is itself an indication of continued commitment to the market, and the returns from that competitive advantage provide a base from which to invest in a future reputation. It is obviously good strategy for Merck to build a reputation for quality in the pharmaceutical market. Not only is it easier and cheaper for the company to build such a reputation than it would be for a generic competitor, but it has an opportunity to do so while still remaining extremely profitable.

My analysis here owes much to the insufficiently acknowledged arguments of Philip Nelson (1970, 1974, 1975). Developments of this can be found in Kihlstrom and Riordan (1984) and Grant (1986). The "lemons" problem—why, in the absence of reputation mechanisms, markets for long-term experience goods rarely work well—is brilliantly expounded by Akerlof (1970).

A substantial economics literature is concerned with the modeling of reputation processes. Spence (1973) first emphasized the importance of signaling in market processes, a theme developed in Kihlstrom and Riordan (1984) and Heil and Robertson (1991). Schmalensee (1978) related this to advertising, and Schapiro (1982) and Milgrom and Roberts (1986) explicitly tie this to reputation. See also Allen (1984), Klein and Leffler (1981), Kreps and Wilson (1982), and Rogerson (1983). The role of brands and warranties is emphasized by Grossman (1981), Lutz (1989), Weigelt and Camerer (1988), Wernerfelt (1988), and Williamson (1983).

Although writers on marketing are mainly concerned with brands rather than the underlying reputation mechanism, see Jacobsen and Aaker (1987) and Jones (1986).

7

Innovation

Innovation is the third principal distinctive capability, and yet firms often fail to gain a competitive advantage from it. In this chapter, I explain why. I describe the costs and uncertainties associated with the process of innovation and the difficulties that firms encounter in securing the returns to innovation for themselves. What appear to be the rewards of innovation are often really the product of the firm's architecture. Some firms have established an architecture that stimulates a continuous process of innovations. Other firms have created an architecture that enables them to implement an innovation particularly effectively.

The process of innovation often involves complex interactions among firms. Two common problems are those in which the innovator can often scoop the pool (patent races) and those in which success for all depends on the establishment of common technical standards (standards battles). This chapter introduces the problems of achieving a competitive advantage that is sustainable and appropriable. I discuss these issues—which apply to all distinctive capabilities—more extensively in Chapters 11 and 12.

*B*usiness history is full of stories about firms that innovated but failed to turn that innovation into a sustainable competitive advantage. For instance, the new electronics industry was pioneered by Texas Instruments and National Semiconducter. Bowmar produced the first handheld calculator. The first commercial jet airliner was made by a European firm called de Havilland. Atari created video games, but it was Nintendo that created a profitable market. SmithKline introduced the first effective antiulcerant, only to lose market leadership to Glaxo. EMI developed the CAT scanner, only to be forced to sell what was left of its loss-making medical electronics business to GE. (The same company had previously led innovation in computers and in television, neither of which it now makes.) Apple, DEC, and Wang first created small computers; Xerox invented the personal computer; and IBM was a late entrant to that market.

This catalog itself demonstrates that there is no single cause of failure to derive commercial success from innovation. The reasons that it is difficult to create a competitive advantage through innovation fall into three categories. First, innovation is, by its very nature, costly and uncertain. It follows that even an innovation that is technically successful may not be profitable. Second, the process of innovation is hard to manage. The direction of innovative companies requires special skills, as does the control of innovation in firms whose market position does not rest principally on their technology. And third, the rewards of innovation are difficult to appropriate. Returns must be defended from competitors, suppliers, and customers and may accrue to groups within the firm rather than to the organization itself. This chapter is concerned with these issues—the process of innovation, the management of innovation, and the appropriability of innovation. The problem of appropriability is a recurrent theme running through every aspect of innovation in business.

The Process of Innovation

Managing innovation is costly and risky. New products may fail because there is no demand or insufficient demand. This is true of more fundamental innovations than the "new" brands of candy or detergent that fast-moving consumer goods markets insist on. Battery-operated cars, three-dimensional cameras, and holograms are more than the brainwaves of the mad inventor caricatures but less than commercial products. The uncertainties go in both directions. Xerox succeeded brilliantly with photocopiers but pioneered both facsimile machines and personal computers only to conclude, quite mistakenly, that these were not commercially viable products.

   If innovation is costly and uncertain, it is nevertheless competitive. The attempt to innovate looks like the game of Figure 7.1, a Chicken-type game. Perhaps there are no winners because everyone holds back. Maybe electric cars would succeed if a major automobile producer devoted enough resources to the venture. The potential gains are very large. If several firms attempt to develop the same innovation, then the effect will be to drive down the returns for everyone, as has repeatedly happened in the aircraft market. The greatest prizes can come from developing a technology that others have rejected. Xerox developed electrostatic reproduction when its potential competitors had concluded the market potential did not justify the investment.

   Chicken structures are most apparent when the innovation is highly appropriable, so that the innovating firm is in a race in which the winner takes all. This is frequently the case in the pharmaceutical industry. In every Chicken game, potential participants need to consider carefully

Firm 2

If innovation succeeded . . .

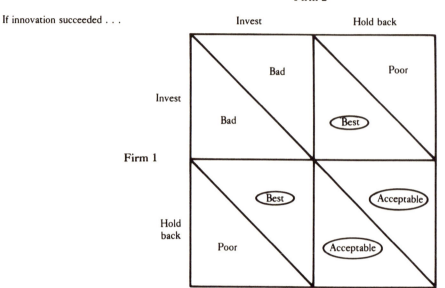

And if it failed . . .

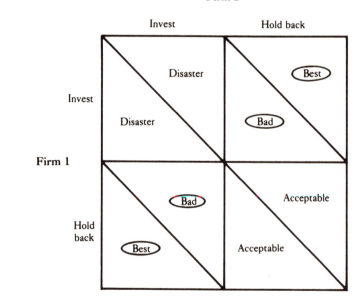

Figure 7.1.   The Innovation Game

whether they wish to play at all. If there are many players, it is quite possible that their combined expenditures will exceed the value of the prize for which they are competing. But if there are few entrants, then large prizes may be available for low stakes.

A variety of strategies are available to escape these difficulties. There is *commitment*—the tactic of pulling off the steering wheel and throwing it out of the window, so that your rivals cannot doubt your intention to stay in the game. The problem of commitment, as the extravagance of this example illustrates, lies in making the commitment credible. The preannouncement of innovative products that have certainly not yet been put in marketable form and may not have even reached a prototype stage has been a regular feature of the recent evolution of the computer industry. It has been such a regular feature, in fact, that such announcements are no longer taken very seriously and so have lost their strategic value. It is difficult for firms to make commitments sufficiently credible, short of legally contracting to supply a product that has not yet been developed. This is a decidedly risky strategy, although it is one adopted by the aircraft industry, in which there is little doubt that the product can be manufactured and uncertainties relate mostly to its cost.

The essence of Chicken is that someone needs to swerve, but there is nothing in the game to tell us who it should be. Often in real-life versions of the game, however, there is something to tell us who it should be. Costs may be lower or potential rewards higher for one of the participants. Inexperienced players are very unlikely to be the victor in a game of Chicken unless they bring some attribute that clearly distinguishes them from the incumbents. New entrants to the pharmaceutical industry have seldom been successful. Boeing and Airbus will minimize the risk of mutually destructive competition if they focus, as they have done to a degree, on aircraft better designed to meet the needs of the American and European markets, respectively; head-on competition could be enormously costly for both.

A reputation as a tough player is a powerful weapon in Chicken games, but it may be very expensive to establish, since it militates against abandoning unprofitable lines of inquiry. It is not the strategy that successful long-term players have chosen to follow in markets to which innovation is critical and research and development costs dominate the total costs, such as Merck, IBM, and Boeing. Failing all else, the best approach is the "mixed strategy"—try some leads, do not follow all, keep your rivals guessing.

These competitive issues are much less critical when the process of innovation is specific to the individual firm. This is usually the case when the technology is generally available but the application in a particular context requires heavy expenditure. The implementation of information technology in the financial services industry provides a good example.

The general principles are well known and well established. But substantial investment is required for their development and implementation by any particular firm or institution. The use of robotics in the automobile industry has similar characteristics.

Firm-specific innovation normally rests on the local application of generally available knowledge or technology. Leadership in this, although advantageous, is unlikely to create a sustainable competitive advantage unless the firm creates an architecture enabling it to implement systematically the technology in advance of, or more cheaply than, its rivals. This is what underpins the success of Bank One in regional banking.

Firm-specific investment is necessarily appropriable—the benefits of it accrue to the firm that undertakes it. If innovation is not firm specific, it may or may not be appropriable. Product innovations in fast-moving consumer goods industries are rarely appropriable. Once you have seen *fromage frais* in one supermarket, many producers can make it and everyone can stock it. Innovative software, such as Lotus 1-2-3, is easier to protect. Such appropriability may be, as in this case, the result of legal protection through copyright or patent, or it may be the product of strategy.

Protecting and Exploiting Innovation

The issue of appropriability is fundamental. The central characteristic of a distinctive capability is that it cannot be easily replicated. A basic weakness of innovation as a source of competitive advantage is that usually it *can* be easily replicated. The result is that the innovator may be exposed to the costs of innovation and the risks of development and introduction, only to see its competitors share—or perhaps dominate—the fruits of success. Public policy has long recognized the problem of appropriability. The results are potentially inefficient as well as unjust, since the prospect of replication reduces the incentive to innovate in the first place. Patent and copyright laws therefore protect innovators, and much innovation is publicly funded—including virtually all basic scientific research.

Patent law has been unable to keep pace with the range and complexity of modern innovation, and it is almost a matter of accident whether or not a specific innovation can find effective patent protection.

Such protection works reasonably well in pharmaceuticals, although even here there is a well-known science of molecular manipulation, based on the attempt to invent around a patent by identifying a compound with essentially the same properties but a distinct chemical composition. In other areas, patents may be used strategically. The innovation is surrounded with patents of doubtful value in the hope that legal costs will deter later entrants. In many areas of innovation—such as product innovation in manufactured foods or financial services—patents are generally useless. Most innovations—from calculus to junk bonds to flavored yogurt—cannot be patented.

If an innovation cannot be protected by law, it sometimes can be protected by commercial secrecy, although this is almost never true of a product innovation. You cannot advertise new goods to your customers without at the same time advertising to your competitors. But for modest process innovations, secrecy may aid the innovator. Mostly, however, reverse engineering—working back from the final product to the initial design—gives the imitator an equivalent opportunity.

If neither law nor secrecy is sufficient to allow an innovation to be turned into a competitive advantage, then strategy must be used instead. This is why appropriation is sometimes unexpectedly feasible. The Sony Walkman is an ingenious concept, but there is nothing about it that the innovator can protect. Any electronics manufacturer in the world who has seen it can make it. Yet Sony continues to be the market leader.

The most effective way of turning innovation to competitive advantage is generally to deploy it in conjunction with another distinctive capability. Innovation and reputation, or innovation and architecture, are often potent combinations.

There are few innovations in the financial services sector that cannot be copied rapidly by competitors. But a reputation for innovation attracts customers, who can gain access to the latest products without having to shop around. Salomon Brothers has benefited from this. The reputation of the supplier may also induce customers to try innovations that they might otherwise view with reluctance. Coca-Cola did not sell a low-sugar product until the availability of aspartame enabled the company to manufacture a good-quality diet drink. Diet Coke then quickly gained an acceptability that drinks with other artificial sweeteners had not achieved, and it established a new segment of the soft drink market in the process. Coke similarly established disposable cans in the marketplace without itself being the leader in this innovation.

Those firms with another distinctive capability are generally the best placed to derive a competitive advantage from an innovation. But even if this is not possible, an innovation may yield a competitive advantage with the aid of other strategic tools. Distribution and manufacturing capabilities are generally important, and there is no reason that the innovative firm should be the one to possess these particular attributes. If it does, then it is relatively well placed to appropriate the returns from the innovation. If the innovative firm does not have these complementary assets, it will need to acquire them. This can be attempted by building them up from scratch or by establishing partnerships.

Standards

In some markets, goods require the use of complementary equipment. For example, an increasing number of new technologies associate hardware and software. Videocassette recorders need videotapes; computers use software and operating systems; and satellite television programs require matching dishes. One of the most important standards issues of all will arise in the coming market for high-definition television, in which there are three competing technologies, originating in Japan, Europe, and the United States. Yet standards also come into play when no particularly advanced technology is involved: The use of a credit card requires both cardholder and accepter, and the Visa and MasterCard networks define the two dominant world systems, thereby increasing the pressure on Amex's older but less widely accepted standard.

Figure 7.2 illustrates two standards game. In reality there are many decision makers, but two players are enough to illustrate the essential dilemma. If both customers choose either VHS or Betamax, there will be more software available to them than if they make different choices. Neither has any strong reason to choose one or the other. The important thing is that they should make the same choice.

These games are readily recognizable as Battles of the Sexes—they are problems of coordination. Like Battles of the Sexes, they do not have an easy solution. More precisely, they have too many solutions, and so there is a real possibility that no satisfactory outcome will be reached. In some markets, no standard evolves, as anyone who has bought a replacement windshield wiper blade knows. For a while, this seemed likely to be true of operating systems for small computers, and it seems likely that it will be true of operating systems for large computers. The adoption of high-definition television is probably unstoppable, but the existence of divergent standards will certainly delay it.

As in the Battle of the Sexes, it is not clear that prior discussion helps. There is no strong reason to choose one outcome rather than another—the important thing is to choose *some* outcome. Since all partici-

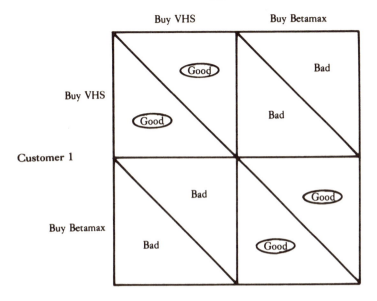

A worse standards game, in which there are slight preferences

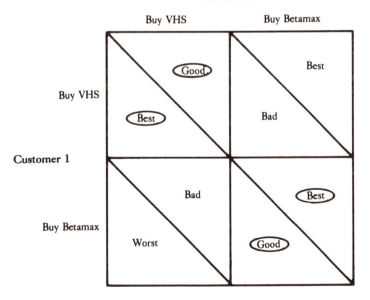

Figure 7.2. Two Standards Games

pants probably have slightly different preferences, their discussion may well continue for a long time. Attempts to establish agreed standards are often protracted. The widespread use of EFTPOS—electronic payment systems as a substitute for cash and check transactions—has been much delayed by precisely this type of difficulty. As with the issue of who goes through a door first, talking about it—after you, after you—does not necessarily resolve the dilemma.

Means of dealing with Battles of the Sexes were described in Chapter 3. Hierarchy is one method. If someone has authority, a standard can be imposed. Sometimes governments or standards institutions have this authority, but with the growing internationalization of the world economy, the Battle of the Sexes often reemerges as a game among different governments. Commitment helps, and a belief that one standard will win often ensures that it does win, regardless of the origin of that belief or the technical merit of the standard in question.

That means that it is rare for more than one standard to survive in the long run. More software is developed for the leading standard, and this in turn leads new purchasers to prefer the leading standard, creating a cumulative process. Technical quality plays little part in the choice. VHS is certainly no better than Sony's Betamax format. Two elements are critical to standards battles: the rapid achievement of an installed base and the credibility of the supplier. Sony mistakenly believed that its dominance of the professional videocassette market would be translated into equal dominance of the consumer market. JVC instead pursued an open licensing policy that ensured that there were quickly more VHS than Betamax machines in operation. Although the denouement took a decade, its outcome was inevitable from an early stage.

The most important standards battle of the last decade has been the fight for control of the personal computer market, described in Chapter 1. Credibility was the characteristic that IBM brought to the market, and this enabled it to quickly establish its standard (and in particular MS-DOS, its operating system) as dominant, although by common consent the IBM PC was not in any way a technically outstanding product. Apple's graphical user interface, which made personal computing accessible to the most incompetent of users, was an outstanding and innovative product but could make only limited headway in a market in which MS-DOS was the dominant standard. Microsoft's Windows was an overwhelming success, not because the interface was superior to Apple's, but because it was designed for an MS-DOS environment. The repeated lesson of standards markets—difficult for the technically minded to accept—is that an installed base and credibility matter more than the quality of the product.

Architecture That Supports Innovation

Often what appear to be competitive advantages based on innovation are in reality the product of distinctive capabilities based on architecture. There are two common types. One is the architecture that allows a firm to generate a continuing sequence of innovations. Even if the individual innovations themselves are inadequately appropriable, a stream of temporary competitive advantages, if repeated, will become a sustainable and sustained advantage. The second is the architecture that enables a firm to adopt, quickly and effectively, generally available technology. The first is architecture directed to the innovation itself, and the second is architecture directed to the appropriation of the innovation.

In many high-technology industries—especially those associated with electronics, pharmaceuticals, or advanced transport equipment—technology is central to competitive advantage. This does not imply that innovation is the only source of competitive advantage—indeed, even in these industries, it is remarkable that the most successful firms are not necessarily the most innovative—but a flow of innovative activity or a quick response to innovative pressure is an essential requirement. Successful high-technology companies are generally characterized by their extensive networks of relational contracts. They reflect the requirements of architecture described in Chapter 5. Organization structures are informal remuneration structures that are flat and related to the performance of the organization rather than to that of the persons in it. The shape of the firm is built around the requirements for speed of response and the free sharing of information—the characteristics that technological adaptation require and relational contracts facilitate.

The success of classically innovative firms like Hewlett-Packard rests less on any single innovation than on the architecture that enables them to derive a succession of innovative products. The continued lead enjoyed by solid-state logic in the manufacture of synthesizers for recording studios rests not on the quality of its technology alone. Rather, it is combined with a set of customer relationships that permits it both to respond to its customers' needs and to secure its products' distribution.

Sony's architecture allows it to generate a seemingly endless series of innovations in consumer electronics. But Sony's reputation also is important. Customers will buy untried Sony products because of the strength of Sony's innovative record, whereas imitators have the nearly impossible job of replicating the architecture and the reputation rather than the relatively simple one of reproducing the innovations.

In other industries, innovation and technology support other competitive advantages rather than direct causes, and architecture may be a necessary complement to innovation-based advantages. Take a financial services firm, for which the lack of innovation can destroy competitive advantage but innovation cannot create it. You can be the worst bank in the world if your technology is bad enough, but no amount of technical innovation will make you the best bank in the world; that is simply not the nature of competitive advantage in this market. In markets of this type, to which technology is not *central*, it is almost inevitable that the contract between those who manage the firm and those who manage its technology is essentially classical in nature. It is credible that the value system of a small producer of high-performance engines revolves around success in technology and that such innovation will be recognized and rewarded. You will not become chief executive of a bank by making its computer system work, nor should you. Instead, you will look for a more explicit reward structure, and the management of the bank, unable to monitor your performance easily, will focus on those indicators it can control. Inevitably, the contract will become more classical in form.

As is generally the case with choosing contract structures, the different arrangements have both advantages and disadvantages. Firms to which technology is not central, which articulate the relationship between the innovator and the organization within a more conventional framework of hierarchical control, minimize the risk that technological enthusiasm will run away with corporate resources. The cost of this is a much more limited capacity to integrate the technology into the rest of the organization.

The issue of integrating innovation technology into the organization is almost as critical as that of appropriability. In a sense, it is an aspect of appropriability—can the firm effectively "own" the technology it deploys? In organizational terms, such ownership requires the effective integration of technology into the firm. In commercial terms, it requires that the value added by the innovation should accrue to the firm rather than to a subgroup within it or outside it.

Innovation as a Competitive Advantage

General Motors, faced by increasingly intense Japanese competition in the 1980s, saw a technological leap forward as its best response. "Technology leadership is what will keep us ahead in world competition," announced Roger Smith, its new chief executive (*The Economist*, August 10, 1991). This vision was enacted by the company's purchase of Hughes Aircraft, Ross Perot's Electronic Data Systems, and the development of the most advanced automobile plant in the world in Hamtramck, near

Detroit. But GM's inability to reproduce its Japanese rivals' architecture—their structure of relationships with their workforce and their suppliers—proved as much of a disadvantage in the new high-tech robotic plants as in the traditional assembly lines. Too often, innovation is perceived as a means of compensating for other sources of competitive weakness.

Technology is often seen as a response by lower-wage countries to low-cost competition. In industries as diverse as the European cutlery industry and the U.S. automobile industry, the belief that competitive disadvantages can be redressed through nonappropriable innovation has been shown to be false.

Innovation may be the distinctive capability that gives rise to competitive advantage, but this outcome is actually quite unusual. More often, what appears to be the return to innovation is in fact a return to a combination of competitive advantages. The most powerful are those deployed by firms such as Sony, which marshal all three distinctive capabilities—architecture, reputation, and innovation—and use each to reinforce the others. Firms less strongly placed may nevertheless give innovation a primary role in their competitive armory, but unless they are favored with regimes of high appropriability, the translation of innovation into competitive advantage requires the strong support of associated elements of strategy.

This chapter owes an obvious debt to David Teece (1986, 1987), whose ideas on the relationship among innovation, technology, and strategy are central. Also outstanding in a quite different way is McKinsey's man in Tokyo, Ken-ichi Ohmae; see, for example, Ohmae (1989) for a lucid discussion of these issues in a Japanese context. The central issue of appropriation is developed in Levin et al. (1985).

The very large literature on the business applications of innovation and technology falls into several categories. One strand of thought identifies patterns of innovation and diffusion. Schumpeter (1961) is invariably cited as the originator of this. More recent analyses in this tradition are by Abernathy and Utterback (1978), Griliches (1984), Landes (1969), and Mathias and Davis (1991). The Science Policy Research Unit at the University of Sussex has assembled very large empirical databases (Henwood and Thomas 1984).

The relationship between organizational structure and technological capabilities is a second central theme, begun by Burns and Stalker (1966) and Woodward (1982). See Abernathy and Hayes (1980), Kay and Willman (1991), McCann (1991), and Willman (1986) for more re-

cent contributions. The game-theory issues relate principally to standards and to patent races. The discussion of standards is mostly empirical and case-related. David (1986) deals with perhaps the most famous standards issue of all—the QWERTY typewriter keyboard; Gabel (1987) is a useful collection of essays; and David and Greenstein (1990), Farrell (1990), and Grindley (1990) offer clear expositions of the issues. On patent races—the Chicken-type problems—most contributions are theoretical; Dasgupta (1988) and Harris and Vickers (1985) are examples.

The economics of technology and innovation is surveyed in Geroski (1993) and Stoneman (1983), whereas broader surveys of its role in business are Butler (1988) and Shaw (1990).

8

Strategic Assets

Some competitive advantages are based not on the distinctive capabilities of firms but on their dominance or market position. These are the strategic assets for the firm concerned. Strategic assets are of three main types. Some companies may benefit from a natural monopoly because they are established in a market that will not readily accommodate more than one firm. In some other markets, incumbent firms have already incurred many of the costs of supply, but entrants have not. In these, the firms' cost structure may give them a competitive advantage. Still other firms benefit from market restrictions that are the product of licenses and regulation. What distinguishes all these from true distinctive capabilities is that any other firm that had entered the industry at the same time or had already made that expenditure or held that license would have enjoyed the same competitive advantage.

Firms that benefit from strategic assets are generally engaged in activities in which government regulation is an important influence on business behavior. Fully one-third of business takes place in industries that are owned by the government, that are extensively regulated by the government, or that mostly sell to the government. Sometimes the government creates, or reinforces, strategic assets; at other times or at the same time, the state may limit the firm's ability to add value from them. The establishment and exploitation of strategic assets are often restricted by regulatory and antitrust policies. In the final section of this chapter, I outline the main rules governing American companies.

*D*istinctive capabilities enable companies to produce at lower cost than their competitors can or to enhance the value of their products in ways that put them ahead of their rivals. Distinctive capabilities are the product of the organization or the firm itself—its architecture, its reputation, or its success in innovation. Yet some firms enjoy an advantage over their potential competitors, even though there is nothing they can do that these other firms, if similarly placed, could not do equally well. These may be firms with a license that is not available to other firms, or they may be firms incumbent in a market that will not readily support more than one competitor. Their competitive advantage follows from the structure of the industry or the market, rather than from their own distinctive capabilities. These firms hold strategic assets.

Strategic assets, and the creation and exploitation of strategic advantages, raise issues about the proper conduct of business in ways that rarely arise when a competitive advantage is based on architecture, reputation, or innovation. When a distinctive capability gives rise to superior performance, the private gains made by the firm and its stakeholders generally correspond to equivalent gains for society as a whole. When strategic advantages are derived from legal privilege or market dominance, this equivalence of private profit and public good may not follow. The view I take in this chapter is that the firm may do what it is legally entitled to do, and what it is legally entitled to do I discuss in the concluding section, which deals with antitrust policy. The subject also raises wider questions of public policy and the ethics of business behavior, which are considered further in Chapter 15.

Natural Monopolies

Some markets are natural monopolies, and it is unlikely that more than one producer will serve such a market. There is a natural monopoly if there are economies of scale and the market is too small to support more than one producer of efficient size. In aircraft construction, and perhaps in mainframe computers, the world market is not big enough for more than a small number of producers to manufacture competitively. But even in industries in which there are substantial scale economies—such as the assembly of telecommunications-switching equipment and automobiles—there will always be several firms. There are not many natural monopolies in manufactured goods industries in which there are few obstacles to trade and to global sourcing and production. Unless regulatory or other barriers to foreign sourcing prevent companies from creating a truly international industry (as was true for many years in telecommunications switching), trade will destroy monopolies. Real monopoly is possible only if the market is defined very narrowly, as with certain kinds of specialized machinery or in service or utility industries in which the geographical boundaries of the market are restricted.

The most striking examples of natural monopoly can be found in the regional distribution networks of utilities. It would cost nearly twice as much to have two alternative supplies of gas, electricity, or water in residential areas as to have a single one, and this may also be true of road and rail networks. There may be a natural monopoly, too, when the market is particularly local. Newsagents and bakers serve perishable products to customers in their immediate neighborhood, and often an individual market can accommodate only one such producer. Sometimes a natural monopoly is created when a firm fills a narrow market niche. The *Wall Street Journal* is a profitable product, but there is probably not room for more than one such paper in any geographical market, and smaller countries do not have comparable daily financial papers. "There is only one Harrods" is a well-chosen slogan because it is not clear that there could be more than one Harrods.

Standards can also create a natural monopoly if the market requires a compatibility standard and that standard is proprietary. Although compatibility standards exist in many markets, few of them belong to individual companies. The owner may have to adopt an open licensing policy in order to establish a dominant standard (as with the promotion of VHS recorders by JVC). Or antitrust restrictions may prevent the owner from using the standard to establish a natural monopoly (as has happened repeatedly—explicitly or implicitly—to IBM). But within the computer industry, Microsoft and Lotus have succeeded in establishing particularly strong positions in their narrow market segments.

In some markets, customers are strongly attracted to the producer that already has the largest number of customers. At its simplest and starkest, the best computer-dating agency is the one with the largest number of dates on its books.[1] In telecommunications systems, the advantage of being number one is so great that competition in network provision is virtually impossible unless producers are forced to offer access to one another's systems. Few people would trouble to use alternative networks if they could call only those customers who were themselves subscribers to the alternative network, and then there would be even fewer subscribers. Network operation favors incumbents in many other industries, particularly in transport systems such as busing or airlines. In financial services, the "thickest" market—the one with the highest volume of dealings—is the one most likely to have a willing counterparty, which explains London's dominance in many commodity markets and Chicago's in many derivative securities. In pool betting, the most popular pool can offer the largest prizes, which enhances the attraction of the pool—and in turn its value.

A natural monopoly is a game with Chicken characteristics—no more than one player can win, but two can lose, either through head-on competition or by mutual failure to recognize and exploit a market opportunity. In some natural monopoly markets, one player has ulti-

---

[1] Although even here specialization allows many niche players to survive; that is, who matters as well as how many.

mately decided to swerve. Lockheed has withdrawn from the civil aircraft market, and McDonnell Douglas is now a minor player. In other
markets—like the London bond market—most players have been willing
to stay around.

Commitment is a key element in Chicken games, and it is the con-
spicuous nature of an incumbent firm's commitment that gives it a powerful advantage in a natural monopoly. In the original version, the new-
comer, James Dean, was at a perceived disadvantage relative to an
opponent who was an experienced player with a tough reputation. But
as in the movie, newcomers can displace incumbents if they have a competitive advantage, a stronger commitment, or a more effective strategy.
Sony believed, wrongly, that its dominance of the professional video
market would win the VCR battle. Then JVC entered, and won.

The Experience Curve and Sunk Costs

A natural monopoly becomes a far more sustainable competitive advantage if it is combined with a strategic advantage based on sunk costs.
The advantages of incumbency are often expressed by reference to the
experience curve. This concept—popularized by the Boston Consulting
Group—relates costs to cumulative output. It is claimed that costs fall by
around 15 percent with each doubling of overall output (Figure 8.1).
This analysis conflates many different factors. The observed relationship
reflects the influence of learning that is specific to the firm and of learning that is general to the industry. It includes both costs that fall with
the cumulative scale of output and costs that fall with the rate of output.
It brings together the effects of technical progress in the economy at large
with technical progress in particular firms and industries.

These distinctions matter a great deal in understanding the implications of an experience curve. Figure 8.1 shows experience curves drawn
from industries as varied as airframe manufacturers and broiler chickens.
The apparent similarity is remarkable, but the causes and the implications are entirely different. The falling costs of the B-29 are truly the
result of learning by experience—learning that is mostly specific to Boeing and largely specific to that particular aircraft. This phenomenon underpins Boeing's position in the world's aircraft market.

The only similarity between chickens and aircraft is that both have
wings. The industrywide adoption of mass-producing chickens (as opposed to free-range chickens), supported by the use of antibiotics, turned
chicken from a luxury product into a commodity staple. The market for
chicken grew rapidly. Whereas in one case the causality runs from out-

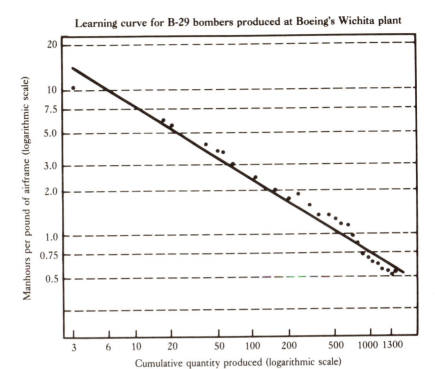

Learning curve for B-29 bombers produced at Boeing's Wichita plant

Source: Scherer and Ross (1990).

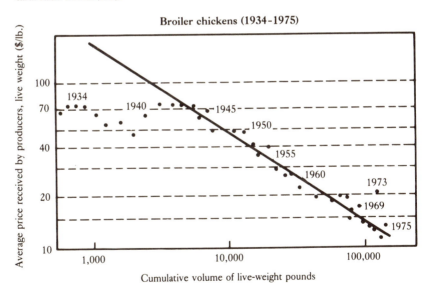

Broiler chickens (1934–1975)

Source: Abell and Hammond (1988).

Figure 8.1. The Experience Curve

put to costs, in the other it runs from costs to output, a difference critical to the strategic implications. The world's aircraft market is, and is likely to remain, dominated by Boeing. The market for broiler chickens is, and is likely to remain, both local and fragmented. Anyone induced by the experience curve to aspire to be the Boeing of the broilers would be sadly misled. We need to look at what drives costs in particular industries.

The degree to which incumbency—already being in the market—establishes a strategic asset depends on the structure of costs in specific industries. Boeing's experience is a good example of a strategic asset that favors the incumbent firm. This strategic asset is the sunk cost of serving a market. An entrant aims to secure an established long-term position in a particular market. The costs incurred are of many kinds—building a plant, establishing a distribution network. Perhaps the market is one in which a credible supplier must build a reputation. Certainly, the firm needs to draw customers' attention to the qualities of its products. The measure of sunk costs is the proportion of the expected costs of supplying output that would still be incurred even if that output were not, in the end, sold.

The Channel Tunnel will have cost around $15 billion once it is completed, and its operating costs are estimated at around $300 million per year. Discounting these operating costs to the end of its franchise at 10 percent, some 80 percent of the total costs of the tunnel, in perpetuity, will have been incurred before it earns a penny of revenue. This is an extreme example of an industry in which a high proportion of costs are, literally and metaphorically, sunk. If no vehicle, no train, or no passenger ever passes through the tunnel, then more than $15 billion will in any case have been spent, a sum that is frightening to the Eurotunnel's bankers. If traffic reaches the expected level, then 80 percent of the costs of supplying a customer will have been incurred before that customer

Illustration 8.1.   The Channel Tunnel (Eurotunnel)

The tunnel under the English Channel between Britain and France, which opened in 1994, is the world's largest civil-engineering project. About thirty miles long, the main purpose of the tunnel is to transport both trucks and automobiles on a fleet of specially designed trains across the Channel in thirty minutes, thus linking the British road system with that of Continental Europe. The tunnel will also allow a high-speed rail link to be established between London and Paris (which are closer to each other than New York and Washington are).

The tunnel was built and is operated by Eurotunnel, a corporation formed for that specific purpose. The company raised finance from a banking consortium, and its shares are quoted on the London and Paris stock exchanges.

arrives, a proportion that is frightening to the Eurotunnel's competitors. It is for this reason that the tunnel will eventually be fully utilized, even if it is for the benefit of the banks rather than the original owners.

Sunk costs are often confused with economies of scale, but they may predominate in industries in which there are few economies of scale. An efficient, modern electricity-generating plant would be a combined-cycle gas turbine plant with a capacity of 700 megawatts. This is roughly equal to the demand of a medium-size town and its associated industry. More than one thousand such plants would be needed to satisfy the U.S. demand for electricity. However, at current gas prices, the costs of constructing such a plant would amount to about 30 percent of the total costs of electricity generation over the twenty-year life of the plant. There are no economies of scale to speak of in electricity generation—or rather, they are exhausted at a very low level—but the sunk costs are very large. This gives incumbents an advantage over entrants.

Capital-intensive industries are often those to which sunk costs are important. But not always. Transport activities—such as airlines, shipping, and busing—also are capital intensive. But there are active second-hand markets for aircraft, ships, and buses, and it is easy to lease a ship or a bus for a fixed period. The sunk costs of entering these markets are relatively low. Such industries differ from cement and electricity because unlike cement plants or power stations, planes and ships do not have to be dedicated to particular markets. If market entry fails, you can fly your plane elsewhere or sell it, and this is what unsuccessful firms in the airline business have regularly done. But there is not much else you can do with your cement works or your generating plant except to produce cement or electricity and to produce them for a particular market. The critical point is not just that capital expenditure is important but that capital expenditure is specific to a particular market. The cross-channel market provides a clear illustration of the distinction. A ferry operator has the option of using equipment on a different, and more rewarding, route, but the Eurotunnel can operate on one route only. That is a problem for the Eurotunnel, but at the same time it makes the firm a very powerful competitor.

When sunk costs are associated with capital investment, their value as a strategic asset depreciates over time as the capital equipment itself does. An electricity-generation set declines in efficiency; a cement works needs to be replaced; even a tunnel under the English Channel ultimately depreciates. In industries in which there are several firms, sunk costs are almost always larger for some firms than for others, depending on the stage of the investment and the product life cycles that have been reached. The firms whose plants are oldest are always those that are most vulnerable to entrants with a competitive advantage. The combination of size and time fixes the upper limit of the size of the strategic asset that the incumbent firm can enjoy. But a strategic asset in the form of sunk costs enables the established firm to hold its own against a potential entrant as long as the entrant's competitive advantage is less than the entrant's sunk costs.

The sunk costs easiest to identify are those associated with an investment. Yet other, less tangible, sunk costs are often more important. Advertising expenditures are a sunk cost, as they are specific to a market and cannot be recovered if the firm leaves that market. Other expenditures on market recognition also are sunk costs: For an airline or a bus company, the cost of informing potential customers of your timetable is a substantial sunk cost, and public knowledge of your schedules and route network is a substantial strategic asset. The costs of establishing a reputation are largely market specific. These types of sunk cost do not depreciate in quite the same way that capital equipment does. So incumbents in these markets may hold even more powerful strategic assets than do firms in capital-intensive industries.

Strategic assets derived from sunk costs are valuable only if competitors must sink them too. Raising sunk costs in a market—such as through advertising—may be an effective strategy for deterring entry, but only if the resulting market structure imposes similar obligations on competitors. Technological change may eliminate strategic advantages based on sunk costs, such as when the position of established steel producers was undermined by the introduction of low-cost minimills.

Licensing and Regulation as Strategic Assets

In many markets, firms gain a strategic advantage through licensing and regulation. There are fewer such markets than there once were, but there still are many.

The distribution networks of utilities are mostly natural monopolies, for which it would be costly to have more than one supplier. A high proportion of costs are sunk—literally so in many cases, as they correspond to wires or pipes in the ground. In these industries, local, state, or national governments have intervened to offer an exclusive license to a favored or incumbent supplier. In most cases they have at the same time regulated the prices that the licensee can charge. If the resources are scarce, access is often controlled through a licensing process. Examples include offshore oil exploration rights and broadcast franchises. Sometimes the scarcity is itself the result of government action, as with gaming licenses.

Licensing and regulation may create strategic assets in industries in which there are no scarce resources or natural monopolies. Entry to the financial services business has been inhibited in many ways. The Glass-Steagall Act, which prohibited interstate banking, prevented the emergence in the United States of the national banks that operate in most other countries and so preserved the regional franchises of state banks as strategic assets. The regulation of civil aviation, introduced to protect consumers, came to be operated as a cartel on behalf of established carriers, so that route licenses became valuable strategic assets. So are the medallions held by licensed New York cab drivers.

In other countries, many of these strategic assets are held by publicly owned companies. In France and Germany, for example, the nationalized carrier still has an almost complete monopoly of telecommunications services. Around the world, many of the water, energy, telecommunications, broadcasting, and financial services industries are in the hands of the government, and almost all of them are subject to government restriction.

All this is changing, however. Aviation was one of the first subjects of deregulation, as it became apparent that the main effects of regulation were to inhibit competition and to ossify the structure of the industry. The results were dramatic, as firms with no competitive advantage other than the strategic assets that deregulation had removed from them were suddenly exposed to competitive forces. But over time, new strategic assets emerged in this industry. Computerized reservation systems gave advantages to the airlines that devised them and that offered them to travel agents on favorable terms. The dominance of hubs created a new form of natural monopoly for established carriers.

In utilities, too, strategic assets are being steadily eroded. Competition in telecommunications came first from alternative suppliers of long distance services, such as MCI and Sprint. This required access to AT&T's networks, but when given that access, various new kinds of competition in these services became possible. The changing technology means that there soon will be no natural monopolies in telecommunications, and if deregulation keeps pace, companies will increasingly have to rely on competitive advantages rather than strategic access. Supply competition based on network access is equally applicable to other distribution utilities such as gas or electricity. The limitations on bandwidth, which were the historic rationale for controlling access to broadcasting, have largely disappeared, and the rationale of regulation in other industries, such as financial services, is increasingly being questioned. Privatization is a policy being adopted around the world, and liberalization usually comes with it. Few companies whose strategic assets are derived from licensing and regulation can feel confident that these will survive for long. As in airlines and telecommunications, however, other strategic assets may emerge to take their place.

Antitrust Policies

Strategic assets may arise from a natural monopoly, from licensing and regulation, or from action to establish market dominance and sustain incumbent advantages.

In two of these three categories—natural monopoly and regulation—the government plays a central role. And in the third—in which strategy itself creates the strategic asset—government also frequently intervenes, through antitrust policies, to correct real or imagined abuses. When market power is found, or suspected, government and its agencies are seldom far away.

Government confers market power, but it also restricts its exercise. The Sherman Act makes it illegal to monopolize, or to attempt to monopolize, any part of the trade or commerce among the several states. The scope of that prohibition is wide and confers liability to personal criminal penalties as well as exemplary treble damages in civil litigation.

But what is prohibited has varied widely, reflecting the changing climates of popular opinion, judicial stance, and attitudes toward enforcement by both government agencies and private litigants. In the spectacular early days of Theodore Roosevelt's trust busting, the courts dismantled the Tobacco Trust and Rockefeller's Standard Oil. A proposal to break up U.S. Steel was rejected. Although the Alcoa case marked the revived interest in antitrust in the later days of the New Deal, it was not until the 1970s that the government again made a determined attack on dominant firms. The landmark cases were those against IBM and AT&T.

Both cases were resolved in 1982, with very different outcomes. The Reagan administration abandoned the suit against IBM, and the AT&T case ended with an agreed settlement that split the company's long distance lines and Western Electric equipment business from the provision of local telephone service, thereby establishing the regional Bell operating companies. The key factor differentiating the outcomes was a perception that IBM's dominance, even if defended by a variety of exclusionary practices, was ultimately the product of its competitive advantage in a contestable market, whereas AT&T's even stronger market position was the result of the strategic assets it enjoyed through licensing and regulation. Thus these two judgments marked a watershed in U.S. antitrust policy. What was under attack was not bigness or dominance as such, but bigness or dominance resulting from strategic assets rather than competitive advantage.

That distinction, and its implications, is much less apparent in cases in which what is at issue is not the existence of the strategic asset as such but the practices in which the firm engages in order to establish or support it. Actions alleged to involve predatory pricing or market foreclosure are sometimes the subject of a suit by the Federal Trade Commission or Justice Department, but actions are often brought by private firms seeking remedies and damages. In these areas also, however, both government agencies and the courts are increasingly inclined to look behind the specific practices that are the subject of complaint and inquire about the origins of the market power that the firm enjoys or seeks to enjoy.

Other countries have their own antitrust policies. After World War II, the occupying powers imposed legislation against monopoly and cartels on both Germany and Japan. The principal motivation was concern for the relationship between concentrations of economic and political power rather than consideration of economic efficiency. The United Kingdom established its Monopolies Commission at around the same time. Now the most important antitrust authority outside the United States is the European Union. Its authority derives from Articles 85 and 86 of the Rome Treaty to which all the union's members are signatories. These provisions prohibit actions that restrict or distort competition within the Common Market established by the treaty or that represent the abuse of a dominant position within it. The parallels with U.S. legislation are fairly clear and extend to the mechanisms of enforcement. These include administrative action by the European Commission or private action by the aggrieved parties in the courts of individual member states or in the European Court of Justice. Whereas the Sherman Act outlaws monopolization, the Rome Treaty allows the creation or maintenance of a dominant position, proscribing only its abuse. This distinction is clearer in principle than in practice. The European approach, like that of an earlier generation of U.S. policymakers, focuses principally on the effect of actions that are the subject of complaint from customers and other firms.

Any actions that firms might take, or contemplate, to use market power or deter entry are governed by these legal restraints. No firm would wish to adopt strategies that break the law, and it is clear that actions such as price-fixing agreements with competitors or predatory pricing whose clear objective is to drive a competitor from the market are illegal and may lead to penalties or civil damages. More generally, however, what constitutes abuse of a dominant position or a restriction or distortion of competition is a matter of opinion and one on which lawyers and economists can honestly disagree. Moreover, actions may often simultaneously restrict competition and benefit consumers; for example, vertical integration may often have these consequences.

These legal provisions must always be in the minds of firms managing strategic assets. Apart from obvious prudential considerations, antitrust enforcement is frequently the result of complaints, and strategies can frequently be recast in ways that either take them clearly outside the scope of legal restriction or are less likely to arouse the hostility of competitors or customers. It is often the antitrust proceedings themselves, rather than the ultimate consequences, that are damaging to the firms involved.

The creation and deployment of strategic assets center on natural monopoly, sunk costs, and licensing and regulation. Most of the literature concerning these issues was written by economists, and their general perspective is that of public rather than business policy. Their interest is that of the concerned citizen rather than the business adviser. A fine overall treatment with this perspective and a wealth of examples is Scherer and Ross (1990). Yao (1988) covers the issues of this chapter with a business policy orientation. The relationship between sunk costs and market structure is innovatively described in Sutton (1991).

Natural monopoly and concentrated market structures are based on entry barriers, scale economies, and the experience curve. Bain (1956) and von Weizsacker (1980) are classics on barriers to entry. See also Ghemawat and Nalebuff (1985), Salop (1979), Schmalensee (1981), and Spence (1977). Emerson et al. (1988) and background papers provide a wide-ranging assessment of scale economies in European industries. Boston Consulting Group (BCG) (1072) and Henderson (1973) describe the experience curve. See also Abernathy and Wayne (1974), Alberts (1989), and Andrews (1980). Sharkey (1982) is a broader survey of issues in natural monopoly. First-mover advantages are analyzed by Lieberman and Montgomery (1988).

The emphasis in this chapter on sunk costs is closely associated with the theory of contestable markets, an approach that, if less revolutionary than sometimes suggested, has nevertheless influenced thinking on industrial structure considerably in the 1980s. Baumol (1982) and Baumol et al. (1982) are the seminal contributions; a good critique is Shepherd (1984). For the European experience of privatization and reg-

ulation, see Bishop and Kay (1988), Kay et al. (1986), and Vickers and Yarrow (1988). International antitrust policies are annually reviewed by the OECD (annual). The account of U.S. policy here owes an obvious debt to Scherer and Ross (1990). The intellectual background of antitrust policy is described in Williamson (1987), and Bork (1978) is a critique that proved influential in U.S. policies. Calori and Lawrence (1991) and Jordan and Richardson (1987) are other sources on the relationship between business and public policy.

IV

FROM DISTINCTIVE CAPABILITIES TO COMPETITIVE ADVANTAGE

Part III defined and identified the principal distinctive capabilities distinguishing successful firms—architecture, reputation, innovation—and explained how firms succeed by creating or exploiting strategic assets. The subject of Part IV is how these distinctive capabilities are applied to specific markets to create a competitive advantage, and the problems that arise in ensuring that these competitive advantages can be sustained and appropriated.

This appears to leave a gap—or so it seemed to many readers of the European version of this book. They recognized that outstanding corporate performance derives from distinctive capabilities. "But how," they asked, "are distinctive capabilities established?" Surely this must be the central question in determining strategy for the corporation?

How distinctive capabilities are created is a good question, but it is not, I believe, the central question of corporate strategy. Distinctive capabilities of real commercial value are hard to create. This almost goes without saying, since if they were not hard to create, they could not remain distinctive for long. What is even more important is to recognize that they are almost never created as the result of a conscious process of strategic choice. This is true for essentially the same reasons. Deciding what distinctive capabilities it would be good, and profitable, to have leads inescapably down the path of wish-driven strategy. A firm may formulate an objective in terms of a distinctive architecture, reputation, or innovation. But in the absence of some unique attribute that enables this firm to achieve that objective ahead of others and more comprehensively, whatever architecture, reputation, or innovation is established can quickly be replicated. The search for distinctive capability is simply taken to a different level.

The question that a firm should ask itself is, "What distinctive capability do we have?" not "What distinctive capability would we like to have?" Most large firms have some distinctive capability or capabilities—they could hardly have survived otherwise. Most small firms have some distinctive capability, too—it is their founders' perception or possession of what brought them into existence. The point is not that distinctive capabilities cannot be, and are not, created but that creation is rarely achieved as a deliberate act. If there is a single central fallacy in much modern strategic thinking, it is the notion that the act of will is the most important element in corporate achievement.

It is not often rewarding to think about creating distinctive capabilities, and so it may be more useful to think about creating strategic assets. Strategic assets can be developed or acquired, and the process of doing so may well be both conscious and profitable. Large firms may enjoy market positions based on strategic assets even if they have no distinctive capability. Small firms may achieve modest profits from local strategic assets—the corner shop, the well-respected local trader. Many firms have successfully maintained their strategic assets for long periods of time, as Chapter 11 explains. But firms may be very vulnerable if that strategic asset is eroded, as various privatized and deregulated firms have discovered. Strategic assets are often less secure sources of competitive advantage than are distinctive capabilities.

The first part of our analysis of the firm's strategy is a description of its distinctive capabilities. The next requirement is matching these to the appropriate markets. This matching is the subject of Chapter 9, which details the principles by which a firm should define its core business. One means—often the principal means—of securing markets is merger and acquisition, the subject of Chapter 10. Chapters 11 and 12 are concerned, respectively, with the sustainability and appropriability of competitive advantages, and Chapter 13 takes the analysis back to the criteria of success developed in Chapter 2 and describes how sustainable and appropriable competitive advantage may add value.

9

Markets

This chapter is concerned with how successful firms choose markets to make the most of their distinctive capabilities. It answers the question, "What is the core business?" which has been a central strategic issue for many firms in the last decade.

I begin with the important distinctions among markets, industries, and strategic groups. Markets are bounded by the ability of consumers to substitute one product for another. Industries are determined by the way in which production is organized. Strategic groups are defined by the way in which firms compete against one another. So there may be—and often is—a global industry in which production is sourced internationally but has many different local markets and several distinct strategic groups. The key issue for the firm is its choice of markets—in both product and geographic dimensions—and its membership in industry and strategic groups follows from that.

A distinctive capability applied to a relevant market becomes a competitive advantage. For each distinctive capability there is a market, or group of markets, in which the firm holding it may enjoy a competitive advantage. For some distinctive capabilities—such as those based on reputation or on some kinds of architecture—it is the nature of the demand for the product that identifies the appropriate market. For other distinctive capabilities—such as most innovations—it is the technical characteristics of the product that define the markets in which they yield a competitive advantage. Similar issues influence the choice of a product's position within a given market.

A distinctive capability or a strategic asset becomes a competitive advantage only when it is applied to a market or markets. A competitive advantage is intrinsically relative. A firm can enjoy a competitive advantage only by reference to other suppliers to the same market, other firms in the same industry, or other competitors in the same strategic group. Correctly matching activities to capabilities is perhaps the most important single element in establishing a competitive advantage.

In the last decade, most companies have recognized the importance of this issue. "What business are we in?" is a starting point for every discussion of strategy. Few chief executives' statements have not included some reference to focusing on "the core business." "Sticking to the knitting" has become a catchphrase.

When the baby Bells left the nest, AT&T was freed from the restrictions that had previously limited its diversification, but it also was faced with the issue of what its "core business" actually was. Some of its executives considered it to be the integrated provision of information. But what does such a provision mean? Should it take the company into computers or into publishing? Should the corporation provide telephone service in other countries or complement its fixed links with mobile communications? A decade later, the answers to these questions, and the criteria by which they should be answered, still are not clear.

"What business are we in?" is a badly formulated question because the term *business* conflates three important and distinct concepts. Sometimes the word *business* describes the *market* that a firm serves—the needs of its customers and its potential customers. More often it relates to the *industry* that a firm is in—a group of products associated by common technology or supply or distribution channels. Sometimes the business refers to the *strategic group*—those firms that the company identifies as its primary competitors.

Demand factors determine the market, and supply factors define the industry. Cunard Line and American Airlines both serve the same *market*—for people who want to cross the Atlantic Ocean—but they are in very different industries. Singapore Airlines is in the same *industry* as Southwest Airlines, but since there are no routes on which both offer services, they are in different markets. From a technical point of view, both washing machines and refrigerators are white boxes with motors in them, and they are distributed through the same channels. But washing machines are useless at chilling food, and refrigerators do not clean clothes. The markets are for laundry services and food storage, and although there is a domestic appliance industry, there is not a domestic appliance market.

The strategic group and the strategic market define the competitive battleground. The strategic group is determined by classifying together companies with similar strategies. Coke and Pepsi, with similar approaches to the market, form a strategic group; whereas Pschitt, a French soft drink company whose aspirations to global branding must necessarily be limited, is differently placed, with a different competitive strategy. In France, Pschitt is in the same market as Pepsi and Coke, but in a different strategic group.

It is important for firms to identify all these—the relevant market,

Illustration 9.1. Markets and Industries

The market

Defined by demand conditions
Based on consumer needs
Characterized by "the law of one price"

The industry

Determined by supply conditions
Based on production technology
Defined by the markets chosen by firms

The strategic group

Defined by the strategic choices of firms
Based on distinctive capabilities and market positioning
Subjective in determination

the relevant industry, and the relevant strategic group—but it also is important to understand that they are not necessarily the same. The Allegis Corporation was formed in 1987 to combine the friendly skies of United Airlines, the comfort of Westin Hotels, and the ubiquity of Hertz car rental in a "total travel experience." But the skills required to manage an airline were very different from those needed to run hotels or control a car rental franchise, and the Allegis Corporation lasted only weeks. There is a *travel* market but not a travel *industry*.

Stung by Theodore Levitt's charge of marketing myopia and concerned with the future of the oil market after the 1973 Arab–Israeli war, several oil companies redefined their business as energy supply and diversified into coal. But the management of coal mines could hardly be more different from the management of oil exploration. Few of the diversifiers still retain their coal interests, although many more are still in gas, for which the required capabilities are not so different.

The activities in which the firm's distinctive capability can offer a competitive advantage can be related to the markets, the industries, or the strategic groups in which the firm competes or might compete. The firm defining its core business should look at all of these, but its primary focus should be on identifying those *markets* in which it can effectively deploy its distinctive capability. The industry and the strategic group are defined by the choices that other firms have already made. Concern for the market focuses attention on the customers' needs, and competitive advantage often rests on using distinctive capabilities to meet these needs in new ways.

The Boundaries of the Market

A market was once an event that occurred in a particular location at a particular time. Consumers would go there to meet suppliers and evaluate their alternative offers. This is still true of some markets. Buyers and sellers meet every day in the pit in Chicago. But these physical markets are now the exception rather than the rule. Even by the nineteenth century, the term *market* had assumed a more abstract meaning. "Originally a market was a public place in a town where provisions and other objects were exposed for sale; but the word has been generalized to mean any body of persons who are in intimate business relations and carry on extensive transactions in any commodity" (Jevons 1871, chap. 4). But like these historic markets, the modern market continues to have a product dimension and a geographic dimension; accordingly, we talk of the New York cab market or the world oil market.

The definition of the product and the geographic dimensions of the market have received an unusual amount of attention because the issue arises in almost every case in which competition policy authorities are involved. The key question in determining the boundaries of the market is the consumers' opportunity to substitute one product for another. They no longer have to walk between market stalls appraising one supplier's price and quality against another's. But if they still have information about alternative offers and the opportunity to choose one source rather than another that the traditional marketplace provided, there is a single market.

If a market is defined as the area within which consumers can readily substitute one good for another, it is often a narrow one. The existence of a single market, rather than distinct markets, is suggested by relative price uniformity and demonstrates whether movements in the price of one good greatly affect the sales of the other. Applying either of these tests confirms that the "American vegetable market" must be divided into many product segments and many geographic areas. A potato in California is not in the same market as is a potato in New York, because buying a potato in New York is not a realistic option for California consumers. Nor is a California potato in the same market as a California tomato, because very few consumers see the two products as alternatives.

One of the more common confusions of the last decade was to mistake the globalization of industry for the globalization of markets. A multidomestic market—one in which the same product is sold in many different markets around the world—is very different from a global market, in which customers are free to buy in any geographical location they like and prices are equalized worldwide. There are global markets for goods such as tin or aircraft, but rarely for manufactured consumer goods or for services.

This "law of one price" is a means of defining the boundaries of a market. "The more nearly perfect a market is, the stronger is the tendency for the same price to be paid for the same thing at the same time in all parts of the market" (Marshall 1890). This criterion is particularly useful in identifying the geographic boundaries of the market. The European Union (EU) implemented a "single market" among western European states at the beginning of 1993. Its objective is to create a European economy as integrated as is that of the United States, and to do this, the EU has removed most of the artificial barriers to trade. Although that is necessary for economic integration—a single market—it does not, in itself, establish it. That will be achieved only when the border between France and Germany becomes as irrelevant to the behaviors of producers and consumers as the border between Connecticut and Massachusetts is.

Table 9.1 shows how the prices of some commonly traded commodities vary across the European Union. There may be a single European market for oil products but not for automobiles, pharmaceuticals, domestic appliances, or life insurance. This is true, even though for all these products, except life insurance, sourcing is done on a Europe-wide basis, and the goods concerned are extensively traded across national borders. Although there is a European industry, it is not the same as a European market.

Despite Europe's espousal of the cause of economic integration and much talk about a single European market, Europe remains far more fragmented than the United States. There are no price differences between New York and California similar to those shown in Table 9.1, and if they were to emerge, organized interstate trading would soon eliminate them.

Table 9.1. Prices in European Markets (Belgium = 100)

	German Cars	Pharmaceuticals	Life Insurance	Domestic Appliances
Belgium	100	100	100	100
France	115	78	75	130
West Germany	127	174	59	117
Italy	129	80	102	110
Netherlands	NA	164	51	105
United Kingdom	142	114	39	93

Sources: Commission of the European Communities (1988); Nicolaides and Baden Fuller (1987); dell'Osso (1990).

Strategic errors can be made by companies that define markets either too widely or too narrowly. Eveready was a market leader in the provision of dry batteries for small appliances in the United Kingdom. In 1975 the company decided to adopt a global branding strategy but was inhibited because it did not have the worldwide rights to its powerful brand name. So it decided to change both its brand name and its corporate identity to Berec. The strategy was not a success: The benefits of the Eveready name were large and those of global branding negligible. The company lost market share in its traditional geographic markets and failed to make corresponding gains elsewhere.

At the same time, long-life alkaline batteries, until then mostly confined to specific applications, were making inroads into the zinc–carbon segment in which Eveready specialized. These batteries had already come to dominate the market in some of the overseas markets that Eveready had targeted. Duracell, Eveready's principal competitor, focused its marketing efforts on long-life batteries, but in order to facilitate its global branding strategy, Eveready delayed the launch of its own competitive products. It had assessed the geographic dimensions of its market too broadly and the product dimension too narrowly. Eveready's profits plummeted, and the company was acquired by Hanson, which redressed these errors, restored the original brand identity, and has since made the battery business one of the most profitable parts of its corporate portfolio.

Matching Markets to Distinctive Capabilities

The question, "What is our core business?" should be reformulated as, "What markets are best enabling us to translate our distinctive capability into a competitive advantage?" The narrow market definition adopted here implies that most firms must expect to compete in many different markets, both product and geographic. The boundaries of the firm are determined by the markets it selects. The boundaries of the industry are determined by the markets that similar firms select. The basis of that selection should be the maximization of competitive advantage, and the key to that is the nature of the firm's distinctive capability itself.

Reputation is most obviously of value in those markets in which that reputation has been created. The *Oxford English Dictionary* has an immensely powerful reputation for comprehensiveness and accuracy. But not many people want twenty-volume dictionaries, so that in its own market the reputation is not worth what it costs to create. Revenues from sales of the dictionary do not defray the expenses of maintaining and updating the databases from which it is derived.

The profitability of the activity depends on exploiting the distinctive capability—the reputation of the OED—in other markets. The most obvious markets are those for other dictionaries. A single-volume Oxford dictionary is not much better than—or even very different from—several other single-volume dictionaries. The underlying lexicographical knowledge is generally available, and fine nuances of scholarship matter little in a one-volume dictionary. But the reputation of Oxford books is very valuable in selling single-volume dictionaries. For this to be true, two conditions must be fulfilled. The dictionary has to be a long-term experience good, which it is—accuracy and comprehensiveness are key features of a dictionary, and it is not easy to assess these by browsing through it in a shop. And the Oxford reputation has to be credibly at stake on the one-volume dictionary, which it is: If the single-volume dictionary is found to be full of errors, then the standing of the principal dictionary will be damaged.

This reputation can be extended to English language–teaching materials and helps sell other reference works, and these are successful Oxford businesses. But it is less valuable for classic novels, which are search rather than experience goods, although publishers try to differentiate their products by adding introductions, notes, and bibliographies. You can tell in a bookstore that a book with *Pride and Prejudice* on the cover is indeed *Pride and Prejudice*. But only experience will tell you whether you will like it, and the publisher offers no warranty on that.

Reputation is of value in the market in which it is created and in related markets for long-term experience goods. A well-managed reputation can gradually be extended to other products, which makes it a particularly powerful form of competitive advantage, since its value increases over time. The matching of *architecture* advantages to markets depends on the specific advantage. Hanson's competitive strength rests on a system of tight financial controls negotiated between its small corporate center and the management of its individual operating business. Such a structure works best for dominant firms in mature and clearly defined markets. It is less successful when the industry requires substantial long-term expenditures to support research and development, in which the payoff is delayed or uncertain and management has only limited influence over time or outcome. Does tobacco—now Hanson's largest single operating business—meet the criteria of dull maturity? Or do the requirements of long-term brand development, emphasized by other successful players in the market such as Philip Morris, make this a less appropriate market in which to deploy the Hanson architecture?

The particular strength of the architecture of Liz Claiborne and Benetton is the rapid response time that their systems facilitate. This style is suitable for a fashion business but not for other types of franchise operations—such as fast food—in which consumers' tastes do not change rapidly and product standardization, rather than product differentiation, is important to consumers. Within the clothing sector itself, the nature of the competitive advantage implies a market positioning—neither down market, where fashion is less important to selling goods, nor at the top, where tastes are more stable and volumes are lower. Both companies have positioned themselves accordingly.

For innovation advantages, the market is generally indicated by the nature of the innovation itself. Often it is the identification of the market that prompts the innovation. It was obvious for many years that there was a large market for an effective antiulcerant, and the problem for the pharmaceutical industry was not that of identifying the market but of devising the product to meet it. Less commonly, the innovation is independent of the market, and the competitive advantage goes to the firm that identifies the application. It was never difficult to manufacture low-quality adhesives, but 3M succeeded in finding a use for them in Post-it notes, in which the product's limited efficiency (the adhesive is not permanent) was actually a virtue. Modern innovations often are applicable across a wide range of product markets. Enabling technologies—for example, in electronics or optics—have allowed firms like NEC or Canon to become strong competitors in apparently quite disparate lines of business.

Product Positioning

The position of a product is a means of defining its relationship to other products in the same market. In the car market, a Honda Civic is positioned differently from an NSX. In newspapers, the *New York Times* occupies a market position different from that of the *Washington Post.* We might choose instead to say that the Civic and the NSX, the *New York Times* and the *Washington Post,* are in different markets. The distinction has only semantic significance.

The term *positioning* is also widely used in a broader sense. Sometimes positioning describes not just the position of the product in its market but also the relationship of a firm's whole strategy to that of its competitors. For example, Michael Porter has written extensively (1980) about positioning in this way and has warned of the danger of being "stuck in the middle." Porter is right to warn of the dangers of a confused strategy, but those writers who have misinterpreted him as advising against adopting a mid-market *product* position have been led into serious error. Many of the world's most successful firms have adopted product positions that are firmly stuck in the middle. Budweiser beer is neither the strongest nor the weakest. Sony equipment is neither the cheapest nor the most sophisticated. American Airlines caters to a broad range of passengers. For these firms, as for many others, a mid-market position has proved the most successful way of exploiting their competitive advantage. Since mid-market positions commonly offer the greatest density of customers, this is hardly surprising.

Newspapers such as the *New York Times* or the *Washington Post* are described as "quality newspapers." The phrase is a useful starting point for thinking about precisely what that quality means. Here is a possible definition: One good is of better quality than another is if more people would buy it if the prices of the two goods were the same. A fine bordeaux is of better quality than a bottle of table wine. Many more people buy the table wine, but they do so because it is cheaper. If both wines cost the same, however, most people would choose the bordeaux. If they would not, then it is hard to know how we could say that the bordeaux was of higher quality, and it is much less likely that it would command a higher price.

This definition is not without its problems. It suggests that Coke is a higher-quality product than Pepsi is. But no one believes that Coke is made of better materials or is manufactured under more closely controlled conditions, and the evidence of blind tasting seems to be that, if anything, consumers prefer the Pepsi flavor. But across the world, people drink more Coke, and this concept of quality asserts that taking the product, its history, and its marketing together, Coke is perceived as being of higher quality.

The *Washington Post* poses a similar difficulty: It is, by any standards, a fine newspaper, but it is not a paper that more than a small minority of newspaper readers would wish to buy. Arthur Hailey is not as good a novelist as Jane Austen is, even though his books sell in larger numbers. For products like these and to some extent for all commodities, there is an objective standard of quality that is not necessarily reflected in the marketplace. But it is the market's assessment of quality that determines profitable and unprofitable positions. That is, we might prefer to read Jane Austen, but we would rather publish Arthur Hailey.

Underlying this are two distinct factors determining the nature of the product space. Within the same market, buyers look for different products partly because they disagree about what they prefer (horizontal differentiation) and partly because even though they agree about what they prefer, they differ in their capacity to afford it (vertical differentiation). Consumers have variable requirements partly because their tastes or needs differ and partly because their willingness to pay differs.

The term *down-market products* refers to both goods bought by low-income households (such as discount retailing) and products that, although not of low quality, cater to tastes that are not well regarded (such as tabloid newspapers). Many managers instinctively shy away from down-market positions, from a sense that price-based competition is unlikely to be profitable or from an understandable reluctance to be associated with products that they would not themselves wish to buy. There are many markets in which this has given scope to very successful down-market entry—Wal-Mart, Motel 6, the growth of fast-food restaurants. Early buyers of Japanese cars were attracted by their price rather than by their luxury, style, or prestige.

The view that "quality is king" is so prevalent that many readers will have already found for themselves rationalizations suggesting that these successful products are really of high rather than low quality. Yet few people would have wished to buy them had they not been cheap. This is another example of confusion between the market position of the product and the strategy of the firm. The quality of goods and services is distinct from the quality of the strategy, management, or organization of the firm that manufactures it. Motel 6 units are not good hotels, but they are good hotels for $30 per night, and Motel 6 is a highly effective organization.

Down-market positions require particularly strong management discipline. To minimize costs while maintaining standards acceptable to consumers requires close control of the product's specification. This is characteristic of companies as different as Wal-Mart and McDonald's. Down-market positions carry the further danger that increasing incomes or the evolution of more sophisticated tastes will steadily erode the size of the segment. Woolworth developed down-market retailing with great success only to see its market develop away from it.

Matching Position to Distinctive Capability

Just as the choice of market reflects a firm's distinctive capability, so must its choice of market position be matched to competitive advantage. When the source of competitive advantage is innovation, then the innovation may itself dictate the product's position. The quartz watch can be placed down market only because the important feature of the innovation is that it offers, more cheaply, a capability for accurate timekeeping that was previously available only at a higher cost.

Sometimes architecture dictates a market position. The distinctive capabilities of BMW or Mercedes necessarily place them toward the top

Illustration 9.2. Markets, Market Positioning, and Distinctive Capability

Basis of distinctive capability	Basis of choosing market and market position
Reputation	Reputation is created in a specific market. Add related markets if consumers think you can transfer attributes and you know you can. Usually implies up-market position (but need not).
Architecture	The nature of relationships—internal, external, network—or their result—flexible response, organizational knowledge—often dictates market and position. Otherwise, seek mid-market.
Innovation	Product innovations usually imply market and position. Process innovations often do—otherwise seek mid-market position.

of the market. In other cases, the architecture may be of value anywhere—such as for Wal-Mart—and the most attractive position is the one attracting the largest number of customers. Sometimes the same competitive advantage is best deployed in different positions in different markets. Marks & Spencer, the British retailer, is famous for its value-for-money, mid-market clothing range. Yet it also sells food of very high quality at prices much higher than those charged by rival supermarkets. Its position in the food market thus is very different from the one it adopts in clothing, and it caters, in large measure, to different groups of customers. The underlying rationale is that the company's distinctive capability—in particular, the architecture of its close and continuing supplier relationships—yields the greatest benefit in different ways in food and in clothing.

When a competitive advantage is based on reputation, a price and quality position toward the top end of the market is usually appropriate because it is where the six major accounting firms, or the international car rental firms, are located. Yet a "value-for-money" reputation may be achieved with a mid-market position—this was the strength of Sears's position for decades—and a reputation may even be gained in down-market positions, where the supplier's reputation assures the customer that despite the low price, the product is of acceptable quality. This is the concept behind Motel 6. More commonly, however, reputation advantages are deployed toward the upper end of the spectrum of product quality—more so than for other primary distinctive capabilities. The addition of a reputation to a capability based on innovation or architecture may therefore imply a move to a more up-market position. This has been a repeated characteristic of Japanese entry strategies.

This discussion shows that distinctive capabilities are frequently, although not necessarily, used most effectively in mid- or up-market positions. This is reflected in the average returns earned (Figure 9.1), but it does not imply that any particular firm can expect to earn more profit by moving up market or that a down-market position may not be the best way of exploiting a particular competitive advantage. The choice of market position must always be a reflection of the firm's distinctive capabilities. Sometimes the distinctive capability is, like reputation or architecture, one that naturally suggests a position at the top of the market. When it is not, a mid-market strategy should always be considered first.

Positioning When Products Have Many Attributes

Most products have multiple characteristics. This is strikingly true of both newspapers and supermarkets. A newspaper contains many different news stories. It probably has features, editorials, and perhaps a cross-word puzzle. It may list racing results, stock prices, the weather forecast, and radio and television schedules. When you buy a newspaper, you buy the package, but when you buy groceries, you buy only a few of the thousands of items that a supermarket stocks. The attractiveness of the supermarket depends on whether that product range meets your specific

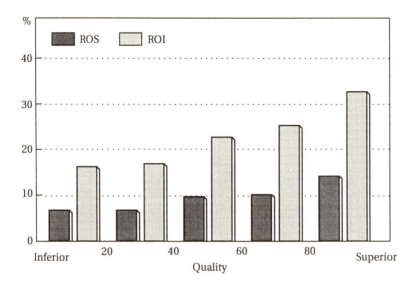

Figure 9.1. Quality and Profitability

needs. You may also be influenced by the cleanliness and layout of the store, the attitude of the sales staff, and the speed of the checkout procedure, as well as by the prices.

Any product can be defined as a bundle of characteristics, each of which can be valued. Consumers look at the speed, acceleration, comfort, and reliability of a car. The price that each of these characteristics commands in the market establishes the "going rate" for any particular specification. The profitability of a product position then depends on its value relative to its cost and on the demand for the product at that price.

Often the value of one characteristic is dependent on all the others. Buyers of a Honda Civic may not be willing to pay much extra for leather upholstery, but purchasers of a Lexus may regard it as essential. A *focused* product is one whose bundle of characteristics is well targeted to a certain market segment. Readers who are interested in gossip about radio and television personalities are probably not interested in analyses of the political situation in Latin America, and vice versa. Newspapers that combine both of these risk being unfocused products. Customers who buy fresh fruit in a supermarket may also demand fresh bread and a variety of cheeses and have high expectations of the quality of the store's layout. Buyers of canned fruit may be more willing to buy prepackaged bread and cheese and to pick products out of cardboard boxes. To satisfy some of these attributes without satisfying them all may lead to an unfocused market position. This means that the cost of the product will be too high relative to the value of the characteristics bundle that is offered.

The importance of focus depends on the number of products available in the marketplace. An unfocused product is one that might be everyone's second or third choice but no one's first. This is viable, however, and may indeed be optimal if few first choices are available. Henry Ford's unfocused Model T was exactly right for an early stage of development of the car market but became steadily less successful as the demand for automobiles grew and the product choice expanded. Focused television channels specializing in sports or music can be sustained only when the number of programs available is relatively large; when few frequencies are available, all channels are typically unfocused. Focused airlines—specializing in business travelers or backpackers—have not succeeded because the density of traffic on most routes is insufficient to support frequent, economic, focused services. Yet if the number of products in the market is very large, focus again becomes less critical, because there will be some customers for almost any bundle of characteristics. A restaurant that provides gourmet food on plastic tables with paper napkins may find a clientele for whom that is precisely the product they require. Such restaurants do survive in New York, although less frequently in smaller towns.

Matching Competitive Advantage to Geographic Market

A distinctive capability needs to be matched to a set of geographical markets as well as to a set of product markets. It is rarely possible to extend reputations outside the geographic market within which they are created—they must be built afresh. Citibank's attempts to build retail-banking networks in Europe have been repeatedly disappointing. The Citibank name, however well known in New York and in (global) wholesale money markets, has little significance to European retail customers.

Reputation most frequently travels when customers do. Hotels, car rental, and professional services all are extensively bought by purchasers whose normal residence is elsewhere. International reputation is powerful in these markets, and reputation is the driving force behind the internationalization of the industry.

A firm with a competitive advantage in one market may find it advantageous to serve other markets even if it has little or no competitive advantage in them—no innovation to offer, no reputation to bring, architecture that is valuable only elsewhere. This will be true if there are economies of scale or economies of scope. *Scale economies* exist when the costs of providing a common product decrease with the volume of output; *scope economies* exist if the cost of providing two distinct goods and services from the same firm is less than the cost of providing both separately.

Scale economies dictate that many producers of manufactured goods serve a range of geographic markets. It is now impossible to be a viable automobile producer on the basis of one geographic market alone. So there is a world automobile industry, even though the Japanese and American automobile markets are very different. There is a world market in aircraft—aircraft are particularly easy commodities to transport—and a viable producer of large aircraft must serve the whole of it. For these firms, the geographical boundaries of the market and the industry coincide. But just as the car industry is one in which the boundaries of the industry are wider than the boundaries of the market, so the boundaries of the industry may be narrower then those of the market. Although there is a world market in cut diamonds, there are no scale economies in diamond cutting, and so the industry is local and fragmented. In general, the more important the scale economies are, the wider the dimensions of the industry will be relative to those of the market.

Scale economies will encourage firms to produce in different product markets if these have important common components. This is true of the automobile and aircraft industries, and it may be true of domestic appliances also. Even though refrigerators and washing machines are in different markets, since both are white boxes with motors, there may be scale economies in combined production, and Fiat's strength in the manufacture of small motors for these appliances was a factor in Italy's dominance of the European white goods industry. The use of common distribution systems was a much more important common factor for these different types of appliances, which is a characteristic instance of scope economies. The distribution of both refrigerators and washing machines together is cheaper and more effective than the distribution of either separately.

These scope economies arise because the products share retail outlets. Closely related scope economies arise when consumers wish to buy bundles of commodities. Xerox's competitive advantages relate to the provision of photocopiers, are modest in relation to the supply of toner, and are nonexistent in the handling and distribution of paper. Yet consumers need all these things to make their copiers work, and if they want to buy service packages, there may be scope economies in serving all three product markets.

Scope economies are common where networks exist. The advantages of interlining and hub-and-spoke operations benefit airlines that operate multiple routes from a single airport over those that offer only one. For this reason, it may pay airlines to operate on routes that would not be profitable on a stand-alone basis because they contribute to the value of a route network taken as a whole.

These extensions to other geographic or product markets are effective only if the firm enjoys a competitive advantage—from reputation, innovation, architecture, or possibly an exclusive franchise—in at least some market. Neither scope nor scale economies can compensate for the absence of competitive advantage, since scale and scope are essentially replicable attributes. This issue is discussed in more detail in Chapter 11. Scope and scale are characteristics that can enhance competitive advantage, but they cannot substitute for it.

The Industry, the Strategic Market, and the Strategic Group

The choice of market is the most important element of strategic choice. But industry matters to the company in several ways. The criteria that statisticians use when determining industry boundaries and organization are similar to those that firms themselves should employ when determining their strategic business units. The principles to be applied—common enabling technologies, relatedness of markets, extension of competitive advantage—are broadly the same.

The scope of the industry offers a guide to how other firms perceive related markets. So it may suggest other ways in which a competitive advantage might be used. Often, of course, the competitive advantage of these different firms is not the same, and they are right to pursue a different set of markets. Coke and Pepsi have strengths in soft drinks quite different from those of the local companies against which they compete everywhere, and it would be a mistake for a local company to think it should try to match either their range of products or their geographical scope.

Although it is important for a firm to identify its competitors, it is no less important to identify competitors with different strategies than it is to identify those with related strategies. Indeed, the concept of the strategic group risks diverting attention from the first task of competitive strategy—the identification of distinctive capability. "How can we be different?" is ultimately a far more important question than "Who are we like?" There are few number twos that do not aspire to be number one, but setting out to imitate number one is only occasionally the way either to be number one or to make the best of being number two.

The strategic market is the minimum area in which a firm can successfully compete. It is a combination of economic markets drawn together by economies of scale and scope. Sometimes the boundaries are narrowly defined, associated with fragmented industries in which innovation is rare or inappropriable—as in many service industries. Sometimes, as in aircraft manufacture, the imperatives of scale and scope are such that the strategic market is the world market. The successful firm dominates at least one strategic market.

Any firm's core markets are those to which its distinctive capabilities, or strategic assets, are directly relevant. Without some such markets, there is no prospect of adding value. But the firm's added value can be leveraged by the addition of other markets in which—even if it has no direct competitive advantage—the economies of scale and scope associated with its key markets allow it to serve that market more effectively or at lower cost. It is these factors taken together that answer the question, "What business are we in?" with which this chapter began. Firms with true distinctive capabilities generally serve their market using these in a unique combination.

The history of markets, literal and metaphorical, is described by Agnew (1986). More recent analysis of the issue falls into two quite distinct groups. One is designed as a guide for marketing managers. The dominant figure here is Levitt, whose principal contributions are reproduced in Levitt (1986); see also Curran and Goodfellow (1990). A specialist literature is concerned with defining the market for purposes of antitrust policies. The major contributions here are Landes and Posner (1981), Scheffman and Spiller (1987), and Stigler and Sherwin (1985). Kay (1990) is a further exposition of some of the concepts in this chapter. A focus on the "core business," much emphasized in the 1980s (Abell 1980), was popularized as "sticking to the knitting" by Peters and Waterman (1982). For further discussion of the European Union's 1992 program and the relationship between American and European concepts of economic integration, see Davis, Kay, and Ridge (forthcoming).

There is now a very large literature explaining the strategic advantages of up-market positioning. Crosby (1979) was an influential early contribution; a more recent discussion is Dale and Plunkett (1990). Empirical support is drawn from PIMS; see Buzzell and Gale (1987). Davis (1990) is concerned with the analytic and empirical issues.

10

Mergers

Mergers and acquisitions are the most common means of entering new markets and play a central role in all discussions and formulations of corporate strategy. In this chapter I argue that this role is frequently overstated. Mergers can, and do, add value, when they enable distinctive capabilities to be exploited more widely or more effectively, and I describe how this can be done. Yet a review of studies of merger performance suggests that the effect on performance is more often negative than beneficial. Frequently the reason is that corporate activity is not based on a clear view of the firm's distinctive capability and an identification of the markets to which that capability can be most effectively applied but is the result of financial objectives—the pursuit of a balanced or diversified business portfolio—or simply the thrill of the chase.

In recent years, joint ventures, strategic alliances, divestment, and management buyouts have given companies many more tools for restructuring their activities. In this chapter I explain some of the reasons that alliances, like mergers, so often fall short of the hopes of their promoters. Nonetheless, the evidence so far encourages a more hopeful assessment of buyouts and divestments. I also discuss the variety of ways in which government policies influence the process of merger and the different attitudes toward mergers that prevail around the world.

*I*n Chapter 9 I considered how firms should identify their markets. In practice, the most common way in which companies enter new markets is by means of acquisition. Mergers play a central role in most discussions of corporate strategy, and increasingly over the last two decades, so has divestment. At times, it is easy to think that corporate strategy consists of little else and that the task of the CEO, like that of an investment manager, is supervising the corporate portfolio.

You would not get that impression, however, if you followed the histories of the ten "winners" identified in Chapter 2. Merger and acquisition did not play an important role in the success of any of these companies. In only one—Philip Morris—did it feature centrally in the firm's strategy, and in a second—Liz Claiborne—did it play a subsidiary role.

As I explain in this chapter, evidence regarding the performance of merged firms demonstrates that the overall record of mergers has been disappointing.

There have been three—perhaps four—great waves of mergers in American business history, and in the changing role that mergers have played, we can see the changing preoccupations of American managers. The first large mergers occurred in the latter part of the nineteenth century, when buccaneering figures such as Rockefeller, Duke, and Carnegie put together combinations that dominated single industries in an unashamed pursuit of monopoly and economic power. Political hostility to these men's ambitions created antitrust policies. The Sherman Act, which, quite simply, prohibits monopoly and monopolization, was passed in 1890 and led to the dissolution of Standard Oil and American Tobacco.

A smaller wave of merger activity came in the 1920s and 1930s, reflecting the consolidation resulting from the development of mass production techniques and rationalization in response to the Great Depression. After World War II, enforcement of antitrust legislation by the Federal Trade Commission and Justice Department made mergers between large firms in the same line of business virtually impossible. Accordingly, the merger wave of the 1960s centered on conglomerate mergers—the acquisition and control by a single company operating businesses in many different industries. Beatrice Foods bought 290 different companies between 1950 and 1978; other major acquirers included ITT, W. R. Grace, LTV, Litton Industries, and Teledyne. It was no accident that this phase coincided with the development of interest in strategic management. The conglomerate was a logical development of the view expressed by businessmen such as Alfred Sloan and business historians such as Alfred Chandler, which emphasized the distinction between the strategic role of the corporate center and the tactical decisions required in individual operating units.

The revival of merger activity in the 1980s was, in large measure, a reaction to the mistakes of that era. For the first time, divestiture became as significant as acquisition, and the takeover activity served to reduce industrial concentration as well as to increase it. Although there had been some hostile takeovers in the 1960s, these became more and more common in the 1980s as bidders stressed their ability to make corporate assets work more effectively than the incumbent management had. The emphasis was on financial reconstruction in order to maximize shareholder value.

There is a reaction again today against the excesses of that era, and it is difficult to believe that figures such as Donald Trump and Robert

Campeau were once regarded as serious businessmen. The element of fashion in merger activity is evident from the changing motivations of those who pursue it, and later I consider why, despite the adverse evidence, portfolio management continues to play such a central role in corporate strategy. My primary concern in this chapter, however, is to identify the conditions under which mergers add value.

Adding Value Through Mergers

It is this ability to add value that justifies a merger. Value is added only if distinctive capabilities or strategic assets are exploited more effectively. In assessing a merger, the first requirement is to define the distinctive capabilities of the firms concerned. A merger will add no value if all that is acquired is a distinctive capability that is already fully exploited, since the price paid will reflect the competitive advantage held. Adding value requires some "synergy," which may be obtained from matching distinctive capabilities or strategic assets, winning access to complementary assets, or deriving economies of scale or scope related to the core business.

Mergers and acquisitions may be a means of entering a new market in which an established distinctive capability has not yet been deployed. Marsh & McLellan's competitive advantage rests on its architecture—its organizational knowledge and its relationships with its corporate clients' financial officers. The company's acquisition of William H. Mercer, employee benefits consultants, enabled it to use these relationships to sell more services. Philip Morris's acquisition of the Miller brewery raised more complex issues. If Philip Morris's distinctive capability lies simply in the strength of its Marlboro brand, it is irrelevant to the beer market— the company did not intend to rebrand Miller as Marlboro Beer. If, however, Philip Morris's distinctive capability is not just Marlboro but, rather, a set of marketing skills—the organizational knowledge that has made Marlboro such a success and that has been enhanced by it—then the acquisition was a means of gaining leverage for the firm's competitive advantage. Philip Morris's success with Miller suggests that this may have been true.

Mergers may add value if the distinctive capabilities of the two firms are complementary. The integration of good local firms into the "Big Six" international accounting firms has achieved this. The national firm has a local reputation but fails to maximize its value because it has difficulty conveying that reputation to international customers. The international firm is well known to its international customers but can extract value from that reputation in the local market only if it can attract the best local practitioners. The combination of the two reputations therefore raises the value of each.

Sometimes an acquisition can add value if one firm has assets that complement the competitive advantage of the other. Marsh & McLellan bought not only Mercer but also Bowring, a British insurance company with strong connections in the London insurance market, enabling it to sell Lloyd's policies and other European products more effectively to its U.S. clients and to offer its U.S. contacts to a European client base. Sony has a strong position in the development of high-definition television. Because there are potentially alternative Japanese, American, and European systems, the evolution of this market will depend both on the actions of broadcasters—who are subject to extensive government regulation—and on the behavior of suppliers of prerecorded material. Sony's purchase of Columbia Pictures gave the company—at enormous cost—control of one of the largest film libraries available.

Or a merger may be justified by cost savings based on economies of scale or scope. If there is cost savings based on excess capacity, a merger may allow a more rapid and less costly means of reducing capacity than would be possible through the operation of market forces alone. Deregulation of the airline industry led to expansion by many firms and overcapacity. Mergers and the acquisition of failing firms by their stronger rivals have been the principal means of reducing capacity.

Merger can be used to create or extend strategic assets as well as to enhance distinctive capabilities. The most familiar route—the one adopted by Rockefeller, Duke, and Carnegie—is to reduce competition and increase market power through the acquisition of a direct competitor. In addition, by inhibiting entry, acquisitions can sustain exclusivity or maintain the value of a competitive advantage. Ownership of well-located gas stations by oil companies makes it more difficult for new wholesalers to get access to the market.

Or a merger may be a means of appropriating or defending a competitive advantage or added value against the demands of suppliers or customers. British financial institutions were concerned that real estate brokers were likely to become increasingly important distributors of their retail products, especially mortgages, insurance, and other services associated with buying a house. In order to defend their own added value, the financial institutions bought chains of real estate brokers. But because they lacked the right kind of management skills, they lost a great deal of money in the process and would have done better simply to have relinquished some of that added value.

Financial Issues in Mergers and Acquisitions

Corporate diversification is often sought as a means of reducing corporate risk. "Diversification is therefore a necessary type of corporate insurance which sound management must achieve on the behalf of its stockholders, so that the risks of separate sectors are pooled" (Harold Geneen, for many years the dominant influence in the U.S. conglomerate ITT, cited in Lamb 1984). Such diversification is not, however, a means of adding value. The reason is simple. Diversification is something that shareholders can—and characteristically do—achieve for themselves. They do not need the corporation to do it for them.

In practice, there are two important reasons for thinking that the diversified corporation is likely to be a bad substitute for a diversified-share portfolio. It is much more expensive to buy whole companies than it is to buy stakes in companies, because of the bid premium that must be paid to persuade *all* shareholders to part with their holdings. When the tobacco company R. J. Reynolds diversified by buying Nabisco in 1985, it paid a premium of around 30 percent of the market price before takeover speculation affected the stock. Any RJR shareholders who wanted to spread the risks of the tobacco business by buying into cereals could have done so much more cheaply than by having the Reynolds management do it for them.

Many Reynolds shareholders may not have wanted to invest in a food company. Diversification means that it is impossible to buy shares in the company that makes Camels without also buying shares in the company that makes Ritz crackers. As a result of acquisitions by tobacco companies, it is now impossible for an investor who believes that the market's wariness of the industry's long-term prospects is exaggerated to support that judgment, since there is no way to buy a tobacco stock without also buying a portfolio of extraneous interests.

By forcing prospective purchasers of tobacco shares or food shares into a fixed-proportions package of tobacco and food that they may not especially want, the imposed combination may subtract rather than add value. An extremely competitive market, through collective investment funds, offers prepackaged diversified portfolios to those who are not able, or do not wish, to create such a package themselves.

Such diversification, although often incorrectly rationalized as serving shareholders' interests, is principally in the interests of the diversifying companies' management. This is not a negligible or disreputable consideration. It is harder to motivate the management of a declining business and difficult to sustain an architecture that entails lifetime commitment to the firm if its long-term prospects are uncertain. This is a relevant consideration for Japanese companies whose lifetime employment underpins their architecture, and it supports the structure of diversified groups that has traditionally been characteristic of Japanese industry.

Markets often find conglomerate companies difficult to assess, especially since companies are not required, and are often unwilling, to break down their overall performance into that of the different operating entities. There is a tendency to attach the price–earnings ratio characteristic of the main business to the company as a whole, so that a diversified tobacco and food company may well attract the low stock market rating applied to a tobacco firm rather than the higher figure applied to food manufacturers. For the combined RJR Nabisco, the result was that it was worth little more than its tobacco business alone, and this led to a bitter takeover struggle and the breakup of the corporation.

The battle for RJR Nabisco was the most dramatic of the many corporate restructurings of the 1980s. As a result of the development of creative methods of financing, particularly Michael Milken's invention of junk bonds, it became possible to visualize financial reconstructions and hostile bids for even the largest corporations. Some of these deals were, as the RJR one was, a reaction to the excesses of conglomerate acquisitions in earlier decades. Others were, as the RJR one was intended to be, management buyouts of existing, established businesses. The rationale of these is the belief that a higher ratio of debt to equity and a larger management shareholding will ensure better performance. Such leveraged buyouts may also enhance the value of corporate equity by downgrading the security of corporate debt. A more skeptical view is that such transactions enable senior managers to extract for themselves the value of their inside knowledge of the company's operations and the substantial costs of removing them from corporate office. Thus there is a conflict of interest at the heart of any management buyout. All these things appear to have been true in the RJR Nabisco case.

Although publicly contested takeover battles for entire companies, such as that for RJR Nabisco, attracted much attention, more such transactions involved the sale of individual operating businesses. Many of these firms disposed of what they no longer regarded as their "core businesses" to other corporations that *did* see the activities concerned as part of their "core business." Others involved selling a division of a conglomerate to its own managers.

These transactions add value to the extent that the new financing or ownership structure leads to improvement in business performance. Although most of them appear to go in the right direction—closer scrutiny of management by shareholders, greater financial involvement by management, and the removal of redundant layers of corporate supervision and corporate ownership—the improvements in performance needed to justify many of the transactions in question would have to be remarkable indeed. RJR Nabisco was finally auctioned for almost twice its value before the company came "into play"—an increase in value of around $10 billion—and the fees to the various parties to the transactions added substantially to the $16 billion price tag. If the improvements needed to justify these figures really are possible in the management of large, well-established corporations, this raises fundamental questions about the current state of American business. It also invites consideration of whether there are alternative, and less costly and traumatic, methods of achieving the same results. Transactions of these kinds are virtually unknown in other countries, including most of America's successful industrial competitors. I return to this issue in Chapter 16.

The Success of Mergers

It is too early to make any firm pronouncement on the long-term consequences of the merger and acquisition activity of the 1980s. But whatever that judgment turns out to be, it should be seen in the context of a large body of evidence from the United States and elsewhere suggesting that taken as a whole, mergers add little or no value.

The most effective way of analyzing the performance of mergers is to analyze the pre- and postmerger profitability of the firms concerned. The most extensive study of this kind is an analysis by Ravenscraft and Scherer (1987) of around 6,000 acquisitions made between 1950 and 1976. They found that the acquired firms had, overall, significantly better than the industry's average profitability before acquisition but that by the end of their period of analysis, the profitability of the merged business was broadly in line with that expected for their industry. Put simply, the acquirers bought better-than-average performers and turned them into average performers.

This somewhat grim verdict is, however, not out of line with that suggested by other similar studies (see Mueller 1986 for a survey of earlier work). Analogous results have been found in other countries: Meeks (1977) reached the same conclusion for the United Kingdom, and a wide-ranging review of merger performance across the European Union reached the verdict (the most favorable to emerge from this type of analysis) that "no consistent pattern of either improved or deteriorated profitability can therefore be claimed across the seven countries. Mergers would appear to result in a slight improvement here, a slight worsening there."

Evidence from the stock market is more favorable to merger. (Jensen and Ruback 1983 provide a survey of these "event studies.") Acquirers almost invariably pay a bid premium, so that merger announcements lead to an increase in the acquired firm's market value. Sometimes the share price of the acquirer rises, sometimes it falls, but for a selection of merger stocks taken as a whole, these broadly balance out so that merger announcements are, on average, neutral in their effect on the acquirer's share price. The implication is that mergers do add value, that the merged concern is, on average, valued more highly than is the sum of the two merging companies. On average, the whole of that gain goes to the shareholders of the company that is acquired.

There are, however, some problems with this interpretation of the data. Acquired firms tend to have done worse than the stock market in general in the period before (though not immediately before) acquisition, and acquiring firms usually have done a bit better. When the stock market performance of the acquiring firms is measured over a longer period of time than that of the merger announcement, the average pattern is one of underperformance. That is, a portfolio of newly merged companies can be expected to do worse than the market. The stock market's initial assessment (perhaps like that of the managers of the companies involved) seems to be unduly optimistic.

The most likely explanation of these facts, and their reconciliation with accounting data, is that the timing of acquisitions tends to reflect valuation anomalies. Mergers tend to be consummated when the acquirer's share price is relatively strong and the acquiree's is relatively weak. The apparent gains from merging reflect the correction of these discrepancies rather than the added value from the merger as such. None of this evidence should be interpreted as indicating that no merger is ever successful. Clearly, some mergers, including many of those discussed in this chapter, have been effective in adding value to the businesses that they brought together. But the implication that both managers and markets substantially overestimate the gains from a merger is very clear.

Why do managers continue to devote so much attention to a process that appears to add little value? The reasons are remarkably similar to those explaining why people gamble despite the overwhelming evidence that on average, gamblers lose. First, the exceptions are striking and everyone tends to overestimate the probability that they will be one of the exceptions. Most people and companies that have made large amounts of money quickly have done so by purchasing undervalued assets. Second, the process itself is enjoyable. Few corporate activities generate as much immediate publicity for a CEO as a major takeover, and many derive pleasure from the thrill of the chase or the "art" of the deal. Third, a substantial legal and investment banking business thrives on merger, acquisition, and divestiture transactions and so has strong incentives to promote them, whatever their value to the companies involved is.

Public Policy and Mergers

Antitrust policy came into existence to restrict the growth of giant combinations right across American business at the turn of the century. Today, the main instrument of merger control is the Hart-Scott-Rodino Act, which requires those companies taking a stake of over 5 percent or $15 million in another corporation to file a report and secure the approval of the Federal Trade Commission (FTC). If the merger would create a monopoly under the Sherman or Clayton Acts, the FTC or the Department of Justice—or a private litigant—can challenge in court the legality of the proposed combination.

These antitrust rules were once a major obstacle to mergers between companies in the same industry, and such restrictions were one reason for the emphasis on conglomerate mergers in the acquisition wave of the 1960s. As noted in Chapter 8, however, the enforcement of U.S. antitrust rules has become much less vigorous. In the light of this general approach and the greater openness of the U.S. economy to foreign competition, the position of the courts and federal agencies on acquisitions has become much more liberal. A merger will not now be challenged unless it violates a set of guidelines prescribed by the Department of Justice. These guidelines interpret the legal requirement of monopoly in terms of the Herfindahl index, a measure of concentration in a particular market. A merger is likely to be challenged if the overall market concentration level is above 1,800 (a figure that would be reached if five equal firms controlled the market) and the combination adds no more than 100 to that figure.

Two other forms of public intervention in the merger process have become more significant as antitrust concerns have faded. State legislatures, concerned with blocking acquisitions of local companies, especially by foreign firms, have attempted to put obstacles in the path of the bidders. Closely associated with this is the adoption by most U.S. corporations of "poison pill" defenses, designed to shield the company from an unwanted takeover. Such a poison pill establishes a clear conflict of interest between the managers of the company, who may want to protect their jobs and positions, and the shareholders, who generally are happy to sell out to the highest bidder. The courts have become involved in order to mediate this conflict, and their general approach is to permit poison pills to be used to give the incumbent management time to find the best alternative for shareholders but not simply to reject a better offer or to favor one bidder over another. In these cases, the courts are not trying to establish the consequences of the takeover for the efficiency and competitiveness of the firms concerned or for the national economy, but simply to ensure that their executives properly discharge their fiduciary responsibilities to the shareholders.

Among the major Western economies, only the United Kingdom (where company law and institutional shareholders have prohibited poison pill defenses) has a comparably liberal takeover regime. In Germany and Japan, hostile takeovers are virtually impossible, and mergers and acquisitions of any kind are relatively rare. The changes in management style and structure that in the United States are effected by takeover are achieved in these countries by a less public mix of internal and external pressures on the corporation. Such internal pressure is made possible by the much less dominant role of the CEO in German and Japanese companies, so that changes in strategic direction or the rotation of the senior officers' posts are made by consensus within the company itself. External pressures may result from the much closer links between the banking system and large corporations.

Other countries (particularly including Germany, Japan, and the United Kingdom) have antitrust policies that require large mergers to be appraised by a government agency before approval is given. In 1990 the European Union adopted a merger regulation that provides for the scrutiny of all large mergers within Europe (including mergers between U.S. companies with substantial European operations), to ensure that they are consistent with competition within the European single market.

Joint Ventures, Strategic Alliances, and Minority Shareholdings

It is not just international merger and acquisition activity that has increased. Joint ventures and strategic alliances, particularly those with an international dimension, have also mushroomed. General Motors, for example, responded to the demand for small cars by establishing a joint venture with Toyota at Fremont, California.

But many of these joint ventures have so far mostly fallen short of their founders' expectations. Some alliances are predicated on the belief that they represent an intermediate contract form between the classical and the relational contract and offer the best of both worlds—security and protection against the opportunism of the classical form and the flexibility and information sharing of the relational form. It is necessary only to spell out that hope to see that it is unlikely to be recognized. The two contract types differ by reference to their means of enforcement: Classical contracts are upheld by reference to the terms of the contract, and relational contracts, which are not spelled out in formal terms, are reinforced by the two parties' continuing need to do business with each other. But you cannot have classical enforcement of a relational contract, and although you can have relational enforcement of a classical contract, that is the worst, not the best, of the two worlds.

Joint ventures fall into two categories—"common objective" and "mutually beneficial exchange." The common-objective venture is typically one in which one party's distinctive capability requires the other's complementary asset, or the two distinctive capabilities complement each other. The defeat of Hitler was based on a combination of the United States' technical and material resources, the Soviet Union's manpower, and Britain's convenient island location. Columbus's discovery of the New World was the product of the complementary assets of Queen Isabella's wealth and his navigational skills (although since he was in search of the East Indies, the latter should not be overrated). A mutually beneficial exchange is one in which each partner has a skill or information or expertise that is of value to the other.

Although most joint ventures contain elements of each, the balance between the two varies considerably. When the British company Glaxo brought what is now the world's best-selling drug, Zantac, to the United States, it did so in partnership with Hoffmann-La Roche, the only foreign company previously to have enjoyed (through its tranquilizers Librium and Valium) blockbusting success in the U.S. market. Philips's collaboration with Sony on compact discs is a case of the second. A stylized view of the payoffs in the corresponding games is as follows: In the common-objective game, the result—success or failure—is common to both parties, and the payoffs are symmetric. The example in Figure 10.1, which develops the joint-venture game of Chapter 3, assumes that the overall gains from full cooperation are 10 and those from partial cooperation are 4. In the mutually advantageous exchange game, however, the outcome may be asymmetric. It is possible for one party to gain from the other—and this, of course, is a result that each may try to secure.

It is immediately clear that cooperation is a dominant strategy for both partners in the first game and that holding back is a dominant strat-

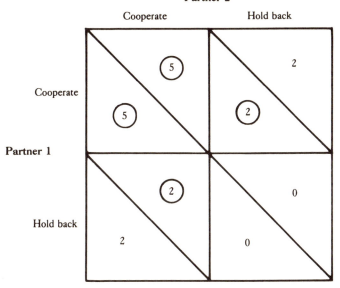

The common-objective venture

Partner 2

The information-exchange venture

Partner 2

Figure 10.1. Joint-Venture Games

egy for both partners in the second game. In the common-objective venture, it pays both parties to put the maximum effort into the common objective (although the parties can, and do, argue heatedly about their shares of the returns). In the information and skill exchange venture, it always is better to engage in strategic maneuvers to get as much as possible while giving as little as possible—and this is true despite the clear mutual benefits from full cooperation. Recall that World War II featured an effective alliance only as long as the objective—the defeat of Hitler— was shared by all its members and that despite the evident advantages of continued cooperation, the alliance collapsed once that common objective had been secured.

This pessimistic view of the outcome of the Prisoner's Dilemma game could be modified if it were played repeatedly. But the key characteristic of that repeated game is that it must be infinite, or at least uncertain, in length. A joint venture that is expected to last for a defined period will incite strategic behavior toward the end of its life, and once the parties realize this, they will behave strategically. This is the unraveling property that undermines many repeated game strategies. Joint ventures based on mutually beneficial exchanges will be effective only if both parties believe them to be of indefinite duration—probably because they are seen as the prelude to a full merger—and joint ventures of an anticipated finite duration are unlikely to work. Most such ventures have left at least one party unhappy with the outcome.

A minority shareholding is created when one firm takes a stake in another that is too small to give it control of, or direct influence over, the other firm concerned. In the United States, such a stake is most often seen as preliminary to a full bid. But in the business environments of continental Europe and, most of all, of Japan, minority shareholdings are common, and their commercial function is different. That is, their purpose is to increase commitment to a relational contract. The holder has made an investment that is virtually useless to it in the absence of a continued trading relationship. (If the shares are readily marketable, then the sunk costs associated with such an investment are low, but usually they are not readily marketable.) The collapse of the relationship leaves the company in which the stake is held with a significant fraction of its shares in what are no longer friendly hands. Thus for both parties the existence of such a minority stake establishes penalties for opportunistic behavior. Like the exchange of gifts in almost all cultures or the exchange of valuable tokens on the occasion of an engagement or marriage, minority shareholdings reinforce commitment in both a real and a symbolic sense.

For surveys of the performance of U.S. mergers, see Jensen and Ruback (1983), Netter (1988), and Ravenscraft and Sherer (1987). Scherer and Ross (1990) provide a survey of the history of merger activity and merger policy. For an analysis of related issues outside the United States, see Bishop and Kay (1993).

The issues of portfolio versus corporate diversification are now covered in most finance texts, such as Brealey and Myers (1991, chap. 33). The performance of buyouts is reviewed by Wright et al. (1993). Joint ventures and strategic alliances are the subject of a burgeoning literature, such as Harrigan (1986, 1988). For the strategic role of minority shareholdings, see Thompson and Meadowcroft (1987).

The "market for corporate control" is a phrase used by Manne (1965), and the concept was most fully elaborated by Jensen and Ruback (1983). Its operation arouses controversy at several levels; see Jensen (1984, 1986) for vigorous defenses. Skeptics can find justification, and entertainment, in Burrough and Helyar (1990).

11

Sustainability

Distinctive capabilities will continue to add value only if both the capability and the distinctiveness can be sustained. In this chapter, I use case studies and statistical evidence to show that many companies are indeed successful in building sustainable competitive advantages from their distinctive capabilities. Of the principal distinctive capabilities, reputation is generally the easiest to sustain, and innovation is the most difficult, but each poses its own problems. Strategic assets can often be defended over very lengthy periods but may be suddenly at risk when regulations or market conditions change. For a firm with strategic assets, skills in handling public policy may be as important as those of business management.

In the second part of the chapter, I use the test of sustainability to explain why some factors that are often cited as sources of competitive advantage rarely yield substantial added value in the long run. I look at the role of scale, of market share, of business portfolio diversification, and of market positioning in achieving corporate success. Sometimes size or scale is itself the product of distinctive capabilities. Sometimes diversification or positioning reflects them. But if factors such as these are not based on distinctive capabilities, then the competitive advantages derived from them will seldom persist in the face of entry by firms that do enjoy true distinctive capabilities based on architecture, reputation, or innovation.

*T*he fluctuating fortunes of IBM, Apple, and Microsoft clearly raise the question of the sustainability of competitive advantage. For those who believe that corporate success is based on "excellence" or on the talents of the CEO, such fluctuations are paradoxical. How can IBM, for so long one of America's most respected corporations, now be performing so badly? "Sculley—chump or champ?" asked *Newsweek* (July 26, 1993), puzzling over the fact that the man who presided over Apple's successes of the 1980s was also the man in charge when it failed to sustain those successes through the 1990s.

Apple succeeded in the 1980s because it pioneered the graphical user interface (which Sculley did not invent), and it encountered difficulties in the 1990s because Microsoft developed a similar product (which Sculley was powerless to prevent). Corporate success depends not on the mood of the CEO but on distinctive capabilities applied in appropriate markets. Apple's success faded because its distinctive capability became less distinctive. IBM's success faded because even though its distinctive capability remained, the market evolved in a way that made it less valuable. Some competitive advantages prove sustainable over long periods, whereas others are only transitory. The outcome depends on the nature of the distinctive capability and of the market to which it is applied. The ability to sustain a competitive advantage is partly within the control of the corporation. But it is often contingent on aspects of the environment over which it has little control.

In most industries, the sources of competitive advantage shift backward and forward. After the creation of the European Union in 1957, the domestic appliance industry was one of the first to market consumer goods extensively across the member countries' frontiers. The automatic washing machine was a new and widely sought product, and the demand for it grew rapidly. Italian manufacturers, led by Indesit and Zanussi, came to dominate European markets, achieving long production runs on individual models and common scale economies in sourcing components and competing aggressively on price.

The market matured. As incomes rose and the cost of machines fell relative to those of other products, cheapness became a less powerful selling point. The development of flexible manufacturing processes reduced the advantages of large-scale operation. By the early 1980s, Indesit and Zanussi were effectively bankrupt. Their names survive thanks to the Italian government and the Swedish company Electrolux (which acquired Zanussi). The most profitable producers in this industry in the 1980s were not those with large multidomestic marketing operations, but those—like Hotpoint in the United Kingdom and Bosch in Germany— that focused on machines designed for their own domestic market and sold them through a distribution network over which they enjoyed substantial influence.

Disney's distinctive capability is clear and enduring. From 1965 to 1984 the corporation failed to make the most of that distinctive capability, but in the 1980s it did. The changes in that company's fortunes resulted from changes in the effectiveness with which it has exploited its distinctive capability. But it is, in an obvious sense, a static capability. The Disney repertoire is fixed; there are few untapped markets available to the company (although the invention of new forms of publishing will create more). Like the utilities discussed in Chapters 2 and 8, Disney is a successful company, but the limits to the rate of growth that success can sustain are clear.

Honda has not only extended its distinctive capability to other markets but has also added new distinctive capabilities. The company entered the automobile industry in 1967. Its first cars were the automotive equivalent of the supercub—simple, low-powered, functional urban transport. Subsequent models were positioned across other market segments. Most recently, the Honda NSX is intended to compete with Ferrari and Lamborghini. Honda has added reputation to its critical distinctive capability. By specializing in engine technology, it has achieved some success in innovation as well. The company has chosen a positioning somewhat up market of its principal Japanese rivals and has supported its entry into most major geographic markets with a plant in the United States and a relationship with Rover in Europe.

Sustaining a Competitive Advantage

Competitive advantages fade for one of two reasons. The distinctive capability may itself decline and become less distinctive, or the markets to which that distinctive capability is applied may shrink or otherwise become less valuable.

Innovation, as Chapter 7 showed, is generally the most fragile of distinctive capabilities. Most innovation advantages are transitory because the successful innovation is quickly copied. Financial services markets provide neither copyright nor patent in innovation. Sometimes an innovation can be protected if proprietary knowledge can be kept secret—as with the documentation needed to establish a new financial instrument. But usually this becomes public or can—like most production innovations—be reverse engineered. An innovation yields a competitive advantage only for as long as it takes an imitation to be effective, even if an innovation is protected by a system of tight appropriability. Xerox reaped handsome benefits from its innovation when it could fully appropriate its benefits but has since faced intense competition from other suppliers. Even a patented innovation is vulnerable to a new technology.

Innovation advantages are most frequently sustainable when they are supported by other distinctive capabilities or are protected by complementary assets, because then the imitation of the innovation itself is no longer enough. It often happens that the competitive advantage from an innovation goes not to the innovator but to the follower with the strongest set of supporting distinctive capabilities. This is how Matsushita (with the brand names of Panasonic and National) has managed to maintain an innovative lead in several of its principal markets, even though new developments have often been pioneered by smaller companies.

Competitive advantages based on architecture can be sustained over long periods, but not easily, as they must be nurtured. Organizational knowledge needs to be refreshed and replenished, and a cooperative ethic requires continual reinforcement. Yet some firms with a strong architecture, like Procter & Gamble, have maintained their advantages decade after decade, adapting their organizational knowledge and redeploying their relational skills in different market sectors.

But architecture is also easily destroyed. For many years, retail banks derived a competitive advantage from architecture. For example, the quality of a loan portfolio emerges only over time. Successful banks built a structure of long-term relational employment contracts that protected their employees from the temptation to emphasize short-term performance. Customers are naturally inclined to give their bankers an optimistic account of their financial prospects, and the successful banks overcame this by drawing up relational contracts with their customers.

In the 1970s and 1980s, many banks overrode these relationships in pursuit—as they saw it—of a more performance-based internal culture and a more aggressive external marketing perspective. Spot and classical contracts were substituted for relational ones, internally and externally. "Transactions banking" replaced "relationship banking," and in due course, the institutions concerned paid the price in bad loans and bad debts.

Organizational knowledge is typically market specific and may lose its value if the market changes. The depreciation of the value of the organizational knowledge accumulated over centuries in the Swiss watchmaking industry is a remarkable, if extreme, case. Likewise, organizational knowledge can often be conservative and fail to see these market shifts occurring or refuse to acknowledge their relevance when they have occurred. The craft skills of American shipbuilders or cutlers were once the basis of strong competitive advantages but ultimately came to have a negative value. The custodians of organizational knowledge knew a great deal about their industry that was no longer true.

More than any other distinctive capability, the sustainability of architecture rests on the skills of senior managers. Recognizing the nature of the company's architecture and its function in the markets the firm serves is a necessary first step. Architecture is certainly not created, and not much sustained, by the proliferation of identity and communication programs of the last decade as chief executives and their consultants unveiled the expensively orchestrated "corporate culture." These programs often confused the symbols of architecture with the substance and failed to acknowledge the degree to which architecture must grow with, and from, the organization. Architecture cannot be imposed, and if it could, it would be replicated.

An alternative danger is that the company—or its new management—does not fully appreciate the elaborate structure of implicit contracts that created its distinctive capability. It always is possible to earn immediate gains by imposing a better set of spot contracts, as Carl Icahn did when he acquired TWA. If you treat each game as if it were the last round of a repeated Prisoner's Dilemma, you will not derive the potential gains from repeated game strategies. Sometimes, of course, you *may* be playing the last round (and in the end, it turned out that Icahn was, as TWA slid into bankruptcy and he lost control).

Reputation advantages, although slow to build up, are often persistent and sustainable. Indeed, we use the phrase "living on a reputation" to describe the process of sustaining a competitive advantage with a modest current input. Reputations can be eroded—the mismanagement of reputation by Hilton hotels was described in Chapter 6—and occasionally, it may be best to consciously milk a reputation. Reputation advantages often fade as the market in which they are established declines. Yet because a reputation in a declining market is evidently a diminishing asset, it is correspondingly less powerful when applied to a new one. The transfer thus must be made well in advance. Accountants, seeing their audit base under pressure, have wisely chosen to use their reputation to establish positions in related markets for other services.

The Sustainability of Strategic Assets

Strategic assets fall into three broad categories. First, some companies enjoy a natural monopoly. Second, a firm may have a license, benefit from regulatory restrictions on entry, or otherwise enjoy special access to scarce factors. Third, the cost structure of the industry, with a substantial component of sunk costs, may confer incumbent advantages. How well do these assets meet the test of sustainability?

A natural monopoly ensures that there will be only one firm in a particular market, but it does not tell us which one it will be. A firm with a modest competitive advantage can easily knock out an incumbent whose only strategic advantage is a natural monopoly. Even a natural monopoly may have no strategic advantage in a contestable market. So a natural monopoly on its own may be difficult to sustain. This is, however, a result of more theoretical than practical interest, although the concept of contestability has been much discussed and widely cited in regulatory and antitrust discussions. In reality, almost all natural monopolies are also associated with sunk costs, and a natural monopoly in a market in which most of these costs are sunk is readily sustainable, as is evidenced by the absence of competitive threat to local utilities and the substantial difficulties encountered by prospective entrants to telecommunications even in the face of regulatory support.

Sunk costs are a depreciating strategic asset if the costs that are sunk today need to be sunk again and again. There are substantial sunk costs in the automobile industry, but they need to be replenished with each model cycle. So the entry fee to the world automobile industry, although large, is one that companies with strong competitive advantages have found possible to pay. But in aircraft, in which the model cycle is much longer and the benefits of learning by doing are enduring, entry has been feasible only with state support.

Changes in the structure of regulation can transform the environment within which a firm operates. AT&T had to face, first, the licensing of competition for its long distance business, over which it had enjoyed an almost total monopoly, from new entrants such as MCI and Sprint and, second, the complete restructuring of its business as a result of its agreed divestiture of regional operating companies. Airlines were deregulated in the 1970s. Some long-established market leaders, such as Eastern Airlines, failed to cope with the new competitive environment and thus disappeared. Others, such as Braniff and PeopleExpress, saw opportunities in that environment but were overoptimistic in exploiting them. And still others, like American and United, reinforced their leading positions.

For utilities, and other companies operating in regulated markets, sustaining strategic assets requires the careful management of public affairs as well as a competitive strategy. Companies vary widely in the sophistication with which they handle public policy issues, and this is particularly true in the changing environment created by market liberalization and changes in the structure of regulation. Too often, issue management is perceived as a part of public relations, and corporate rewards go either for fire-fighting activities or for the preparation of self-congratulatory documents for which there is no external readership. Preventive action is often much more effective than a vigorous response to an issue that has become the subject of political controversy.

The Persistence of Profitability

Competitive advantages may increase or diminish. The evidence from Western economies is that competitive advantages do persist, but as they persist they diminish. The best measure of the sustainability of competitive advantage is the extent to which a firm continues to make above-average profits year after year.

Table 11.1 brings together studies of the erosion of above-average profitability in a number of different countries. Its basic finding is that firms with high initial profitability at the beginning of the period studied (twenty-three years) can be expected to have higher-than-average profitability indefinitely, although the strength of the relationship varies considerably across countries, as does the dispersion of profitability. Above-average profitability is less sustainable in Germany and Japan and is easiest to maintain in France and the United States. In all countries, initial profitability rankings were a good guide to longer-term profitability rankings.

Over an even longer period, an analysis of around 250 British firms (Cubbin and Geroski 1987) suggested that even during that period a minority of firms enjoyed excess profits that showed no sign of erosion. Such persistence was more likely for small firms than for large ones—indicating that a sustained competitive advantage is more beneficial for focused businesses—and more likely for firms that did not engage in acquisition activity during the period than for those that did—suggesting that acquisition served more often to dilute competitive advantage than to reinforce it.

Are competitive advantages more, or less, persistent today than in earlier periods? This is an impossible question to answer systematically, but an intriguing insight is provided by Scherer and Ross (1990) (Figure 11.1), who measured the stability of the list of top 100 U.S. corporations year by year over the century. From 1909 to 1940, this measure of turbu-

Table 11.1.   The Erosion of Above-Average Profitability

	Initial Difference Between Most Profitable[a] Group of Firms and the Average of All (%)	Long-Run Difference Between Most Profitable Group of Firms and the Average of All (%)	Correlation Between Initial and Long-Run Profitability (all firms)
France	8.5	6.4	0.36
Germany	4.6	0.5	0.24
Sweden	14.3	4.1	0.60
United Kingdom	9.1	1.9	0.34
United States	5.5	4.7	0.58
Japan	3.4	0.7	0.31

[a]"Most profitable" are those in the top sixth by initial profitability.
Source: Odagiri and Yamawaki (1990).

lence showed a continuing downward trend, plateauing in the postwar period. Yet in the last decade, there has been a sharp reversal, and exits from what is now the *Fortune 500* list between 1977 and 1987 matched the rates at the beginning of the century. Over the century as a whole, the tendency for large firms to increase their control over the economic environment in which they found themselves was widely observed. But there also are clear indications that the greater internationalization of the world economy and a volatility of economic activity greater than that during the previous fifty years have seriously challenged that control.

Other indicators confirm this conclusion. The degree of industrial concentration measures the large firms' share of economic activity, and it is commonly measured for both whole economies and individual economic markets. Although throughout the twentieth century, the trend has been one of increasing concentration, this now seems to have been halted and reversed. The check seems to have occurred in the United States around 1960. In the United Kingdom, the merger boom of the 1960s increased concentration substantially, reaching a peak at the end of that decade. Since then, the average size of large firms and their share of total output have dropped markedly. In Germany and France, some increase in concentration seems to have continued into the 1970s.

Table 11.2 shows the international pattern of concentration. The leading companies of Europe and the United States are, on average, much larger than those of Japan, although this picture must, to a degree, be modi-

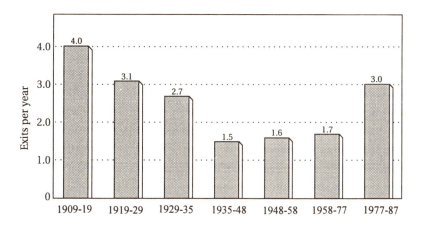

Figure 11.1. The Average Number of Exits per Year from the Top 100 U.S. Corporations

Table 11.2.   The Size of Firms in Europe, Japan, and the United States

	Average Size of Leading Firm (number of employees in thousands)		Leading Firm's Employment as % of All Industrial Employment	
	Top 10	Top 20	Top 10	Top 20
United States	311	220	13.1	18.6
Japan	107	72	7.3	9.9
European Union	311	233	8.9	13.3

Sources: Scherer and Ross (1990); own calculations.

fied by the extensive relationships among groups of companies in Japan. Although industrial concentration is the best documented, similar patterns can be seen in other sectors. The utility sector has become more and more fragmented as measures are taken to introduce competition and, in some cases, to force the breakup or divestiture of established dominant firms. In banking (Table 11.3), the leading banks of twenty years ago have steadily lost market share, although the rise in the Japanese banks' resources means that their overall concentration has risen, not fallen.

Scale as a Competitive Advantage

In many casual discussions of strategic issues, size appears to be viewed as a principal source of competitive advantage. Sometimes the impression is given that size is the *only* source of competitive advantage. Indeed, this increasing focus on a small number of companies in most industries may be many strategists' vision of the future. The verdict of the marketplace does, however, seem to be different. Although large corporations will continue to dominate the international economy, the concentration of business activity in the hands of large firms, which was the most important feature of the industrial landscape in the first sixty years or so of this century, appears to have come to an end.

There is a tendency to confuse the indicators of success with the causes of success. That is, the king may wear a crown, but it does not follow that one will become king by wearing a crown. Likewise, when looking at Boeing or Toyota or IBM, we observe companies that are both large and successful. But the causation runs from their success to their size, not from their size to their success, and it is quite mistaken to believe that by replicating their size, one could replicate their organizational effectiveness.

Table 11.3.   The World's Largest Banks, 1970–1990 (by assets)

Rank	1970	1980	1990
1	Bank America	Citicorp	Dai-ichi kangyō (Japan)
2	Citicorp	Bank America	Mitsubishi (Japan)
3	Chase Manhattan	Crédit Agricole (France)	Sumitomo (Japan)
4	Barclays (U.K.)	Banque Nationale de Paris (France)	Mitsui (Japan)
5	National Westminster (U.K.)	Crédit Lyonnais (France)	Sanwa (Japan)
6	Manufacturers Hanover	Société Générale (France)	Fuji (Japan)
7	Banca Nazionale del Lavoro (Italy)	Barclays (U.K.)	Crédit Agricole (France)
8	J. P. Morgan	Deutsche (Germany)	Banque nationale de Paris (France)
9	Western Bankcorp	National Westminster (U.K.)	Industrial Bank of Japan (Japan)
10	Royal Bank of Canada	Dai-ichi kangyō (Japan)	Crédit Lyonnais (France)
	Share of these in 1970: 24.3%	Share of these in 1980: 22.8%	Share of these in 1990: 27.7%
	Share of these in 1980: 16.6%	Share of these in 1990: 19.8%	Share of these in 1980: 19.2%

Source: Banker.

This is a mistake that is often made, however. In 1967/1968, British Leyland was created by an amalgamation of the principal remaining British automobile producers, under government sponsorship and in pursuit of a strongly held view that the British industry lacked critical mass to compete effectively in international automobile markets. But within seven years the company was effectively bankrupt and was nationalized. Despite the steady stream of financial aid from the British government, the company's market position continued to deteriorate. Today, Rover, a firm that, when established, held about 40 percent of Britain's car market, has a 13 percent market share. Its export sales in real terms are around half of what they were when the company was formed. The company's partial revival in the 1980s rested on its collaboration with Honda. Honda produced its first automobile at almost precisely the same time as Leyland was formed. It did so despite the opposition of the Japanese government, which took the view that the Japanese automobile industry was already sufficiently fragmented. Nonetheless, cars are now Honda's primary business, and the company is one of the largest and most successful manufacturers in the world. The difference, of course, is that Honda held, and still holds, substantial competitive advantages and

Leyland did (and does) not. Without a competitive advantage, Leyland's size did not help it at all; with a competitive advantage, Honda's lack of size did not prove to be an insurmountable problem.

Economies of scale are a measure of the extent to which costs fall as output expands. In assessing how they influence the competitive position of different players, it is necessary to look at the very long run in which all costs can vary. During this long term, the type of plant and its scale of operation can be chosen freely, and the form of corporate organization also can be changed. The mental exercise required to assess the magnitude of scale economies assumes that the industry could plan its output on a blank sheet of paper. To what extent then would average costs vary with the size and scope of output?

I have yet to encounter a firm or an industry whose managers did not initially overestimate the importance of scale economies. One reason is that most firms have many costs that are fixed in the short run and a variety of activities that have excess capacity. It almost always is possible to get more output out of the same inputs by working them more intensively for a short period of time. Many small businesspersons have learned that they are most profitable when they are overtrading. But most successful small businesspersons have also learned that they cannot overtrade indefinitely. Few costs are truly fixed in the long term. Even the chairman's salary, the archetype of fixed costs, ultimately varies with the level of output. The salary of the chairman is systematically correlated with the size of the organization that he (usually) chairs (more systematically, incidentally, than with its profitability). Scale economies are not the product of the more intensive working of existing plant. Nor are they often derived from spreading corporate overheads more thinly over more output: The corporate overheads will grow again, for reasons as good or as bad as those for which they were incurred in the first place. Scale economies are created when there are real technical advantages to larger-scale output. A telephone network can provide the same quality of service for twice the traffic with fewer than twice the number of lines, because the margin of spare capacity needed to ensure service rises less than proportionately with volume. Or scale may allow greater specialization. It was Adam Smith who looked with wonderment at a pin factory, where early versions of mass production meant that one worker was no longer responsible for the manufacture of a single pin. The "two-thirds" rule of process engineers was devised because the material needed to form a container rises less than proportionately with the volume it will hold. The inventory and spare capacity that is required to support unexpected demand or occasional breakdown rises less rapidly than does the level of demand or capacity that is underwritten.

Whereas economies of scale are mostly technical, tangible, and visible, diseconomies are mostly human, intangible, and invisible. As size increases, lines of communication are extended and distorted. Large plants provide a less satisfying work environment, and so workers need to be paid higher wages and are more likely to cause industrial disputes. Information flows are less immediate, and the response becomes less flexible. In an ideal world, these diseconomies of scale would be minimized while technical economies of scale would be fully realized. It is this ideal world that process engineers generally inhabit and into which general managers are frequently drawn. The idealization systematically biases judgment of efficient size.

Yet the relevant question is not what is possible in a perfect world but what can be realistically achieved. At the level of national economies, arguments for central planning are always difficult to resist, since it is clear that an ideal system of coordinated central planning performs better than a chaotic market economy does. The practical issue is not the comparison of ideals, however, but the level of performance that is likely to be realized. In the case of national economies, it does not appear that those systems of planning actually implemented matched the effectiveness of market economies. The same issue applies to the management of large corporations. Some firms do manage to achieve these things—to gain technical economies of scale while reducing, or at least minimizing, the diseconomies associated with human factors. But that achievement (rather than scale as such) is their competitive advantage, and it is quite unusual. The trend toward smaller plants is more marked than is the trend to smaller firms.

There are two main methods of assessing the extent of scale economies. The engineering method is based, as described earlier, on the estimated production costs of hypothetical plants. The survivor method measures how the actual distribution of plant sizes evolves over time, in the belief that a plant of inefficient size will lose market share to those of more appropriate scale. The survivor method therefore attempts to incorporate both diseconomies of scale from human resource management and market responsiveness. The minimum efficient size indicated by the engineering approach is generally much larger than the survivor technique would suggest. The technical economies of scale that the engineering approach identifies are offset by the organizational diseconomies that the survivor method takes into account.

There are some scale economies even in the long term. Some expenditures are truly fixed—such as those on advertising, product design, and research and development. The significance of these costs, together with the degree of product differentiation in the market, determines the maximum number of viable producers. If the product is essentially homogenous—for example, utilities like gas, electricity, and water—then the existence of moderate scale economies will make unviable those structures with more than one seller in a geographic market, which is generally what happens in such industries. Product differentiation tends to increase the number of firms that a market can sustain. The car industry is one in which there are significant unrealized economies of scale. But there is also a considerable variety of tastes, which ensures that the lowest-cost producer does not dominate the entire market. Accordingly, various firms with different products and different market shares continue to coexist, and the market as a whole features higher costs and higher prices than would be feasible if each market segment were devoted to a particular model.

In this way, technology, time, and changes alter the cost structure associated with supplying a market. Changes in telecommunications technology have made what was once a powerful natural monopoly potentially competitive at almost all levels, from international calls to local service. The industry is far more fragmented than it used to be, and this fragmentation is likely to continue. Airlines have developed in the opposite direction. The introduction of hub-and-spoke methods of operation and computerized reservation systems have given major advantages to the larger carriers and so promoted concentration. I described earlier in this chapter the way in which changing tastes and technology in the European domestic appliance market first swung competitive advantage toward size and then returned it to smaller producers.

If scale were the primary source of competitive advantage, then the greatest competitive advantage ever enjoyed by any firm was that held by General Motors in the 1950s. GM was the world's largest and most respected corporation, preeminent in an industry unquestionably characterized by substantial scale economies. Following the failure of Kaiser and Studebaker, it was generally assumed that the automobile industry would center on a smaller number of existing players. The notion that GM's dominance might be challenged by a new entrant to the industry then appeared inconceivable; yet that is precisely what happened, and Toyota, once a maker of sewing machines, succeeded in toppling GM from its one-time preeminence. In fact, in 1991, GM declared the largest loss ever incurred by a corporation. The lesson is that size cannot be a sustained source of competitive advantage. If size is a firm's only source, then it is something that a competitor with a true competitive advantage, based on a distinctive capability, can ultimately replicate.

Market Share as a Competitive Advantage

If size as such is not a competitive advantage, what about market share? The association of high market share and high profitability is one of the clearest empirical findings in business strategy. But just as with the nexus between size and success, it is important not to confuse the manifestations of competitive advantage with its causes. A firm with a competitive advantage is likely to have both a large market share and high profitability, but it does not follow that a firm without a competitive advantage can become more profitable by increasing its market share through price cutting, advertising and promotion, or market development. Nor, for that matter, does it follow that a firm with a competitive advantage can become more profitable by increasing its market share. To use the analogy adopted by Buzzell and Gale (1987), even though height and weight are closely associated, you will not necessarily grow taller by eating more. If you were a malnourished child you might, but you are unlikely to do so as a well-fed adult. The answer must depend, in all instances, on the specific circumstances of the case.

At the very least, however, this analysis suggests that building market share is likely to be part of creating a competitive advantage and that a firm with low market share is unlikely to have a sustainable position. But there is less to this recommendation than it seems at first sight. BMW has little more than 1 percent of the world car market, but if the market were redefined as the luxury car segment, its share would be much higher.

The underlying issue is that almost all successful firms enjoy a large market share relative to their perceived competition—it could hardly be otherwise. The PIMS database, appropriately for its purposes, asks firms to define their "served market" by reference to these perceived competitors. To an outside observer, any firm with a competitive advantage is dominant in some market, suitably defined. If "build market share" means "build market share even if that is not the most effective way of developing your competitive advantage," then the prescription is a misleading one. If it means only "build market share if that is the most effective way of developing your competitive advantage," then it adds little to our understanding of competitive strategy.

Attractive Markets and Market Positions

Chapter 9 analyzed the firm's choice of markets by referring to the application of distinctive capabilities. It did not consider whether the market was intrinsically attractive or unattractive. Yet it is rare to hear a strategy discussion that does not center on that issue. The search for attractive markets was at the heart of the portfolio planning that was a dominant theme a decade ago, and it still has a considerable influence on corporate behavior. The Boston Consulting Group's matrix assesses the quality of businesses according to two criteria: market share and market growth.

Here, too, the measurement of market share requires care in the definition of markets. Indeed, anyone who has used these portfolio-planning structures will recognize that if the firm perceives a business as successful, the market is always redefined in such a way as to give it a large market share. The particular contribution of this and other portfolio-planning techniques is its emphasis on the objective attractiveness of the industry—here measured by market growth.

At first glance, it is apparent that rapidly growing markets, such as those for financial services or electronics, are more attractive than are declining markets, such as those for steel or tobacco. Yet it is the very obviousness of this observation that is the problem. If these markets are objectively attractive, then they are attractive to everyone, and this will erode the industry's profitability as rapidly as firms can enter the markets. To identify an industry as attractive is to say no more than that Merck is a good stock or the Mexican peso is a weak currency. It does not follow that a firm should enter an attractive market any more than investors should buy Merck or sell pesos. The issue is how much of that attractiveness, or lack of it, has already been discounted.

Correctly perceiving the attractiveness of markets like financial services or electronics, many firms have entered them, and many have lost money doing so. Often the largest money losers are firms with no relevant competitive advantage, which see the appeal of a growing industry—observe Exxon's losses in the small-computer market or GE's problems with Kidder Peabody. At the same time, firms like Hanson and BTR have built highly successful businesses by targeting acquisitions in industries that other firms regarded as objectively unattractive.

The PIMS shows some relationship between market growth and return on investment, but the effect is small. In Buzzell and Gale's analysis (1987), the difference between the return on investment in the fast-growing industries (averaging 11 percent growth per year) and those of shrinking industries (averaging 4 percent decline per year) is about two points. This small effect actually overstates the impact of growth on profitability. Accounting profitability most frequently exaggerates true profitability when growth is rapid. For instance, the pharmaceutical industry, in which the true amount of capital employed is greatly under-represented because R&D expenditures are expensed, is an example of an industry in which the reported profitability overstates the true rates of return. And growth that is faster *than expected* almost certainly has a positive outcome on profitability, and fast-growing markets inevitably include many in this category.

This is one aspect of a greater statistical problem. Industry profitability has strong cyclical elements—it is quite common for there to be good or bad years for all firms in the same industry. Once these cyclical effects are removed, very little of the difference in firms' profitability can be explained by what industry they are in. For the sample of firms from which the "top ten" of Chapter 2 was selected, only around 10 percent of the overall variance of added value could be accounted for by industry factors, with the balance relating to factors specific to the firms themselves.

Only one source of data allows a systematic decomposition of the variance of profitability by firm and industry and also by the contribution of firm and business unit effects: the FTC line of business data compiled for a sample of U.S. corporations in the 1970s. The evidence from these is striking (Table 11.4). Not only are the industry effects small, but the firm effects are found almost entirely at the business unit rather than the corporate level. Neither the choice of industry nor the choice of corporate parent adds materially to the profitability of U.S. corporations. Value is added at the level at which competitive advantage is created—the individual business unit—not by portfolio planning.

The efficiency of markets ensures that market selection is not a basis for competitive advantage, except when it provides a means of exploiting a distinctive capability specific to a particular firm. The same proposition must follow for positioning. Yet the PIMS shows that high returns are associated with quality positions. These are not simply returns to market position as such, for if one position were more profitable than another and equally attainable, the others would adopt it, and accordingly the returns from it would drop. Rather, the high returns from quality positions reward the underlying competitive advantage—reputation

Table 11.4. Contributions to the Variance of Profits Across Business Units (%)

Corporate ownership	0.8
Industry effects	8.3
Cyclical effects	7.8
Business unit–specific effects	46.4
Unexplained factors	36.7

Source. Rumelt (1991).

in some cases, in others a distinctive capability in innovation or architecture—and this allows that firm, but not others, to attain a high-quality position. These firms' competitive advantage is best exploited in a high-quality position. But it does not follow that the same position would produce the same returns for other firms, and it cannot be expected that it would. That is, the success of Mercedes does not mean that it is possible, or sensible, to recommend the same market position to Hyundai. Each should select positions that reflect its—quite different—sources of competitive advantage.

The confusion between good positioning and competitive advantage is a particularly common management error in markets for fast-moving consumer goods. The case of one British retailer—the Next Group—provides a chastening example. Next successfully identified an underdeveloped market for fashionable clothing of moderate quality for women aged 20 to 35, and sales and profits grew very rapidly. Mistakenly believing that its good fortune rested not on its market position but on its competitive advantage in retailing systems, the company diversified into mail order, interior design, and financial services, with a marked lack of success. At the same time, established retailers with strengths in retailing systems invaded its market niche and brought the Next Group to the verge of collapse.

Positioning is unlikely to provide a sustained competitive advantage because positioning is rarely appropriable. Most market positions can be replicated, and if they are profitable, they will be. Some market positions—such as that of Mercedes—are truly hard to emulate, and this demonstrates that the true competitive advantage lies in their quality of engineering and in their consumers' recognition of it, rather than in their position as such. An exception to this general rule can be found when a market niche is sufficiently small that it can support one profitable incumbent but not two. Although CNN is replicable, it probably would not be profitable to replicate it.

Sources of Competitive Advantage

The final sections of this chapter examined factors often identified as sources of competitive advantage—size, market share, market selection, and market position. None of them is a *sustainable* source of competitive advantage because they all are characteristics that given time and expenditure, other firms could replicate. In this they differ sharply from the primary distinctive capabilities: innovation, reputation, and architecture. Often, of course, a distinctive capability enables a firm to achieve a large size, take a dominant market share, or be best applied in a quality-market position. But these factors are the outcome of that firm's competitive success, not the source of it. Confusion between manifestations of success and its causes is one of the most widespread errors in strategic thinking.

Many of the references cited in this book are relevant to the issues covered in this chapter. See, in particular, public policy management and the maintenance of strategic assets (Chapter 8), scale economies (Chapter 8), product positioning, and product quality (Chapter 9). Ghemawat (1986) is a general discussion of sustainability.

Cubbin and Geroski (1987), Jacobsen (1988), and Mueller (1986) are particularly useful overviews of the persistence of profitability. The performance of market leadership is covered by Davies et al. (1991). The importance of market share and the interpretation of empirical findings related to this issue have been widely discussed; see especially Buzzell and Gale (1987). Early accounts of the portfolio-planning approach are Day (1977), Hedley (1977), and Hitchens et al. (1978). Critical surveys are Coate (1983) and Hapselagh (1982). See Oster (1990) for an "efficient market"–based critique of this approach. For the history of the Next Group, see Cronshaw and Kay (1991).

12

Appropriability

If a competitive advantage is to form the basis of corporate success, it must also be appropriable. Appropriability is a firm's capacity to retain the added value it creates for its own benefit. Adding value is an objective for a not-for-profit organization just as it is for a corporation. But whereas a tennis club or a university may be content to see that added value distributed to its members or community, the successful corporation must be concerned with appropriating it for the benefit of its shareholders.

Only if a firm adds value does it have something that it can distribute to its various stakeholders over and above the minimum necessary to persuade them to work for it, invest in it, supply it, or buy its products. When a firm successfully adds value, the government generally seeks to obtain part of that added value through taxation (and, conversely, for those companies not successful in adding value, there is no sustainable corporate tax base). Shareholders are the residual claimants of added value, and in the United States, they also are the principal claimants of added value. This primacy of shareholders is less clearly true in other countries and other cultures.

Who benefits from the firm's success in adding value depends partly on the decisions of the firm, partly on the structure of the markets in which it participates, and partly on the sources of the added value itself. To sustain distinctive capabilities based on architecture and reputation, it is generally necessary to share at least part of the returns among all the stakeholders in the business and to achieve their agreement, or at least their acquiescence, in that distribution. The returns to strategic assets, in contrast, generally are fought over by the different stakeholder groups.

The Appropriability of Added Value

Adding value is not an objective only for profit-making institutions. The purpose of a university, or a tennis club, also is to add value, just as the objective of Disney or Microsoft is to add value. All these organizations seek to create an output that is more valuable than the cost of their inputs. The test of their effectiveness is whether they have made better use of these resources than would have been the case if the same resources had been deployed elsewhere by another organization.

It is easier to assert this objective for a corporation—and to determine whether it has been achieved—because measuring the output of a corporation is much simpler than measuring the output of a university, which is certainly not captured in any financial indicator. Likewise, the product of a tennis club is the value that its members attach to its facilities, which is not at all the same as the dues they pay. If those who run universities or tennis clubs do not use financial measures of success, it is in part because they correctly believe that the result will emphasize those aspects of output that are easy to measure, at the expense of less tangible dimensions, which are of equal or greater importance.

It is not only the objective of adding value that is common to every activity that yields useful output—commercial or noncommercial. The structure of strategy is not so different for not-for-profit organizations. The university and the tennis club should define their distinctive capabilities, identify the markets to which these are most effectively applied, and review their positioning in relation to their competitive advantages and those of their competitors. The pitfalls of wish-driven strategy are as real and as prevalent for noncommercial organizations as they are for companies.

There is a critical difference between corporations and other organizations, however. For the successful company, the *appropriability* of the value it adds is a key issue for management. The success of the corporation depends on its ability to retain much of the added value it creates and to prevent it from being dissipated among its workers, suppliers, and customers. But the university or the tennis club has a responsibility to a very different group of stakeholders. The successful university distributes its added value to its customers—its students—and if it is truly successful, it will allow the added value to spill over into the wider community. The appropriation of added value is thus wholly antithetical to its purpose. The tennis club similarly seeks to create added value for its members. The corporate chief executive correctly points to the company's profits as a measure of its success. If the dean of a university or the captain of a tennis club were to do the same, we would conclude that they had fundamentally misunderstood the purposes of the organizations for which they were responsible.

In some organizations, the firm is no more than the aggregate of its members; the added value it creates is appropriated by the members; and when they depart so does the added value of the firm. This challenge of appropriation is particularly clear for the professional service firm.

Drexel Burnham Lambert was briefly the most profitable firm on Wall Street. But the added value it generated was largely the creation of Michael Milken and his associates, who appropriated a large part of it. Then, when Milken was arrested and put into prison, the firm ceased to prosper and, soon afterward, collapsed. Corvath, Swaine and Moore and Goldman Sachs earn more than they would if each of their partners traded as individuals. The added value created is a product of the firm, even though it is then distributed among the partners.

If appropriability against insiders is necessary for continued success, appropriability against outsiders is necessary too. Innovative firms can succeed only if they can appropriate the returns to their innovation. Often this is impossible; innovation is readily copied or can be exploited effectively only with the cooperation of a dominant customer. The value that has been added is real enough, but to prosper, the corporation must create appropriable added value.

Appropriability is the ability to turn added value into profit. Yet it is possible to put too much stress on the appropriability of added value relative to its creation, and this has been a feature of the past decade. Look at the companies that would be near the top of everyone's list of the world's most successful corporations. Such a list might include Procter & Gamble, Volkswagen, Matsushita, Honda, Merck, and Hewlett-Packard. Profits and profitability certainly are important to them all. Yet none of these companies is characterized by an exclusive preoccupation with profit maximization. All would acknowledge a wider set of responsibilities—to their customers and employees, to the communities within which they operate—and this is a significant element in our perception of their success. Nor should this be a surprise. The corporations envisaged by T. Boone Pickens and Milton Friedman are not corporations for which many of us would like to work, and we would hesitate to buy the products of such businesses or lend them money unless we also had the services of a good attorney.

And yet firms with wider concerns, like those just listed, are successful according to all criteria. Procter & Gamble, Merck, and Hewlett-Packard have done well for their shareholders over the decades. The indifference of Japanese companies to the owners of their equity is well known amd is reflected in their negligible dividends and high levels of retained earnings. Yet it is the competitors rather than the investors in Japanese securities who complain about the performance of Japanese corporations. An appreciation of the importance of relational contracts in doing business and of architecture in creating competitive advantage makes these apparent paradoxes easy to reconcile.

The subject of this chapter is the degree to which firms can, do, and should appropriate the added value they create.

Appropriation in Added-Value Statements

Table 12.1 shows added-value statements for two nonprofit institutions: Blue Cross of New York and Harvard University. The Blue Cross statement is the easier one to interpret. Indeed, it looks much like the added-value statement for a commercial company such as Microsoft. Blue Cross reinvests the added value it creates in the development of its business; instead of distributing it to shareholders, it retains it for the benefit of future stakeholders in the business. So, as a matter of fact, does Microsoft, which has yet to pay a dividend.

Harvard University presents more of a problem. At first glance, Harvard does not appear to be a very successful institution. There is nothing in its added-value statement to suggest that it has a competitive advantage over other colleges. The problem is in the way we value Harvard's output. We value Disney's output as what people pay to visit its theme parks, and we calculate Microsoft's added value by reference to what people pay for its software. But Disney World admits anyone who pays the entrance fee, and no test of competence is necessary before you are allowed to buy Windows. The clearest indication that a Harvard education is worth more than the fees its students pay is that Harvard finds it

Table 12.1. Added-Value Statements for Blue Cross and Harvard University (U.S.$ millions)

Empire Blue Cross Blue Shield		Harvard, 1992–1993	
Revenues		Revenues	
Premiums less benefits	607	Tuition and charges (net)	297
Investment of premiums	122	Research income	335
		Other income	200
	729		832
Wages and salaries ⎱	529	Wages and salaries	640
Materials ⎰		Materials	474
Capital costs	49	Capital costs	487
	578		1,601
Added value	151	Added value	(769)

Source: Financial reports of Blue Cross and Harvard College.

necessary to ration access to its places. There would be no problem filling the next freshman class with students, even with a tuition far in excess of what Harvard actually charges. Harvard does not do so because, first, making money is not Harvard's purpose and, second, Harvard believes that it adds more value by accepting only a limited number of students and making sure that these are the best.

Suppose we were to value a Harvard education at $500,000 (and if we look at the lifetime earnings of Harvard alumni, this is probably a conservative figure). This compares with the current annual tuition fee of around $25,000. Thus we would be adding more than $1 billion to the value of Harvard's output. We would then have to turn our attention to Harvard's research output, which is valued at cost. As we all know, much research leads nowhere and is worth less than it costs; on the other hand, many of Harvard's faculty have won Nobel Prizes, and many of the most important innovations of the century originated in their research. Accordingly, if we were to value Harvard's research output at $1 billion per year, we would find that Harvard added more value than did Disney, Microsoft, or General Motors. The difference is that Harvard is unable and unwilling to appropriate the added value it creates. Yet if we were to measure the value, rather than the price, of its output, we would indeed find that Harvard added value and enjoyed a competitive advantage over rival schools.

It also is true that the output of Disney and Microsoft is worth more than it would cost to buy. Disney World would still attract customers if its admission charges were higher, and many would want to go on using Windows even if it cost far more than Microsoft now charges for it. Commercial companies nonetheless want to appropriate as much as possible of the added value they create. As I described in Chapter 1, the appropriation of a higher proportion of that added value was one of the primary achievements of the Disney management in the 1980s, and Microsoft has never been reticent in trying to extract full value for its proprietary products and its intellectual property. Not-for-profit organizations, like Blue Cross and Harvard, share the fundamental objective of adding value but differ in respect to its appropriation. Rather than making distributions to its shareholders, Blue Cross imposes less stringent enrollment requirements than commercial insurers do and offers plans for low-income households. Harvard makes its research freely available in academic journals.

Government-owned companies have particular freedom and responsibilities in the appropriation of added value. Table 12.2 illustrates the issue for two state-owned companies—Electricité de France (EDF), which is the only generator and distributor of electricity in France, and

Table 12.2.   Added-Value Statements for State-Owned
Companies (U.S.$ millions)

	Electricité de France (1989)	Statoil (1990)
Revenues	28,169	13,622
Wages and salaries	1,793	819
Capital costs	15,482	1,722
Materials	17,467	7,789
Added value	(6,613)	3,266

Sources: EDF and Statoil annual reports and accounts.

Statoil, which owns a substantial share of Norway's oil reserves and sells
and distributes oil products in Norway. The government's objective for
EDF is to ensure that any added value created by the organization benefits French consumers of electricity, and it does this by accepting a modest return on its own investment. Customers are intentionally allowed to
secure added value at the expense of EDF. The objective of Statoil is
quite the opposite. The enormous added value created by Statoil accrues
almost entirely to the Norwegian government; indeed, it was for precisely that purpose that Statoil was established.

The government's influence on the appropriation of added value in
Statoil and EDF arises directly from government ownership. But the government also is involved in the appropriation of added value in private
corporations through its role as tax collector. Philip Morris (Table 12.3)
is seen in a different light if the value of its output is measured by the
prices paid by its customers rather than by the revenues received by the
company. Much of the added value that business creates is appropriated
by governments before it ever reaches the company. (This does not lead
us to underestimate Philip Morris's competitive advantage, however, because the same is true for other companies that produce tobacco and
beer.)

Few commodities are subject to taxes of the magnitude that Philip
Morris pays, but the government, through corporation taxes, appropriates from all companies some of the added value they create. Indeed,
because corporation taxes are levied on profits and not on added value,
a firm may pay more than the added value it creates, as United Airlines
has done.

A firm cannot survive in the long run if the government appropriates
more added value than the business generates, since it then will be unable to meet the requirements of its suppliers and customers and the

Table 12.3.   Added-Value Statements for Philip Morris, 1992 (U.S.$ millions)

Version A		Version B	
Revenues (sales at value to PM)	50,095	Revenues (sales at market prices)	59,131
Wages and salaries	12,075	Wages and salaries	12,075
Capital costs	5,964	Capital costs	5,964
Materials	27,440	Materials	27,440
Added value	4,616	Added value	13,652

Version C		
Relationships with	Financial flow	Value
Customers	Revenues (sales at market prices)	59,131
Labor	Wages and salaries	12,075
Investors	Capital costs	5,964
Suppliers	Materials	27,440
Governments	Taxes	9,036
	Added value	4,616

expectations of its investors. Added value sets an upper limit on the range of tax demands that are feasible in the long run, and the analysis of added value is a helpful approach to understanding the strengths and limitations of corporate tax structures. If a firm creates a very large added value—as the activities of Statoil do—then the government can take a major share of that—as the Norwegian government does.

The government is an important stakeholder in almost all the businesses described in this book. And government is in a unique position regarding the appropriation of added value. Because it can legislate, it can demand and will receive. This exaggerates the difference. Firms like Statoil and EDF and even, to a degree, Philip Morris negotiate with governments over what they must pay. The tax structures with which they must deal are the subject of regular discussion. Governments are normally aware both that golden geese must occasionally be fed and that multinational companies have opportunities—through either tax planning or substantive shifts of operations—to create added value in other jurisdictions instead. If the government is not exactly another supplier, providing goods and services in return for a fair price, these firms also are not in the same position as small businesses are, which must work with the tax system as they find it and may believe they receive nothing in return.

The relationship between the firm and the government is an issue for each company, as is the relationship between the firm and its customers, suppliers, employees, and investors. For Statoil and EDF, this is clear and explicit. The state is not only a stakeholder but also the principal investor and the only supplier of risk capital. But for Exxon or Philip Morris, their relations with governments are of almost equal importance. Exxon depends on governments to license its exploration activities; it pays handsomely for these rights when the outcome is successful; and its operations are an important source of government revenue in many of the jurisdictions in which it operates. The effective management of public affairs is at the very heart of the business of these corporations, and the company's success is critically dependent on the competence with which they are handled.

Influences on Appropriability

Usually the division of added value is a matter for agreement, not legislation. Two factors are critical to determining the way in which added value is divided among the various stakeholders. One is the degree to which any or all of them have contributed to the achievement of added value. The other is their negotiating power. How many and how concentrated are they? What alternatives do they have?

The profit-oriented firm often wants to share its added value with other stakeholders because doing so is good business. This is most evident when the firm's competitive advantage is based on architecture or reputation. When its competitive advantage is derived from architecture, there almost always are short-term benefits for individualistic behavior. An individual person always gains—for a time—by confessing, by shooting rather than passing, by holding back what he or she knows. Sustaining cooperative behavior depends on persuading him or her that the long-run gains outweigh the short-term benefits of opportunism. One cannot drive the hardest possible bargain in a relational contract, because to do so would be to destroy it.

The firm whose competitive advantage is derived from its reputation is often in a similar position. This reputation depends not only on the actions of the firm but also on the behavior of many individual employees. This is most true in service organizations, in which the supplier's reputation often is influenced by the customer's experience in dealing with relatively junior employees. Maintaining the firm's reputation requires that individual employees feel that they, as well as the company, own the reputation. And ownership generally implies return.

It is not only the employees who can expect to benefit from architecture or reputation. For those firms that have created external architecture, it is equally essential that suppliers or distributors share some of the gains that that architecture has created. And reputations can easily turn sour if customers feel that too high a price is being extracted. The objective is to be seen as "a good company to do business with."

There is less reason for firms that benefit from innovation or strategic assets to choose to share the value that this innovation or those assets add. But often they must. The problems of effectively appropriating the returns from innovation were described in Chapter 7, and they frequently undermine the effectiveness of innovation as a source of advantage. A firm that enjoys the benefit of the strategic assets, incumbency, and exclusivity often finds that its position confers equally powerful strategic assets on its suppliers, its distributors, or its employees.

Even though a firm may often, rationally, choose to share the value it adds, it also may be forced to do so. Its distinctive capability—innovation, reputation, architecture—is its own. Its strategic assets may be under its control. But in turning that distinctive capability into competitive advantage in a market, the firm must deal with customers and suppliers, and the structure of the markets it faces in doing so determines its ability to retain this added value for itself and its stakeholders.

If suppliers or customers have market power, they will be able to ask for some of the firm's added value, and they will generally succeed in getting it. Table 12.4, drawn from the PIMS database, shows why the influence of unions and the importance of purchases to customers are among the most significant variables affecting profitability. The growth of supermarket chains has enabled multiple retailers to appropriate some

Table 12.4. How Supply and Purchase Conditions Influence Profitability

	Impact of Factor on Return on Investment Relative to Average (%)	
	Unattractive[a]	Attractive[a]
Market growth rate	−1.2	+1.1
% of purchases from top three suppliers	−0.8	+0.8
% unionization	−2.4	+2.9
Purchase importance[b]	−3.0	+1.8
Purchase amount[c]	−4.0	+5.2

[a]Unattractive means in the worst 20% by reference to this factor; attractive in the top 20%.
[b]Measured by proportion of customer's inputs from this supplier (high importance is unattractive, 75%).
[c]Measured by average order size.
Source: Based on Exhibit 4-10 of Buzzell and Gale (1987).

of the rents that previously accrued to the manufacturers of branded foods. This development both reduced the value of food brands and gave a further competitive advantage to the multiple retailers themselves.

Strategic assets are often particularly vulnerable to appropriation by other stakeholders. There is no commonality of interest in sharing strategic assets—all players work for what they can get, and this is often a lot. Some of the most striking demonstrations of this have occurred when the strategic asset itself has eroded. Pilots shared in the cartel profits earned by regulated airlines. Deregulation was followed by acrimonious labor disputes and reductions in earnings—as at Continental Airlines and TWA, or in the protracted strike surrounding liberalization in Australia. In the newspaper industry, profits were for decades appropriated by print workers in inefficiency, overpayment of employees, and featherbedding, rather than by proprietors, who have often been quite happy to lose money in order to retain their own vanity. The introduction of new technology has increased competition and forced management to reappropriate the added value that successful newspapers create, thereby prompting a series of battles between workers whose traditional skills are no longer required and a new and often more commercially minded breed of newspaper executives.

In all these cases, added value is the subject of negotiation. The key to the outcome of negotiation is the best alternative that each party has to a negotiated agreement. The outcome of such a bargain depends on the number of parties or possible parties and the range of their options.

How Numbers Influence Outcomes

Sometimes there is no other contractor, and the two parties must do business with each other or not at all. The alternatives to such an agreement are perilous. Sometimes there are strikes or interruptions in supply, or supplies are delivered on an interim basis while a new contract is hammered out. Stores may stop stocking products, or manufacturers may refuse to supply their usual outlets. Usually these are only temporary outcomes. Almost always, there is some agreement, and usually many feasible agreements, that would leave both parties better off. The breakdown of the relationship reflects a misjudgment by both parties of the firmness of the other's resolve. Or one party may see value in establishing a reputation in a repeated game.

In defense industries, there may only be a single likely buyer for a product innovation. The owners of global brands, such as Coca-Cola or McDonald's, often need the approval of Third World governments before they can sell their products in these countries. In some parts of the world, business can be done only through local brokers. In these cases, the other party involved may have contributed nothing to the added value in question. The international reputation of Coca-Cola owes nothing to the government of Zaïre. In one-to-one negotiations over the distribution of added value, who created it may have very little influence on the final outcome.

This dependence on a single customer, supplier, or distributor may leave the firm in a vulnerable position, especially when a distinctive capability is developed for a particular supplier relationship and is of little use outside that relationship.

A subcontractor may develop an innovation specific to an individual product. Nissan UK was an independent distributor and was awarded the franchise for Nissan cars when Japanese products were virtually unknown in Western markets. Nissan UK's founder, Octav Botnar, built up an extraordinarily committed network, which made the United Kingdom the only important world market in which Nissan far outsold its Japanese competitors. But the value of Nissan UK's architecture depended entirely on the continued supply of Nissan cars. Although Botnar had created much of the added value, Nissan was in a position to demand a larger share. Relationships between the parties became more and more strained until Nissan finally terminated its agreement and established its own distribution network. The relationship ended in acrimony and civil and criminal legal proceedings.

A more common situation is one in which a firm has a choice of exclusive relationships. The manufacturer of a consumer good must find a distributor in an overseas market. A retailer wishes to select a private label supplier. A specialist subcontractor is needed for a specific component. The availability of alternatives means that the firm is in a much stronger position than it is in one-to-one negotiations, as it can effectively conduct an auction among alternative suppliers or distributors.

Thus in any relationship, there may be one, few, or many possible parties on each side. Table 12.5 defines the matrix of possibilities that this generates. In a one-on-one negotiation, any division of the added value from the transaction is possible, and both parties would be better off agreeing to it than not doing so. The range of feasible outcomes—the core of the negotiations—is wide. As the number of partners on each side rises, the range of outcomes narrows, because anyone who attempts to drive too hard a bargain will be disciplined by his partner's ability to seek other counterparties. When the number of partners on each side is large enough, there is only one outcome in the core. This is the competitive outcome, in which each party is rewarded by reference to his incremental contribution to the added value created. If you are a good bar-

Table 12.5.   Types of Vertical Relationships

Number of Buyers	Number of Sellers		
	One	Few	Many
Examples of vertical relationships			
One	Some defense contracting	Specialist subcontracting, private-label retailing	Franchising
Few	Branded packaged groceries	Heavy plant manufacture	Offshore-oil supply
Many	Branded candies	Beer, gasoline	Agricultural commodities and natural resources
Taxonomy of vertical relationships			
One	Bilateral monopoly	Auction	Controlled competition
Few	Negotiation	Oligopoly	Negotiation
Many	Controlled competition	Negotiation	Competition
Outcomes of vertical relationships			
One	"Splitting a pie"	Second-highest bid wins	One takes all
Few	Depends principally on negotiation	Depends on negotiation and relative contribution	Depends on relative contribution and negotiation
Many	One takes all	Depends on relative contribution and negotiation	Determined by relative contribution

gainer, try the bazaar or the used car showroom. If you have a good product, you may prefer the competitive marketplace.

One-to-one negotiation in a situation of mutual dependence is sometimes described as the problem of splitting a pie. (The bakery seems to figure prominently in the analysis of vertical relationships.) If the two parties agree on how the pie is to be shared, they can have it. If they fail to agree, there is no pie. The pie represents the total gains from the contract for the two parties. If there is agreement on its distribution, the contract is effected. If there is no agreement, there is no contract. And since the parties each need each other if either is to compete effectively, there is no competitive advantage for either one.

When the game of splitting a pie is played experimentally, the two players almost always agree within a few seconds that they will divide it equally. Certainly, that is what my students usually do, and they are probably more aggressive than most. Equal division in commercial life would suggest that innovators that depend on government or primary contractors must expect to give up about half their gains or that the governments of less developed countries might look for half the returns that international firms will earn from operating in their countries.

Fifty–fifty sharing is a natural solution to the problem because it has an appearance of fairness. Sometimes real negotiations make explicit this fifty–fifty structure, as with royalties or taxes. Most publishing contracts provide that the value of subsidiary rights not specifically covered will be divided equally between publisher and author. Often, however, sharing the gains from a competitive advantage is implicit rather than explicit, buried in the transfer price of a component or a supply rather than the subject of calculation. Here there is no natural focal point, although a possible approach is to translate an agreed basis for sharing the benefit into a specific price, and this is common practice in subcontracting relationships.

Fifty–fifty sharing is a focal point if the parties see themselves as equals in other respects. If one party baked the pie (or believes he did), then equality is a much less plausible outcome. Equality may also be dismissed if one or the other party wishes to acquire a reputation as a tough negotiator. Usually the prospect of a repeated game makes it easier to reach cooperative solutions, but here it can make things worse. Players may not mind losing a pie or two if they will be able to extract a disproportionate share of pies thereafter. But there is a price to pay for a reputation as a tough negotiator. It is difficult to sustain architecture-based advantages in such a framework, and other parties will be reluctant to enter one-to-one relationships in the first place.

As the number of possible counterparties increases, two cases should be distinguished—when the firm selects one partner for an exclusive relationship (the specialized subcontractor) and when it seeks to secure as many partners as possible (the manufacturer in search of retail outlets). The first of these cases is essentially an auction, with the firm looking for the best bid. At a salesroom auction where a piece of furniture is on sale, the ritual of knocking down lots to the highest bidder has a clear outcome. The object is sold for its value to the second-highest bidder. So long as the bidders are not swept off their feet by the excitement of the salesroom, the winner can wait for all others to drop out and then collect the item for $1 (or $10,000 depending on the units of the auction) more than the highest of their offers. This is a sum still less, and possibly substantially less, than its value to him.

The salesroom analogy cannot be applied exactly to commercial negotiations. The salesroom is an open auction, in which all bids are made publicly and each player can revise her bid in the light of the other participants' bids. But business dealings are rarely like that. Formal auctions are generally conducted by public bodies, to which sealed bids are invited and the lowest is accepted. Although at first glance, it may seem that a mechanism by which upward revisions are permitted would yield a better price, the sealed-bid system forces the initial bids to be realistic, whereas in a salesroom auction, the first bids usually bear no relation-ship to the value of the object. The average outcome is no better, or is worse, than the salesroom system. Most commercial negotiations are intermediate between open outcry and sealed bid. There is some infor-mation and some disinformation about competing offers. There is some scope for revision of bids, but that scope is limited.

Thus the "second-price" rule is a realistic guide to what happens in analogous commercial negotiations. The price you get is governed by what the next-best supplier, or customer, can get. If all suppliers are equally capable, the buying firm can keep the whole value added by the relationship. If one supplier is best, then that supplier will earn a share limited to the amount by which it is best. In a real sense, other firms can appropriate only what they themselves have contributed to the rela-tionship.

The choice of counterparty may be afflicted by "the winner's curse." In a salesroom auction, all agree on what the object is; the bidders differ only in how much they value it. Some commercial negotiations are like that. The specific task to be performed is clear, and the participating firms differ only in their capacity, or their anxiety, to perform it. Other negotiations have a "common-value" property. When oil companies bid for offshore oil blocks, if they all agree on how much oil they contain, they all will bid the same. Their bids differ only because they have made different—and inevitably erroneous—assessments of the attractiveness of the territory. The winner's curse, which was first identified in the off-shore oil industry, strikes because the blocks you get are inevitably the ones whose prospects your geologists have grossly overestimated.

The winner's curse is a particularly serious problem for the rather mechanical tendering procedures often carried out by public authorities. It may afflict both the bidders and the authorities themselves. Business relationships typically have elements of both common and private-value auctions. Firms differ in their abilities to do the job and also in their assessment of what is needed to do it. In choosing partners, it is neces-sary to look behind the apparent differences in prices to their underly-ing rationale.

As the number of potential parties on each side of the relationship increases (Table 12.5), numbers and bargaining power matter less, and contribution to the joint creation of added value matters more. What con-tribution means here is the amount that each party can add to or subtract from the jointly established added value. This may not be at all the same as a measure of the effort that either party expends. The value of a brand is created by its owner. But a supermarket can add to it, or subtract substantially from it, by its decisions whether to stock it at all and how to display it. The result is that each supermarket—and supermarkets in general—can extract a significant fraction of a brand's value and can do so even in a competitive outcome in which there are many supermarkets and many brands. Competitive markets do not solve all problems of appropriability, and competitive prices are not necessarily "fair" prices; they are simply the outcomes of the market.

Appropriation for Shareholders

Harvard adds value for its students, and Blue Cross for its members. EDF adds value for its customers, and Statoil adds value for the Norwegian government. Most successful firms add value for their employees and for the governments of the countries in which they work, through taxes, and for their investors. Along with the addition of value runs the appropriation of added value among these various stakeholders. The degree to which added value is successfully appropriated by any or all of these groups is measured by the difference between what they earn, or pay, under the contract they have with the firm and what they would earn, or pay, under the best alternative contract open to them.

For Harvard, we should attempt to value the education received—in principle, the amount that its beneficiaries would, with hindsight, have paid for it. For EDF we might measure the difference between what French consumers pay for its electricity and the cost of buying it from Germany or the United Kingdom or from new suppliers who contracted to provide electricity in France on a basis that would fully recover their costs in the long run. Or we might look at what a prosperous firm pays its workers relative to the wages and benefits that these workers could earn elsewhere. We might measure the taxes the firm pays. We might weigh what shareholders earn from the company relative to the minimum the company needs to offer in order to attract its capital to the business in the first place.

Once we begin to query the extent to which the prices recorded in an organization's accounts truly reflect costs or values, we open up a wide range of issues. Prices seldom reflect environmental costs, for example, and this may lead to considerable understatement of the cost of electricity. If burning oil or coal contributes to global warming, it may impose costs not reflected in either the price that EDF pays for its fuel or what its customers pay for their electricity. Most of EDF's power is generated in nuclear-powered stations, and the risks associated with nuclear generation, which are not confined to France, should form part of an added-value calculation. A firm that damages the environment appropriates added value rather than creates it. These issues are discussed more generally in Chapter 15.

But among the stakeholders in corporate activity, shareholders have a special place. They have a special place because they have the residual claim on the firm's added value, and in a free market, the firm's ability to generate added value for its shareholders is the test by which it is or is not able to continue operating in the long term. This is why profit—meaning return to shareholders—is often described as the "bottom line" of the measurement of a company's operations.

Shareholders have a special place in the appropriation of added value in all capitalist economies. The degree to which this special place becomes primary varies in different business environments. The shareholders' interest is dominant in the United States. In Japan, shareholders are seen as only one of the stakeholder groups to which the corporation is responsible, and typically a minor one at that. Nonetheless, the relationship between added value and other measures of financial performance is important everywhere, and this is the subject of Chapter 13.

The subject of appropriability pulls together a range of otherwise apparently disparate issues. One important concern is the nature of the corporation's objectives. This has both a normative side—what should the firm's objectives be?—and a positive side—how do firms really behave? The very notion that a firm can sensibly be viewed as a single entity with coherent objectives is challenged in, for example, Cyert and March (1963) and Simon (1964) and also by various theories of the firm that start from objectives other than profit maximization; see Baumol (1959) and Marris (1966).

The normative issues are discussed further in Chapter 15, which addresses ethical issues in business more widely. In regard to the firm's objectives, one polar extreme is taken by Milton Friedman, whose 1970 New York Times article, "The Social Responsibility of Business Is to Increase Its Profits" is widely cited, but this is an issue on which perspectives are particularly distorted by the ethnocentricity of U.S. management writers; see Albert (1991) and Odagiri (1991) for opposing views.

Management issues for nonprofit organizations are considered in Connors (1980) and Espy (1986). Drucker (1977) contrasts profit and not-for-profit management systems, and Kay (1991b) develops the position of nonprofit organizations with the overall framework developed here. Issues in business ethics and corporate social responsibility are covered in Chapter 15.

13

The Value of Competitive Advantage

In this chapter I explain how competitive advantage is quantified, how it is turned into added value, and how added value is reflected in conventional measures of financial performance, such as cash flow, profits, and returns to shareholders.

Competitive advantage is, necessarily, relative—a competitive advantage is something that one firm has over another. When I talk of competitive advantage without making a specific comparison, the implicit comparison is with a normal or representative firm—perhaps the weakest competitor or a hypothetical entrant to the market in which the firm concerned holds its competitive advantage. The expected costs and revenues of that representative firm provide a benchmark against which the competitive advantages of other firms in the same market can be measured. In a contestable market, where it is easy for firms to enter or leave, the value added by each firm is exactly equal to the size of its competitive advantage. But if entry is costly, firms with little competitive advantage may nevertheless succeed in adding value, and if there is excess capacity in an industry, there may be no added value, even for firms that have competitive advantages. These relationships among the competitive advantages of different firms and the ability of any or all to add value are the subject of the first part of the chapter.

In the second part of the chapter, I explain how added value underpins all the principal measures of corporate performance, including cash generation, accounting profitability, and shareholder value. I demonstrate the fundamental equivalence of all these measures in the long run and show how each offers a valid but distinct perspective on corporate success.

The success of corporate strategy is generally gauged by financial measures of corporate performance. There are many alternative financial measures. Some commentators emphasize profitability and earnings per share, and others stress cash flow and returns to shareholders.

These different measures reflect a range of perspectives. The accountant stresses profitability and earnings per share and looks to the strength of the balance sheet. This interests the banker, but so does the cash flow that the business is expected to generate. Economists have always regarded this as central and have urged that projects be appraised on the basis of discounted cash flow techniques. Investors and stock market analysts are concerned with share prices, capital gains, and dividends. The corporate strategist emphasizes the strength of competitive advantage, and so, in one way or another, do observers who attempt to assess the firm's contribution to the international economy.

Profits and earnings per share remain by far the most widely used measures of performance, and despite challenges, accountants retain a dominant grip on the manner in which corporate financial statements are presented. There is a tradition in which advocates of alternative measures shower scorn on one another and particularly accountants. For some strategists, it is the preoccupation with accounting numbers that is at the root of the Western economies' decline. For many economists, accounting information is meaningless mumbo jumbo. One of the most popular movements of the 1980s was the growth of interest in shareholder value. Its advocates argued that accounting profits were not related to returns to shareholders, and they proposed a return to the cash flow basis of assessment.

Much of this disagreement is exaggerated and unnecessary. Cash flow, profits, shareholder returns, and competitive advantage are not different things, but different ways of measuring the same thing, and the different interest groups who are concerned with a company's performance are not pulling it in radically opposed directions but are adopting different perspectives on the same phenomenon. The full exploitation of a firm's competitive advantage serves the interests of every observer and enhances every measure of corporate performance. The later part of this chapter describes this fundamental equivalence and how the concept of added value underpins them all.

Wal-Mart has a competitive advantage over Kmart. The two firms serve very similar markets and are part of the same strategic group; each could see the other as a principal competitor. Does Merck have a competitive advantage over Wal-Mart? Or Wal-Mart over Bloomingdale's? There is a sense in which these statements are true. Whereas $1 of output costs Wal-Mart 82 cents, it costs Merck only 47 cents. But Wal-Mart and Merck are not in the same market. Nor are Wal-Mart and Bloomingdale's, even if statisticians would assign them to the same industry. That is, competitive advantages and disadvantages exist among firms that serve the same customer needs.

A competitive advantage also exists between one firm and another. Kmart is at a competitive disadvantage relative to Wal-Mart but has a competitive advantage over Sears. In any paired comparison, one or the other firm will enjoy a competitive advantage. Any statement about competitive advantage carries with it the implicit or explicit questions, "In what market?" "Over whom?"

Are there natural benchmarks against which to measure competitive advantage? One such benchmark is provided by the position of the marginal firm in the industry—in this case Sears. There are many worse retailers than Sears, including many that are no longer in business. The marginal firm sets the minimum standard that a firm must reach in order to be a viable contender in an industry. *When no explicit comparator is stated, the relevant benchmark is the marginal firm in the industry.*

From Competitive Advantage to Added Value

The definition of that benchmark provides an immediate link between competitive advantage and added value. In a contestable industry—one in which entry and exit are relatively free and not very costly—marginal firms (the Sears of their particular market) neither add value nor subtract it. They do not add value because if they did, others would be tempted to enter the industry. Then either returns to everyone would be bid down, or the marginal firm would be joined by another, yet more marginal, firm over which the original firm had a competitive advantage. In a contestable industry, the marginal firm does not continue to subtract value by earning less from its assets than it would if they were sold and the resources used elsewhere. If that were true, it should quit the industry and, in due course, will. Some other firm would then become the marginal firm, and it would become the new baseline for competitive advantage.

Discount retailing is close to being a contestable industry. Small-scale entry is not difficult. Capital requirements are modest, and the regulatory restrictions are few. Stores can be used for other purposes, so that leaving the industry or reducing capacity in it is less costly than in many areas of business (although the growth of specialized superstores is changing this). No market is perfectly contestable, but this one is workably so, and several firms have entered and left. If others are discouraged from entering, the reason is their perception of the strength of the incumbents' competitive advantages. In a contestable market, as in food retailing, the value added by firms reflects the value of their competitive advantage.

Automobile markets are much less contestable. Entry involves massive expenditures on plant and on model development. It requires the establishment of a distribution network. All these are specific to particular products or groups of geographic markets. Governments are reluctant to let weaker automobile firms contract, and so British, French, and Italian firms, which have generally been among the most marginal players in the world industry, all have received direct and indirect government support. In an industry with sunk costs and excess capacity, the marginal firm earns less than the cost of capital, which drives down added value for all firms.

Treating PSA as the marginal producer in Figure 13.1, Nissan holds a competitive advantage over it of 13 percent. Although this competitive advantage is large, the firm over which it is held is so unprofitable that Nissan adds no value overall. Of Toyota's massive competitive advantage of 26 percent, only around half is translated into added value.

In the long term, PSA's position is not, according to these data, sustainable. The company might improve its performance, thereby diminishing the competitive advantages enjoyed by Nissan and Toyota. These companies would then hold smaller competitive advantages, but they would be more fully reflected in the companies' added value. The world's car industry might reduce its capacity, so that the profitability of the industry as a whole and of each individual company would increase. Or PSA might ultimately exit from the market, leaving a group of leaner and fitter firms among which Toyota's competitive advantage, although still real, would be smaller. Whichever of these outcomes occurs, in the long run the competitive advantage is likely to be translated into added value.

The European banking industry displays a range of outcomes across its various markets (Figure 13.2). In France and Germany, the major

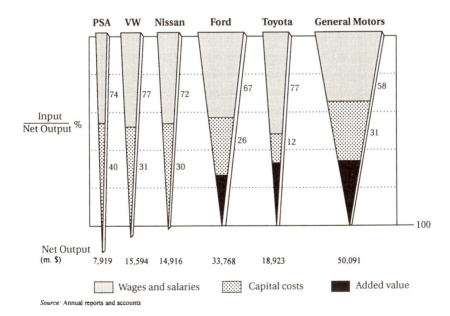

Figure 13.1. Added-Value Statements for Auto Producers, 1989

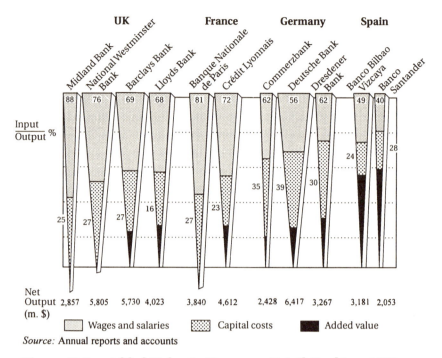

Figure 13.2.   Added Value in European Retail Banking, 1990

banks create small amounts of added value. The established banks do have a competitive advantage relative to that of the entrants to the market, and they perhaps also hold strategic assets. But no bank has a strong competitive advantage over another. In the English market, which is probably the most competitive, there is a wide dispersion of performance. Lloyds has been outstanding. Barclays has a competitive advantage over National Westminster and especially Midland. In Spain, it does not seem that either of the major banks has a significant competitive advantage over the other, but both are extremely profitable. No one would describe the Spanish retail banking market as a contestable one. The added value that Banco Santander and Banco Bilbaō Vizcaya derive is the result not of their competitive advantages. Rather, it is the product of their strategic assets—established positions in a market in which competition is restricted and entry is limited.

As in the automobile industry, but for opposite reasons, this is a situation that is unlikely to last indefinitely. Entry is attractive even for banks that are at a competitive disadvantage relative to that of the incumbents, as most foreign banks entering Spain would be. However, the prospect of such entry is likely to create a more competitive Spanish banking industry, and there are many indications that this is already happening. Here too, added value is likely to be sustainable in the long run only if it is based on real competitive advantage and strategic assets that are impregnable, not merely transitory.

The Measurement of Capital Costs

In order to measure either competitive advantage or added value, it is necessary to charge the firm for the capital employed in the business. This measure of capital costs links the added-value statements of consecutive periods in the life of the business. There are several different ways of measuring capital costs, each corresponding to a different perspective of the firm's operations.

Cash flow is the simplest basis. In this, capital expenditure is simply treated like any other expense of the firm and is charged against the added-value statement as it is incurred. In assessing a stream of cash flows, no allowance is made for depreciation, and no concept of capital value is necessary. In 1990, British Gas spent $2.144 billion on new investment, including fixed assets, replacement, and acquisitions. Each of the other methods of accounting for capital expenditure requires some continuing record of the capital invested in the business. The charge to the added-value statement then falls into two components. There is a cost for the annual depreciation of these capital assets, and there is a capital charge, based on the value of the assets concerned—the amount the firm must pay itself (or pay its investors) for the capital equipment it uses or the funds that they have invested in it.

The customary basis for assessing cost and depreciation begins with the most secure historical facts—what the firm paid for the asset concerned. Historic-cost accounting attempts to spread capital expenditures over the useful life of the asset concerned. Depreciation charges write off that historic cost, generally on the basis of some convention, such as straight line or reducing balance depreciation, that lowers to zero the asset's depreciated value at the end of its economic life. Illustration 13.1 shows the capital costs[1] incurred by British Gas in 1990 on the basis of its historic-cost accounts.

---

[1] Capital employed on a historic-cost basis may be measured by reference to shareholders' funds rather than operating assets. These differ from the value of operating assets to the extent that the company finances its operating activities from borrowings rather than equity, on the one hand, and to the extent that the company invests its shareholders' funds in financial rather than operating assets, on the other hand. One approach stresses the historic operating capacity of the business, and the other looks at the amounts historically contributed by investors. The depreciation charge is the same under both methods. Financial assets and liabilities do not (or should not) depreciate, unlike operating assets, but the charge for the use of capital differs in the two cases.

The historic cost of assets may bear no relationship to what they are currently worth. Inflation may have made historic costs meaningless. Some firms have land and buildings on their books at prices that they paid many generations ago. But prices do not only rise. Telecommunications has been transformed by fiber-optic cables, digital-switching equipment, and satellites, and the historic cost of copper wires and mechanical switches is far above what it would cost to achieve the same results today using modern equipment.

Current-cost valuations are based on the price of a "modern equivalent asset," a measure of what it would cost, in today's money and using today's technology, to undertake a comparable investment. Usually, the effects of inflation mean that the current-cost value of assets is higher than the historic cost, but in businesses related to information technology and electronics, these values are often lower. Current-cost valuations define what it would cost to get into the business now. Illustration 13.1 shows the cost of capital to British Gas on a current-cost valuation basis. (Two approaches are shown that would yield the same answer if British Gas's assets increased in value exactly in line with inflation.)

When prices were rising rapidly in the 1970s, many accountants favored a shift from historic- to current-cost accounting, believing that the continued use of historic-cost accounts misled investors and encouraged imprudent management decisions. Accounting standards based on current costs were promulgated in several countries, including Britain and the United States. As inflation receded, however, the interest in current-cost accounts flagged. British Gas is one of the few large firms still publishing current-cost accounts (which is why its figures are used in this

Illustration 13.1.   Measuring Capital Costs for British Gas, 1992 (U.S. $millions)

1 Cash-Flow Basis		2 Historic-Cost Basis	
Expenditure on fixed assets		Total operating assets	27,027
less disposals	2,8301		
Replacement expenditure	654	Capital charge at 12%	3,244
Acquisition expenditure	203	Historic-cost depreciation	906
Capital costs	3,688	*Capital costs*	4,149
3 Market-Value Basis		4 Current-Cost Basis	
Market value at 31.12.91	17,662	Total operating assets	45,498
Equity charge at 16%	2,826	Capital charge at 7%	3,184
Interest payments	616	Current-cost depreciation	1,861
Capital costs	3,442	*Capital costs*	5,045

Sources: British Gas Report and Accounts; LBS Risk Measurement Service.

example). Historic-cost measures are based on what was invested in the business in the past, whereas current-cost valuations look at what would need to be invested to achieve the same result today. Both of these can, and do, differ from the firm's market value. But this is, in a real sense, a measure of what today's shareholders have invested in the firm.

Another method of measuring capital cost and capital returns is by reference to the current market value, in which the opportunity cost of the shareholders' funds invested in the business is determined by the company's market value. The shareholders can, if they preferred, realize that sum and invest it in another business or deposit it in the bank. The market-based measure of the cost of capital, therefore, looks first at what the shareholders might have expected to earn if they had invested their money elsewhere or put it in a bank. Depreciation is similarly measured by reference to the company's market value: It is the difference between the change in that value (the appreciation or, in this case, the depreciation of the value of its stock) and the amount (the retained earnings) that the shareholders added to the business's funds. This figure does, of course, vary from year to year as the market's assessment of the company varies, just as cash flow–based measures of capital costs change with the company's own expenditure program. Historic- and current-cost estimates of capital charges are more stable.

The market value of a company's shares and its cost of capital together define the return that the firm must provide to satisfy its shareholders. In practice, this firm takes the form of dividends and capital gains (or losses). In any year, the shareholders' returns will be above or below this. In 1990, British Gas's returns were below shareholder expectations. In earlier years, they had been above them. The difference between the actual return to shareholders and the required return is the

Illustration 13.2. Current-Cost Accounting

A current-cost accounting standard was proposed in FASB Statement 33 in 1979. The main elements of the standard were

- Asset values to be measured by the replacement cost of a modern equivalent asset (or recoverable amount where lower).

- Depreciation to be based on these asset values.

- Inventory to be valued at the current cost of equivalent supplies.

- A gearing adjustment to reflect the decline in the real value of the debt.

- As inflation receded in the 1980s the interest in current-cost accounting waned. The standard is not obligatory, and few companies now issue current-cost statements.

excess return, the amount earned by the shareholders over and above what was needed to persuade them to invest their capital in the business.

These different bases for capital charges can be translated into different ways of assessing the value added by the firm. They correspond to

- The net cash flow generated in that period
- The added value in historic-cost terms
- The added value in current-cost terms
- The excess return to shareholders

Historic Cost and Current Cost

Historic-cost accounts are designed mainly to report on the managers' stewardship of the money that has been entrusted to their care. Although historic-cost accounts are often criticized, mostly for not bearing interpretations that they are not intended to bear, this central purpose has caused them to remain at the center of corporate reporting systems almost everywhere.

When using historic-cost accounts, it is important to ensure, as the added-value statement does, that the opportunity cost of capital employed is fully considered. Some of the more strident criticisms of using accounting profits or historic-cost earnings per share to assess performance are made because firms can enhance these measures without adding value. The retention of earnings for reinvestment at rates of return that are below the cost of capital, or the exchange of equity for shares of companies with a lower price–earnings ratio, will increase earnings per share but are of no likely benefit to shareholders or other stakeholders.

Historic-cost accounts provide one basis for the assessment of added value, and a firm that succeeds on this criterion has indeed added value. Historic cost is a measure of the resources that have been invested in the business, and capital charges based on historic costs are an accurate reflection of what could have been earned if these resources had been employed in alternative uses. If a firm earns more than this, it is truly a measure of its superior performance.

But historic-cost accounts do not necessarily indicate the degree to which a firm enjoys a competitive advantage today. If a firm adds value in historic-cost terms but not on a current-cost basis, it is because it bought well in the past. It may have timed its asset purchases well; it may have conserved its capital equipment effectively; or it may simply have benefited from inflation that it might or might not have anticipated.

Its managers deserve credit for at least some of these things. But they all are history. They may be the result of competitive advantages that the firm once enjoyed. They are not a measure of its competitive advantage now. Current-cost accounts look forward from the present, and historic-cost accounts look backward from the present. Both have their own purposes. Competitive advantage is a description of today and tomorrow, not of yesterday.

The measurement of added value in historic-cost terms is an appropriate means of assessing the quality of a management's past stewardship of corporate assets. It may be inadequate in its reflection of what they have built up for the future. It is also no guide to current or future strategic action. It is a mistake to think that a low historic cost of assets can ever be the basis of competitive advantage in a particular activity. It is relevant that a company owns a certain set of assets, but what they cost is irrelevant to how they should be used. There is almost no operating decision to which the historic cost of assets should be relevant. Historic costs are suitable for financial reporting, not management accounting.

The marginal firm—Sears among discount retailers, PSA in the automobile industry—provides one benchmark for assessing competitive advantage. But based on its present costs and revenues, PSA is not a viable producer in the long run. There is some consolation in holding a competitive advantage over a firm whose business future is uncertain, but not enough. When measuring competitive advantage and added value, there is a second benchmark that the firm should use. This benchmark is provided by a hypothetical company that is earning just enough to remain viable in the markets in which the firm is competing.

In a perfectly contestable market, these two benchmarks are always the same. The marginal firm is, in these market conditions, the firm that is earning just enough to stay in business. If it earned more, other firms would enter the market. If it earned less, it would immediately pack its bags and leave. In food retailing, there is little difference between the benchmark of the hypothetical viable firm and that of Sears. But in the automobile industry, from which firms are reluctant to exit, or in the Spanish banking market, into which firms are unable to enter, there is.

This hypothetical benchmark provides a definitive answer to the measure of capital costs to be used in assessing competitive advantage and in determining the long-term viability and success of a firm's strategy. The level of capital costs that needs to be earned to remain viable is given by a current return on the replacement cost of assets. More than that is more than is required. Less implies that assets will not, ultimately, be replaced.

Therefore, even though historic-cost accounts are the measure of a management's stewardship of the company's assets, its current-cost accounts are the key measure of its competitive position and its corporate strategy. Unless the firm enjoys a competitive advantage relative to the replacement cost of its assets, it enjoys no competitive advantage in the long run.

The Measurement of Risk

The purpose of business organization is to add value, but this purpose is not always achieved. If it does happens, then some stakeholder in the business will earn less than she could have elsewhere. But which stakeholder?

When a business operates as a corporation whose shareholders have limited liability, its structure offers a clear answer to that question, which is why the limited-liability corporation has become the dominant form of economic organization throughout the world. Shareholders provide long-term finance for the company, and they make a long-term contract with the corporation in which they are—implicitly—offered an expected yield above the going market rate for safe securities. In return, they accept the risks associated with the company's success or failure. If the venture is less successful than they hoped, they will earn less than a reasonable rate of return.

An organization without shareholders—a mutual financial institution, an agricultural cooperative, or a tennis club—has to deal with these potential problems in some other way. Usually, this is through a combination of accumulated reserves and pledges from some stakeholders. But these often are inadequate, which frequently restricts the growth of these unincorporated forms of organization. But when other stakeholders are bound into long-term contracts with the company—as with the customers of a life insurance company—it is common for them to assume some of the firm's risks.

Thus there are two services to the company—the provision of capital for the business and the bearing of the risks of the business—and when measuring added value, each should be assessed and charged separately. Since the shareholders generally both bear the risk and provide some of the capital for operating the firm, these two costs are closely linked. But the proportions in which they are provided are not fixed. It is entirely possible to increase the capital employed in a business without increasing the uncertainty attached to the business, whereas other firms, such as a professional service business, may have very volatile returns without using much at all in the way of operating assets. In an industry that must maintain solvency reserves—such as a bank or insurance company—the distinction between risk capital and operating assets is evident.[2] In an institution like the Lloyd's insurance market, which depends on risk capital but does not call on it until actually required, the distinction is clearer still.

Since the marginal firm to the industry is the benchmark for measuring competitive advantage, the relevant cost of risk bearing is what it would cost that firm to obtain the risk capital it needs for its business. The price of risk may then be calculated as an addition to the cost of capital applied to the value of current-cost assets.

When the risks of corporate activity are borne by the equity shareholders, the costs of risk bearing are measured by the premium that they earn over the rate of return on safe securities. A series of studies of long-term rewards to shareholders in Britain and the United States concluded that this averages around 8 to 9 percent per year, after taxes. This is an average figure for risk bearing over the corporate sector as a whole.

The capital asset–pricing model is a widely used technique for estimating the cost of risk bearing for individual corporations. The basic idea underlying it is that the riskiness of corporate activity is measured by the volatility of a firm's share price relative to the market as a whole. A company whose shares moved in line with the market (a corporation with a beta of 1) would need to earn an additional 8 percent on capital in order to reward its shareholders for the risks they had assumed. Companies with more volatile shares, relative to the market average, need to pay more to their shareholders to bear these risks, and those with stable share prices, less.

One important implication of this approach to the cost of risk is that firms cannot expect to reduce it by changing their capital structure. Higher levels of gearing enable them to substitute cheaper debt for more expensive equity, but by increasing the volatility of the remaining equity, they increase costs by an amount that precisely matches the apparent savings.

If risk bearing is bound up with the provision of capital to the business, it is also closely associated with its governance structure. It is the equity shareholders who bear the largest part of the risks associated with corporate activity, and these equity shareholders also have a major influence on the corporation's management. In Britain and the United States, such influence is theoretically exercised through the right to elect and reelect directors and, more practically, through the opportunity to

---

[2] Bank regulators distinguish between *free capital* and *infrastructure assets*.

accept or reject offers for control from competing management groups. In Germany, France, or Japan, the shareholders' influence is exercised more privately and less directly. And it is clearly efficient that the responsibility for creating or increasing added value should be associated with those who benefit from it, as it ensures that the pressure to add value is as great as possible. In the same way, the tennis club is controlled by its members, and the university should be accountable to the wider community.

Shareholder Value and Cash Flows

Shareholder value became a popular business term in the 1980s, and by the end of the decade, few U.S. companies failed to include a reference to this concept in their annual report. This new emphasis on generating returns for the company's stockholders had several origins. It became increasingly apparent that many of the conglomerate businesses that were put together in the 1960s and 1970s in pursuit of diversification or synergy diminished or concealed value rather than added it. The interest of managers was considerably heightened when the growth of new and creative forms of financing meant that no company, however large, was immune from the threat of takeover by raiders who promised to deliver more value to the shareholders.

Shareholder value may be measured as the excess return to shareholders—the amount by which the total return they earn, taking dividends and capital gains together, exceeds the cost of capital. Excess returns calculated in this way are extremely volatile, and there is almost no apparent relationship between these excess returns and the underlying effectiveness of the companies concerned. A portfolio of the ten "winners" of Chapter 2 moved more or less in line with the Standard & Poor 500 index in 1992. In fact, six of the ten outperformed and four underperformed, very much what you would expect from a chance selection. Observations of this kind have led some commentators to question the relationship between accounting data and investor returns.

Over a longer period of time, however, the position is very different. Between 1982 and 1992, all ten companies outperformed the market, mostly by very large amounts (Table 13.1). A portfolio invested equally in these ten shares would have yielded a return more than 14 percent per year better than the market average. The longer the period of time is, the closer the relationship between shareholder returns and accounts-based measures of performance will be.

The reasons for this are clear. If historic-cost figures are essentially

Table 13.1. "American Winners":
Share Price Performance (= 100)

	1982–1992 (average)
Abott Laboratories	720
Coca-Cola	1,150
Liz Claiborne	1,900
Disney	1,000
Kellogg	980
Marsh & McLellan	450
Merck	1,140
Nike	725
Philip Morris	1,120
Wrigley	1,400
Standard & Poor 500	260

backward looking and current-cost ones describe the present, market values look to the future. Although Merck earns very substantial added value from its drug portfolio, this is already reflected in the high price of its shares. Changes in the market value of the company today, therefore, will reflect its actual performance relative to its expected performance. Since expectations are high, it is difficult for it to outperform, and in the short term, such reassessments are as likely to be downward as upward. The stocks reported in today's newspaper as the fast-performing stocks of yesterday are not the best and worst companies in the market but the stocks about which new information has become available. But as the period over which we look back grows longer, those we recognize as excellent companies today are increasingly likely to have run ahead of yesterday's expectations, and today's bad companies, to have run behind them. In this way, value shows through in the long run.

An emphasis on shareholder value is particularly associated with cash flow methods of investment appraisal. Although it is impossible to quarrel with this approach, it also is often impossible to quantify precisely many of the elements of a strategic decision. The effective manager must therefore steer a course between the spurious quantification of what are essentially matters for judgment and a common unwillingness to attach even orders of magnitude to proposals that can be justified only by their financial returns. But the capacity to generate cash flow is a primary test of a company's ability to add value through its operations. And it is also the key to the firm's long-term financial health.

The Equivalence of Financial Measures of Performance

Current-cost measures emphasize current performance; historic-cost measures record past achievement. Stock market values look forward; cash flows are the underlying product of profit and the source of shareholders' returns. These measures differ essentially in timing rather than in nature.

Figure 13.3 shows how the pattern of cash flows evolves for a typical activity. During the initial period of investment, the project requires expenditure but yields no revenues. As development ceases and output comes onstream, cash flows turn positive. Toward the end of the activity, net cash flows may diminish as costs rise, revenues fall, or both. These may imply an economic life shorter than the actual physical life of the asset. These types of profile are familiar from activities as varied as product development and capital investment programs.

The objective of historic-cost accounting is to smooth the impact of these varying revenues and expenditures in a way that reflects the effect on the company's performance more realistically in the long term. The company is allowed to capitalize its initial expenditure and then to balance that expenditure against the returns as they materialize. Typically, the cost of the assets concerned is written off before the end of the asset's

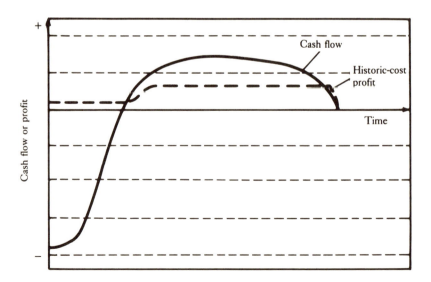

Figure 13.3.   From Cash Flow to Historic-Cost Accounts

useful life, so that in the final stages, profits fall less rapidly than revenues do.

Current-cost accounting came into existence principally because inflation made misleading the use of the historic cost of assets. Relative to historic-cost accounts, current-cost accounts imply lower capital charges in the early years of a project or an activity and higher capital charges taken in its life, when the replacement cost of assets is usually above the historic cost. This effect is offset initially either by the holding gains that the firm earns or by the use of a real rate of return that is well below the nominal rate.

The stock market attempts to anticipate both cash flows and revenues. If the cash flow profile of Figure 13.3 were completely and correctly anticipated, then the value of the company would rise by the whole of the prospective discounted value of the activity on the day it announced its intention. The stock market is neither as prescient nor as trusting as this implies, however, and so it will look for evidence of the successful completion of the development of an activity and for the growth of revenues from sales. It is in these late phases of investment and early phases of realization that returns to shareholders are likely to be greatest (Figure 13.4). Once an activity has reached its steady state, shareholders are unlikely to do better than in any alternative investment.

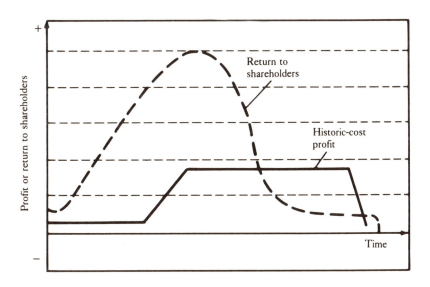

Figure 13.4.   From Historic-Cost Profits to Market Values

Both historic- and current-cost profits allow for depreciation of the capital invested in an activity, but not for the cost of capital itself. The same is true for calculating the shareholders' return. This further adjustment is necessary to derive added value from profits. Its impact is greatest in the first revenue-producing years and diminishes as the capital invested in the activity is reduced.

The four ways of measuring the returns from an activity are shown in Figure 13.5. The four profiles have different shapes, reflecting the different aspect of operations that each emphasizes. *However, the value of the areas under each of these curves is the same.* The approaches to performance assessment differ essentially in timing rather than in nature. Over the life of a firm or an activity, the present value of all these things, discounted at the firm's cost of capital, are equal.

- Net cash flows from operations
- Added value, measured in historic-cost terms, plus gains from the sale of assets
- Added value, measured in current-cost terms, plus holding gains on assets
- Excess returns to shareholders

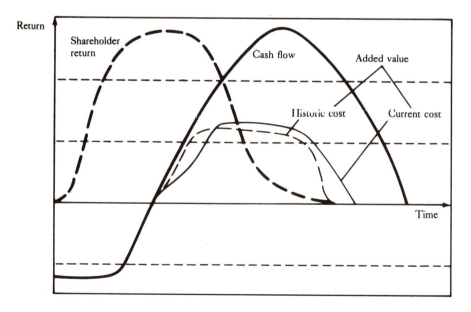

Figure 13.5.   Four Approaches to the Performance of an Activity

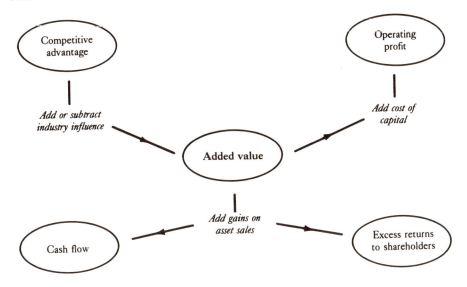

Figure 13.6.   The Equivalence of Measures of Financial Performance

A firm's returns rest on the added value it generates from operations and on any gains it makes on the acquisition and disposal of assets. Figure 13.6 illustrates the basic structure by which added value drives cash flow, accounting earnings, and shareholder returns.

Eurotunnel

Eurotunnel is an unusual company. It was formed to undertake a single activity—the building of a tunnel between England and France—and that activity is particularly well documented. The estimates of costs, revenues, and other operating data used here are drawn from the prospectus issued when the company was floated on the London Stock Exchange and the Paris Bourse in November 1987. Estimates of the company's market value on various dates are based on estimates made contemporaneously by Warburg Securities. All these were later overtaken by events, but since updated information and estimates are not available in equally comprehensive form, we used these 1987 figures.

Table 13.2 shows the anticipated cash flow from the tunnel in various years. It follows broadly the pattern of Figure 13.3. During the construction phase, cash flows are negative but turn around when operating revenues begin. There are some subsequent capital expenditures, but they are small, and cash flow will grow (in money terms) until the firm's concession expires in 2042 when ownership of the tunnel is scheduled to revert to the French and British governments.

Table 13.2. Cash Flows: Eurotunnel (U.S.$ millions)

	Operating Revenue	Capital Expenditure	Net Cash Flow
1990	0	1,363	1,363
1995	1,202	0	1,202
2003	1,723	202	1,521
2020	4,863	0	4,863
2040	15,320	0	15,320

Source: Derived from Eurotunnel plc prospectus.

Table 13.3 looks at the added value created by Eurotunnel in historic-cost terms. As the capital employed in the tunnel diminishes (because depreciation charges have repaid most of the initial construction costs), the added value rises. What is the source of Eurotunnel's added value? Although the company did win its franchise against a number of competing bidders, there is little reason to think that Eurotunnel has much competitive advantage in building and operating tunnels (especially given what is now known about the outcome of its project management). But Eurotunnel enjoys large strategic assets and faces little competition. Entry from competing tunnels is blocked by regulation (Eurotunnel has the first option on any extension of services until 2020) and by the immense political difficulties and costs associated with entering.

Table 13.4 shows the evolution of shareholder returns. Excess returns to shareholders are, in this projection, greatest as the tunnel approaches completion and begins operations. Once the tunnel is established, it becomes a rather dull utility stock, offering relatively poor shareholder returns, and there are large capital losses to shareholders as the concession expires. There is something paradoxical about the concept of predicted excess returns: These projections should be seen as a view of what shareholders would receive if certain events transpired—the tunnel were completed on time and at budget, and the concession expired worthless. But the tunnel was not completed on time and at

Table 13.3. Added Value for Eurotunnel (U.S.$ millions)

	Operating Revenue	Capital Employed	Capital Cost	Added Value
1990	0	5,933	457	−457
1995	1,202	7,367	1,037	166
2003	1,723	5,158	821	883
2020	4,863	−926	346	4,517
2040	15,320	−8,441	−230	15,551

Source: Own calculations based on prospectus estimate.

Table 13.4.   Shareholder Returns for Eurotunnel (U.S.$ millions)

	Market Value	Capital Gain	Net Dividend	Excess Return
1990	7,759	1,644	—	896
1995	15,228	1,518	237	232
2003	30,178	2,383	1,059	−218
2020	77,784	2,663	3,327	−1,604
2040	46,781	28,069	11,749	−16,320

Source: Own calculations based on prospectus and Warburg Securities' estimates.

budget, so shareholders are earning less than this projection allowed. (In consequence, the concession has now been extended.) This pattern of returns is, again, broadly that of Figure 13.4.

Table 13.5 brings together these three measures of performance described. Although the three columns display completely different patterns of returns, they each have the same present value. Cash flows, added value, and shareholder returns all are equivalent in the long term. Each provides a valid measure of the value, over time, of the firm's competitive advantages and strategic assets.

In Chapter 2, I proposed added value as the best measure of corporate performance. In Chapters 5 to 11, I described how corporate strategy adds value. Only in Chapters 12 and 13, however, does the central role of added value become clear. It is the appropriation of added value (Chapter 12) that determines what the successful firm offers to its stakeholders. And it is the calculation of added value (Chapter 13) that determines the returns it offers to its shareholders.

The discussion in the first part of this chapter is closely related to the McKinsey "business system" or the Porter value chain; see Porter

Table 13.5.   Eurotunnel's Performance (U.S.$ millions)

	Net Cash Flow	Added Value	Excess Shareholder Return
1990	−1,363	−457	896
1995	1,202	166	232
2003	1,521	883	−218
2020	4,863	4,517	−1,604
2040	15,320	15,551	−16,320
Present value over life of concession	4,336	4,336	4,336

(1985). The benchmarking process described there harks back to Marshall's (1890) "representative firm"; yet it is hard to find the rank ordering of firms that serve the same market, essential to the discussion here, pursued on either a theoretical or an empirical level. Benchmarking—directly comparing both qualitative and quantitative competitors—is developed in Camp (1989) and Eccles (1991).

The shareholder value movement is closely associated with Rappaport. Rappaport (1986) is the clearest statement, but see Ball (1987) for the most outspoken attack on account concepts, Blyth et al. (1986) for a discussion of their implementation, and Reiman (1989) and Copeland et al. (1990) for the relationship of these concepts to corporate strategy. Shareholder value is closely bound up with LBOs and hostile bids; see the exchange between Jensen (1989) and Rappaport (1990). A long tradition in economics disparages the use of accounting rates of return. Harcourt (1965) and Fisher and McGowan (1983) are classic references. Kay and Mayer (1986) and Edwards et al. (1987) explain some of the relationships that do exist, and the analysis here draws on and extends that argument.

Inflation accounting is well surveyed by Whittington (1983). Most empirical measurements of risk and the cost of capital in the face of risk are based on the capital asset–pricing model, which underpins the discussion here; this is credited to Sharpe (1964) and is expounded in all finance texts.

V

THE STRATEGIC AUDIT

Successful corporate strategy refers to the choice of markets in which the firm's distinctive capabilities yield competitive advantage. In Chapter 14, I describe how firms can begin understanding their distinctive capabilities and how that understanding conditions their strategic choices. This is the process of the strategic audit.

There are dangers in describing the process of strategy formation, because the determination of strategy is not a checklist that can be handed over to the planning department or to a firm of consultants. Rather, it emerges from the firm's analysis of its own capabilities and is part of its everyday decision making. Nor are there recipes for strategy or a menu of generic strategies. Effective strategy, based on distinctive capabilities, is unique to the firm that pursues it.

Chapter 15 asks what light the structure of strategy throws on the competitive advantage not of firms but of nations. This issue falls into two distinct, though related, parts. To what extent does the competitive advantage of individual firms represent the creation of wealth for the national, or international, economy? And when is it simply an appropriation of wealth to the stakeholders of the firm? I go on to consider more directly how the competitive advantage of nations, or groups of nations, rests on their own distinctive capabilities.

14

Strategies for Corporate Success

The subject of this chapter is the way in which firms evaluate their strategy—the process of the strategic audit. I begin by describing some common errors—the confusion between planning and strategy, the pursuit of wish-driven strategy, and the "implementation" that is not preceded by a careful analysis and assessment of what is to be implemented. I describe the process by which firms assess their distinctive capabilities and achieve a competitive advantage by matching them to the markets in which they operate. I also exemplify the issues that arise in assessing the sustainability of distinctive capabilities, and the problems that need to be considered in effectively defending the value of competitive advantage from rivals, customers, and suppliers. The chapter uses real, but disguised, applications of the analysis of the book.

Assessing Strategy

You are succeeding in a corporation when you become sufficiently senior, or sufficiently respected, to be invited to its strategy weekend. The strategy weekend is a ritual observed by many companies in which senior management retreat to the country to contemplate the issues that face them, with a detachment that daily routines render impossible. There are as many methods of conducting these events as there are corporations that conduct them.

One company, like many, began its strategy weekend with a discussion of the corporate plan. Within minutes, there was a heated exchange across the table between the vice-president for strategic planning and the CEO of one of the principal operating businesses. The CEO picked up the firm's planning document. It was not an easy task. The book contained printouts of key financial variables for each division of the corporation over the next five years and numbered several hundred pages.

"What's this for?" asked the CEO. "Is it a forecast? If so, it's not a good one. Does it provide targets? Then why aren't there any penalties for failing to meet them? Four of my staff spent six months preparing the data for this, and I haven't had to refer to them once." The planning vice-president, equally angry, snapped back at him. "You don't really think you can go on running this business by the seat of your pants?" Yet as they later acknowledged, both were right. The CEO had to agree that a longer-term guide was needed for day-to-day operating decisions, and the planning VP had to admit that the corporate plan was not it. Like many other corporations, this firm had begun strategic planning in the 1960s; like many other corporations, this firm had discovered that these elaborate planning documents had little influence on the way it actually conducted its affairs.

Another weekend. This British company had flown in an American facilitator to oversee its weekend. First, he posed for them what he saw as the main issue: "Do we want to be Europe's leading firm in our industry or not?" The assembled executives responded enthusiastically in the affirmative. But the plan to be Europe's leading firm quickly encountered a snag: the firm's weakness in Germany. The solution was clear—a German acquisition. Within half an hour, the discussion had turned to plans for buying a German company, plans that this company subsequently, but unprofitably, implemented. As so many corporations did in the 1980s, this firm discovered that establishing a mission, or creating a vision, is not the same as implementing it profitably.

This emphasis on implementation, so characteristic of more recent strategy discussions, was reflected in another strategy weekend. A consulting group, specializing in the management of change, were introducing their work by means of a video, "The Circle of Quality." The circle of quality ran from higher quality to larger sales, through scale economies to lower costs which, combined with the additional revenues from greater output, would establish a virtuous circle of ever-increasing quality and ever-rising profits.

The firm in question was a water supply business. Improvements in the quality of output would have a negligible impact on its sales. In addition, increased sales imply higher, not lower, costs, because water resources are scarce. Revenues, furthermore, would not rise because most customers paid the company a fixed sum for water, regardless of how much they consumed. Higher quality might be desirable, but for this company, it would inevitably mean additional costs without additional revenues. The video therefore was irrelevant to the point of absurdity for this particular business.

The first company's strategy had become immersed in the numerical detail of its strategic plan. The second was in the process of formulating a vision no different from the vision formulated by many other firms in its business and was no more capable of being realized. The third had fallen victim to the practice of reciting fashionable slogans—"go global," "improve quality," "empower," "reengineer"—without regard to the specifics of the business concerned. What should they have done instead?

Identifying Distinctive Capabilities

Meaningful strategy begins from the question "What are this firm's distinctive capabilities?" It provokes debate no less heated but more structured and more conclusive than "What is our mission?" or "What business are we in?"

When Finserco, a leading retail financial services company, set about analyzing its distinctive capabilities, there was no shortage of suggestions. The marketing group stressed the novelties in its product range; the human resources vice-president argued that its competitive advantage lay in its internal architecture; and the business services division emphasized its information technology. Yet the analysis and debate at Finserco's strategy weekend revealed that these capabilities, although real capabilities of the company, were not truly distinctive.

The firm had made many minor innovations in product design, but those that appealed to its customers were usually quickly picked up by others in the industry, and several of Finserco's competitors were also pushing through these sorts of product changes; no one was really prepared to argue that Finserco had a reputation for innovation. Employee relations were good, it was true, despite some recent problems, but the same was true for all of Finserco's principal competitors. Finserco was in a service business, and the quality of its products relied on accurately processing several hundred thousand transactions every day. In this business, you could not stay among the market leaders unless you had a well-trained, committed workforce, but this very fact meant that it was no one's distinctive capability.

When seeking the company's distinctive capabilities, Finserco's management eventually focused on two features of its business: its reputation and its branch network. Market research confirmed what everyone around Finserco instinctively knew: Its customers trusted Finserco. It was not just that they were sure the company would still be there when they wanted their money back. They also appreciated the quality of its service and its products and believed that the advice they got in its branches was honest and not the biased product of commission-hungry salespeople. Most surveys put Finserco number one or two in its peer group—well ahead, the executive group noted, of firms that today were providing services not very different from Finserco's but that had not, in the past, maintained the same quality of relationships with their customers. And although there was concern about the cost of Finserco's retail branches, it was clear to all that this was a strategic asset. The amount that one overseas bank had been willing to pay to acquire a comparable chain was one good indicator of that, and so was the expenditure that another had been ready to make in an unsuccessful attempt to build something similar from scratch.

Bankcorp, another financial services firm, came to very different conclusions about itself. Whatever the vice-president for marketing and communications might say, Bankcorp did not have a name in the marketplace, outside its narrow regional origins, that rivaled that of Finserco. Bankcorp's rapid expansion had been based essentially on only one element in its market position: It had the lowest cost-processing capability in the business. Some called this an innovation; certainly no one had yet been able to match the quality of Bankcorp's technology. But the CEO, who had come up through the operations group, preferred to emphasize the bank's architecture. It was, he argued, the interaction between the systems people and the day-to-day users in the business (which, he argued, had been possible because Bankcorp was based outside the major financial centers and therefore had a much lower turnover of head office staff), which no one else in the industry had been able to replicate effectively.

Discussion of Universal Airlines' distinctive capabilities began with a long discourse on the importance of the brand, replete with the latest in marketing jargon. The chief of operations, a former pilot, brought the debate down to earth with the same confidence he had shown when he had brought his passengers down to earth. "You know very well," he said, "that the only reason passengers prefer our flights to others at the same price and the same time is our frequent flyer points." The executive group tossed around various possible distinctive capabilities, concluding that there were not many in the airline business. The financial director's laconic observation that perhaps this was why no one seemed to make any money was not regarded as helpful. The firm's main distinctive capability, the group concluded, was its hub—the large regional airport that was its historic base and from which more than half the flights were Universal's.

The CEO of Sonico, who had recently been recruited from the finance group of a large multinational, was all the more uncertain what she had inherited when she saw the senior management group assembled for the first time. She compared the chaotic enthusiasm of the technologists with the arrogant indifference of the salesforce, and she knew that neither would have been tolerated for long in her last company. But she also knew that these two groups represented the distinctive capabilities of Sonico, which made specialized sound equipment for the popular-music business. The creative technical team bubbled with ideas; for people with interests in this area, a job with Sonico offered all they wanted or needed. Occasionally, individual persons or small groups would leave to do their own thing, but there was no team of remotely comparable size or quality. And the salespeople's ability to relate these technical skills to the idiosyncratic and demanding requirements of the users was the other element in Sonico's competitive advantage. The external architecture of its customer relationships complemented the internal architecture that produced its technology.

Popular Energy, like many utilities, was both excited and overwhelmed by the range of opportunities created by the new world of privatization and deregulation. In common with many firms in its position, it had suffered from early ill-considered diversification; now it was emphasizing its core business. But what was that core business? The management of Popular Energy began the search for a definition by identifying the firm's distinctive capabilities.

The company enjoyed the considerable strategic asset of a distribution monopoly within its local area. Beyond that, it was forced to conclude that its distinctive capabilities were limited. Although it had relationships with its customers, they were not deep and could be reproduced by others. Its regional focus might be important: It was the second largest company with a head office in its area; it was well regarded in the community; and it had, in the broad sense of the word, good political connections. It was also a leader, not only nationally, but also internationally, in a specialized technology that had been needed to deal with a particular local problem.

Matching Markets to Distinctive Capabilities

Identifying distinctive capabilities is the first stage of formulating strategy. Matching markets to these distinctive capabilities comes next. Are the markets in which the company operates all ones to which its distinctive capabilities add value? Are there other markets that it has not yet entered, in which they might create a competitive advantage?

Finserco had clearly determined that its distinctive capabilities were to be found in its reputation and its branches, and so its strategic focus followed directly from that. Both Finserco's distinctive capabilities related mainly to its existing customer base, or at least to its existing geographic area. The main choice it faced—whether it should sell a broader range of services to its existing customers or seek by means of geographic expansion to sell its established product range to new customers—was therefore easily resolved. It could add far more value by attaching its name and reputation to new services than it could by selling its old ones in markets in which it enjoyed no competitive advantage.

Although most of the executive group was excited by the prospect of expanding Finserco's product range, there was a group that was disappointed at the brake that had been put on geographic expansion. After all, they argued, if their predecessors had taken the same view, Finserco would still be a company with one branch in a single small town. But a consensus was quickly reached. Everyone agreed to rule out the major overseas acquisition that some advisers had been urging on them. The Finserco name would simply add no value there. But a controlled process of organic expansion that gradually enlarged the area in which the Finserco name was known would be part of its strategy. This process was, they all agreed, one that would take many years to come to fruition.

Bankcorp reached just the opposite conclusions. Its systems could be applied widely; what it needed was the local presence that would bring in the business. Extending its product range would stretch its capabilities, but adding greater volume to its current processing capabilities would increase its cost advantage still further. Bankcorp agreed to form a dedicated acquisitions team to speed up the pace at which new firms in different geographic areas could be absorbed into its organization.

Could it be right that two firms in the same industry could reach such different conclusions about the appropriate direction of its strategy? In fact, it would have been much more worrying if they had reached identical conclusions, because that would have raised serious questions about the viability of both companies' plans. Strategy based on distinctive capabilities necessarily takes corporations in directions as distinctive as their capabilities.

Universal Airlines' analysis emphasized the critical role of its hub, and so its analysis of markets began from there. The markets for business travelers to and from that catchment area were its principal clientele. Universal also catered to the leisure traffic originating in that catchment area and had segmented the market effectively to offer attractive fares to these customers while preserving its premium business rates. The market for leisure traffic to the hub was met much less effectively, and a strategy for tackling that market was assigned as a priority for the marketing department.

The heated debate was over the CEO's plan to move into hotels. He emphasized the intensity of competition in the airline business, argued that greater stability of earnings was essential to the future of the corporation, and stressed the links between the demand for air travel and the demand for hotel services. "Three-quarters of our passengers check into a hotel," he noted. "We're missing a great selling opportunity—and one that our competitors are taking." But when pressed to explain why Universal Airlines' distinctive capabilities were relevant to providing overnight hospitality, he finally conceded that his opponents had the better argument. "Perhaps that's why airlines lose even more money per dollar in hotels as they do in flying," commented the finance director.

Sonico's CEO had come into the business with ambitious plans to use the company as a base for developing the sort of multinational conglomerate business with which she was familiar. But looking around her, she understood that this notion had been a mistake. Her people were currently doing precisely those things that they could do better than anyone else. The scope of the business exactly matched its distinctive capabilities. Her job was to preserve these distinctive capabilities and this match.

And once Popular Energy had focused on its distinctive capabilities, its strategic directions were clear. It agreed to divest its assorted portfolio of worldwide energy ventures just as soon as it could obtain reasonable offers for them. Outside its central utility business, it would concentrate on two niche opportunities. There was a chance both to rationalize and to develop a forest products business in Popular Energy's home area. With its connections in the state capital and the trust of the local people, Popular Energy would encounter little of the local opposition that had deterred others from going ahead. There was some opposition from a group that argued that Popular Energy had no skills in forest products. But they came to realize that skills and distinctive capabilities were not necessarily the same. Skills could be bought; there was no shortage of capable managers in the forest products sector. Distinctive capabilities were another matter, however. (Notice that Sonico answered the same question very differently. Sonico's skills were one of its distinctive capabilities and could not be bought or reproduced by another company.) After a decade of searching, Popular Energy had finally come to terms with what it meant by its core business.

Sustaining and Appropriating a Competitive Advantage

Each company needed to consider how it would sustain its distinctive capabilities and how it would ensure that the resulting added value was appropriated for the benefit of its shareholders. Finserco knew where its distinctive capabilities lay—in its name and its reputation. But these were being threatened. Other, nonfinancial, companies were using their reputation to get into financial services. These were manageable problems, however, and there were strategies in place for managing them.

The most important element in maintaining Finserco's position was that each of its employees who dealt with its customers should remember, every day, the origins of the company's added value—and their profit share. When Finserco's executives finished their discussion with an affirmation of their mission—how they communicated their distinctive capabilities and their strategy to their employees—that issue was at the center of their thinking.

The appropriation issue was central to another of Finserco's discussions. In broadening its range of financial services products, Finserco would be moving aggressively into new business areas, such as insurance, whereas in the past it had been content to collect commissions as a relatively passive seller of other companies' products. How far should it take this vertical integration? One school held that Finserco should acquire an established insurer; another, that it should buy into systems expertise initially as the basis for its own greenfield operations. "What we need," this group argued, "is to earn the manufacturer's profit as well as the distributor's margin."

But when they approached the debate in terms of the analysis of added value, a different perspective emerged. There was no such thing as "a manufacturer's profit"; there was already excess capacity in the insurance industry, and so a new entrant could not expect to earn more than the cost of capital. Why, then, were the financial projections for Finserco's entry into insurance so attractive? They were attractive not because of any "manufacturing profit" but because Finserco could add so much value in distribution. Now Finserco could add that value whether or not it was itself the manufacturer. The best option was to ensure that Finserco had full control over product design and development while shopping around for the cheapest provider of systems and underwriting. Given the excess capacity among insurers and the volume of output that Finserco could deliver, it could drive an exceptionally tough bargain. Against this strategy, the alternative of paying a bid premium for an insurance company looked very unattractive. Finserco had come to understand that as long as it controlled the point in the chain of production at which value was added, it could leverage that to secure the added value from the whole chain without needing to own all of it.

Bankcorp had many more concerns about the sustainability of its distinctive capability. Its systems were the best in the business, its technical team second to none. But retail financial services are not at the leading edge of information technology. There were other people in the industry just as good; other teams had comparable talents, even if they had not yet realized them. Bankcorp was not at a technical frontier, as

Sonico was. Some of Bankcorp's executives projected the recent past into the indefinite future and constructed visions of an even rosier future. The more realistic among them recognized that sooner or later, some of their competitors would catch up. They might even leap ahead. However much they invested in technology, there was little they could do to stop that from happening.

For the enthusiasts, this was defeatist talk. But the wise CEO reminded them that they were in the business of adding value, not winning medals for defying the odds. There were, he suggested, two main routes ahead. "If your distinctive capability may fade, it is time to sell," he commented cynically. Specifically, a merger with a well-established player whose systems were not up to scratch could add value to both companies and could almost certainly be done on terms that overvalued Bankcorp's possibly transitory capability relative to the more sustainable one. The market, not fully appreciating the nature of the different distinctive capabilities, was mistakenly projecting the recent experience of both companies into the indefinite future. Alternatively, the window of opportunity created by the firm's current technical superiority could be used to build a reputation-based distinctive capability that would endure even if the lead in systems faded. This meant racing against time and promoting the firm's name through an extensive advertising and sponsorship program that current levels of profitability could easily accommodate. The firm's merger talks did not work out, however, and the second path is now Bankcorp's strategic priority.

The lesson that Finserco had debated earnestly—how integrated a producer did it need to be to maximize its added value?—was one that Sonico had resolved years before. In Sonico's early days of operations, it used almost exclusively bought-in components. There had been pressure to fabricate an increasing proportion in-house. A consultant's report had advised it that it should make for itself everything that was customized for Sonico's operations or whose quality was essential to the quality of the final product. That, the consultant argued, defined Sonico's "core business."

Sonico had rejected this proposal. It was not practical—it identified components for in-house manufacture that Sonico's technical people did not believe the company could make to the necessary standards without a huge investment. Nor was it necessary; the quality and reliability achieved by some of Sonico's suppliers were enviable. Like Finserco, Sonico did not need to undertake the whole process to extract the added value from it.

The greatest danger to Sonico's position was that one of the giants of the electronics industries would invade its market. Some argued that Sonico's technical capabilities were so strong that no one could do this.

But realism prevailed; if these firms spent enough money, they could. It would not be profitable for them to do that, another argument ran. But it did not matter—in the graphic phrase that had been quoted then and is still remembered around the company, "Being in front of a steamroller is uncomfortable even if the steamroller shouldn't be there."

What was vital to Sonico was to discourage such entry. That meant not being too greedy, remaining on good terms with the relevant technical divisions in the industry's giants, and ensuring that they knew enough about Sonico's business to meet its needs but not enough to make their own entry too easy. These principles had been established three or four years ago, and so far they had been successful in achieving Sonico's objectives.

Universal Airlines had emphasized the role of its hub as its primary distinctive capability. What threats were there to that? The prospect of another airline's establishing a similar operation was remote. The greatest danger was probably that the market would move away from the "hub and spoke," which had emerged as the principal means of airline operation since deregulation in the 1970s. The economics of smaller planes might become more favorable, or business travelers' preferences might move further toward point-to-point services. These were trends that needed to be watched, but problems did not seem imminent.

Universal had scheduling and code-sharing arrangements with a number of commuter airlines that brought passengers into its hub. There was a good deal of resentment at Universal regarding the profits that some of these companies had been making, especially because the airline business as a whole had been going through such difficult times. Universal's operations director was, again, on top of the issue.

"Some commuter services," he pointed out, "were provided by carpetbaggers with an airplane." They would move elsewhere if the returns were better, and conversely, Universal could find equally good operators to replace them. Others were people with real roots and connections in their local community. "Passengers are booking with them, not with us. Sometimes we add the value to the code share; sometimes the other fellow does." Universal had to distinguish carefully between one and the other. "We can deal toughly with the first sort of relationship, but we need to treat the second with kid gloves."

Adding Value

The return on capital employed earned by these five companies varied considerably. Sonico's was the highest. The company added substantial value and used very little capital employed. Subject to some of the dangers that the analysis of its operations had identified, it might continue earning that rate of return for many more years, as the company was one with a genuine distinctive capability. Sonico's shares had been a stunningly good investment for those who had held them for a decade or more (which included many of its senior management group). But today, these shares sold on a price–earnings ratio well above the market average, and its market value was many times the book value of its assets. The good news about Sonico was fully in the price.

Bankcorp and Finserco also earned returns well in excess of any reasonable measure of the cost of capital in their businesses. Finserco's projections showed a steady decline in its ratio on assets as its diversification proceeded, and this worried some of its executives. But they were somewhat reassured when they focused on the fundamental objective of adding value. It is better to earn a 20 percent return on capital than to get 25 percent on a business half the size, was how the argument was put to them. In Bankcorp, by contrast, the return it expected to earn on capital employed continued to hold up as it increased the geographic scope of its operations. Bankcorp could, its executives believed, add as much value to its new businesses as it was doing on the old.

The four ways of looking at the capital employed in a business—current cost, historic cost, cash flow, and shareholder return—were effectively reduced to two for Sonico, Finserco, and Bankcorp. The first three measures of current profitability and cash flow all gave similar impressions of the business, because physical capital was not very important to any of these companies. But even though their financial statements reflected their current position, the market was driven by expectations for the future. All three companies had outperformed the market over the last few years as the stock market had come to appreciate the strength of their distinctive capabilities. Now, all enjoyed glamour ratings. Finserco had the lowest PE of the three, and its management suspected that the market still underestimated the strength of its franchise when applied to a wider range of products. Bankcorp, which had the most doubts of any of these firms about the sustainability of its distinctive capability, concluded that its stock was probably fully valued.

But both Universal Airlines and Popular Energy were capital-hungry businesses. Their returns on capital were much lower, partly because their added value was spread over a much larger base, but more because it was doubtful whether they added much value. Popular Energy earned a respectable but regulated historic-cost rate of return on its assets. As our analysis made clear, its diversification program had raised earnings per share, but these higher earnings had been obtained by using retained profits to generate returns that, although positive, were less than the cost of capital (which measured what the shareholders could have earned by investing the money themselves). Popular Energy's refocusing of its business implied more shareholder value from higher dividends and slower growth, a return, in fact, to something closer to its traditional utility status. Not everyone in Popular Energy found it easy to accept the limitation of its horizons that an analysis of its distinctive capabilities produced. After a decade in which costly strategic and financial advisers had told them that the world was at their feet, the narrower conception of the business seemed constraining. Yet the consequences of buying firms to which they had no real value to add were obvious—they had seen a declining return on capital and a falling stock market rating. As their CEO summed it up, "Running a utility well is one of the hardest management jobs, and now is the time we should start doing it."

The financial appraisal of Universal Airlines was the most depressing of all: "Over the last five years, we would have done better to sell our fleet and put the money in a bank, and our shareholders would have done better to sell their stock and put the money in a sock." Yet Universal Airlines was a well-run business with some real distinctive capabilities. In the equation that says that added value is the sum of competitive advantage and industry conditions, it was industry conditions that had let them down.

Would—could—too many planes go on chasing too few passengers indefinitely? Economic and commercial logic said no, but the experience of the airline industry seemed to suggest otherwise. If, but only if, the business reaches an equilibrium in which the marginal firm is, as we explained in Chapters 2 and 13, just profitable enough to stay in business, will Universal's competitive advantages enable it to add value.

Conclusions

I sat down with my notes to write down what these five companies—Finserco, Bankcorp, Sonico, Universal Airlines, and Popular Energy—had in common. But it is far more important to record what they did not have in common. Take the slogans of the strategy business in the last two or three decades—"stick to the knitting," "go global," "emphasize related diversification," "focus on the core business," "emphasize quality"—and you will find that there were some of these companies to which each was appropriate and others to which each was not. The only extraordinary thing about this statement is that anyone could ever have thought otherwise.

But it would be wrong to conclude that because there are no general solutions to management problems and no valid generic strategies, there are no general principles of good management. The fact that aspirin does not cure every disease does not mean that medicines are useless, and to respond to this discovery by looking for some other compound that will cure every disease is a foolish response. Just as the appropriate medicine is specific to the disease for which it is prescribed, the appropriate strategy is specific to the company that adopts it. It should be no surprise that although Bankcorp and Finserco were in the same business, the moves that were right for one were wrong for the other. Geographic diversification was right for Bankcorp and wrong for Finserco; extending the product line was right for Finserco but wrong for Bankcorp. Bankcorp was right to stress acquisition and even to contemplate being acquired. Both would have been damaging to Finserco. These differences followed directly from the differences in their distinctive capabilities.

Not all firms have distinctive capabilities in all their markets. Indeed, some firms may not have any distinctive capabilities at all. Most of us come to terms with the fact that we are not likely to win Olympic gold medals for anything. It is curious that we find this so much harder to accept in regard to corporations. The most difficult business cases in strategy classes are those of companies whose competitive advantages are inherently transitory—the result of an innovation that others will certainly follow or a position that others will assuredly replicate. The extravagant claims made, if rarely realized, for strategic management and the extraordinary powers attributed to charismatic CEOs make us all reluctant to accept such obvious propositions as that IBM might have to settle for being a lesser corporation than it once was, because there is nothing else that it can do.

A firm's distinctive capabilities therefore are those it has, not those it would like to have. All these companies found it difficult to distinguish the wish from the reality. "If we are number one in processing, why shouldn't we be number one in customer service and number one in investment management?" asked a Bankcorp manager. It was as if the 100-meter gold medalist had asserted that merely because she was a gold medalist, she could just as easily win the 1,500 meters in swimming and the long jump as well. Distinctive capabilities are precious; companies must identify and nurture them but not exaggerate them.

When I ask a class to identify the distinctive capabilities of successful companies, they usually come back with extended lists. Merck, Microsoft, BMW, and Nintendo have extraordinary architectures, outstanding reputations, many innovations, and a series of strategic assets. But companies seldom have all these advantages, and most of what the class identifies is readily replicable and usually replicated. Few companies, however successful, have more than one or two distinctive capabilities. One or two will be sufficient, if the capabilities are truly distinctive, to enable a firm to add substantial value.

Unfortunately, most of the data that went into this chapter must remain confidential to the firms involved.

15

....

Why National Economies Succeed

*Although most of this book is concerned with the implications of my
analysis for business policy, in this chapter I consider the relationship
between business and public policy. What are the connections between
competitive advantage in the firm and competitive advantage in the national economy? The free-market system succeeds when the pursuit of
the former secures the latter, but there is no necessary equivalence between the two. I begin by looking at the reasons that markets may fail
to produce efficient outcomes. I identify these as inequality of information, externalities, and the existence of natural or strategic monopoly.
When these conditions exist, firms may add value for themselves, but
this added value may represent an appropriation of existing value
rather than an increment to national wealth. I go on to explore some
implications for business ethics, suggesting that modern corporations
have both classical and relational contracts between themselves and
the communities in which they operate and that business behavior is
governed by the terms of both types of contracts.*

    *In the second part of the chapter I look at the competitive advan-
tages of nations themselves. The basic sources are the same as for
firms. The competitive advantage of nations rests on the sustainable,
appropriable distinctive capabilities of architecture, reputation, and innovation and on the ownership of strategic assets. Sometimes the value
of these distinctive capabilities is effectively appropriated by individual corporations, but often it accrues for the benefit of the population
at large. But as with firms, the pursuit of national competitive advantage relies on identifying distinctive capabilities, choosing appropriate
markets, and maximizing the value of these capabilities. This has implications for the industrial policies that countries should pursue.
Wish-driven strategies are as unproductive for countries as they are for
firms, and effective industrial policies are directed toward reinforcing
strengths rather than compensating for weaknesses.*

*I*t is not," wrote Adam Smith, "from the benevolence of the butcher,
the brewer, or the baker, that we expect our dinner, but from their
regard to their interest. We address ourselves not to their humanity but

to their self love" (Smith 1776, vol. 1, bk. 1, chap. 2, p. 15). Smith went on to describe the "invisible hand" that drew men to achieve "ends which were no part of their intention." Smith drew attention, more clearly and eloquently than anyone before or since, to the greatest paradox in economic institutions. A free-market system based on the decentralized pursuit of uncoordinated objectives by individual firms not only works but appears to work better than any other form of economic organization yet implemented.

Smith's arguments have been restated in many different if less felicitous ways in the last two centuries. Today, they are reflected in two strands of thought—two different attempts to account for the economic superiority of the free-market system. The "fundamental theorems of welfare economics" describe the conditions under which competitive markets efficiently allocate resources. A competitive market equates prices with costs, with the result that resources are directed toward activities that reflect their value in alternative uses. A different school, often called neo-Austrian after influential proponents such as Von Hayek and Schumpeter, emphasizes competition as a dynamic process. The business environment is endlessly innovative. Most innovations fail, but successful ones persist and form the basis of further development. Natural selection operates among firms, activities, and ideas in the same way that the biological process of natural selection works in nature.

The recent background has produced more striking evidence on the relationship between economic structure and economic performance than any theory could have offered. Early critiques of modern totalitarianism were based on the threat they posed to individualism and personal liberty. The critics did not doubt that these regimes, with their capacity to centralize and coordinate resources, would be successful in economic terms. Experience then seemed to support that. Stalin's Russia had taken a preindustrial society into the age of modern technology in two decades; Hitler's Germany had brought its economy out of recession more quickly than any other had. Finally, however, it was the economic failure of the Eastern European regimes that brought about the collapse of their political systems. Whatever the superficial attractions of central direction and control, in practice it literally failed to deliver the goods. The immediate contrast between East and West Germany provided as close to a controlled experiment as social science is ever likely to see.

The results of that experiment and its dramatic end have established beyond doubt that the dominant form of economic organization in the future will be the privately owned value-maximizing corporation. This makes it all the more important to understand the relationships between added value in the firm and added value in the nation. The first part of this chapter considers the degree to which value created by the firm is and is not translated into wealth creation in the national, or international, economy. The second part is concerned with the competitive advantage of nations themselves and how it is reflected in the performance of individual firms.

Both the welfare economics and the Schumpeterian perspectives are relevant to these questions. The welfare economics approach identifies the conditions under which the maximization of corporate added value makes the best use of available resources. In doing so, it also identifies the circumstances under which the maximization of added value at the corporate level may be inconsistent with that objective. In the Austrian view, those firms that succeed in adding value will prosper and grow, whereas those that fail will wither and decline. From a social perspective, we might ask whether this process of natural selection discriminates between desirable and undesirable characteristics—whether corporate added value is indeed created by forces of enterprise and innovation or is simply appropriated.

Added Value and Wealth Creation

The clear and consistent perspective on the purpose of commercial activity adopted throughout this book is that the objective of the firm is to add value to the resources it uses. Its success in doing so is both the measure of its competitive advantage and the quantum of its achievement. Yet adding value for shareholders or other stakeholders is not always the same as adding value for society. The issue here is once more the *appropriability* of added value. A firm may—most frequently through monopoly—add value for itself, although it has created none. Rather, it has merely appropriated it from consumers for the benefit of its shareholders or other stakeholders. Or a firm may create wealth that it cannot effectively appropriate, such as through innovation it cannot protect. So there is no necessary equivalence between the creation of added value by the corporation and the creation of wealth in the economy as a whole. Although there is a correlation, it cannot be put more strongly than that.

The social benefits of corporate added value depend on its source. When the added value is the product of reputation or architecture, there is a broad identity between the private and social value of corporate activity. The value of a company's reputation can be largely appropriated by the firm that enjoys that reputation. With architecture, too, there is a basic equivalence of private and social interests. Yet when architecture depends on a network of relational contracts, inside or outside the firm, the corporation will jeopardize that network if it emphasizes appropriability too strongly. Firms typified by strong architecture—Procter & Gamble, Hewlett-Packard—also are associated with an emphasis on good working conditions, generous employee benefits, and strong community involvement. These features are very evident in Japan, the home of architecture-based competitive advantage. And the returns from competitive advantage are shared more generally. Firms that make above-average profits pay above-average wages. Contracts with profitable companies are sought after and prized when obtained, and one of the common marks of the successful company is that consumers feel that its products are good buys.

With innovation, the difficulties of appropriation are especially real. For example, Newton's invention of calculus may have been the most important scientific discovery of the millennium, but very little of the benefit accrued to Newton or to his employer, Trinity College, Cambridge. Electricity was probably the most significant product innovation of all time, but Con Edison earns more from it in a week than Benjamin Franklin did in his lifetime. Much innovation takes place within corporations but is ineffectively appropriated, from Xerox's personal computers to AT&T's transistor, and the difficulties of appropriation imply that a good deal of economically important innovation requires public funding if it is to take place at all.

In contrast, there are three kinds of circumstances under which firms may appropriate more value than they create.

- *Externalities.* Market prices do not adequately capture all the costs or benefits associated with particular activities.
- *Information problems.* Inadequate or differing information from buyers and sellers leads to market inefficiency.
- *Monopoly, natural or strategic.* Competition is insufficient to ensure that relative prices are aligned with relative costs.

Environmental factors are among the most important externalities. That is, the price of hardwood may not reflect either the cost of renewing these resources or the costs of their nonrenewal. The cost of electricity does not incorporate the damage from acid rain. When calculating profit and added value based on only the private costs of these commodities, firms may make choices that, from a wider perspective, use too much wood, or the wrong sort, or too much electricity, or generate it in undesirable ways. Added value may seem to be created at the corporate level, only to be destroyed at the national level.

The appropriability of returns to innovation comes under this head-ing too. The fruits of research or experiment can be obtained by both those who have not borne the cost and those who have. Indeed, there is a sense in which all externalities can be seen as problems of appropriability. If someone owned the environment, he could, and no doubt would, stop us from polluting it or make us pay for cleaning it up.

Markets may fail when information is deficient. Reputation is the market's own corrective to the problem of imperfect information. In some markets, however, such as real estate and used cars, product quality is uncertain and good reputations are few. There are others—medicine, airlines, and banking—in which customers and politicians have insisted that reputation is supplemented by explicit regulation. They suspect that in these markets traders may exploit their superior information, as financial swindlers do, or simply behave complacently in light of it. Indeed, concern for reputation may not give all airlines or all doctors sufficient incentive to maintain suitably high standards.

Differences in information often allow the creation of private added value through arbitrage. Knowing that a stock is worth $100 when it is selling for $75 is as profitable as making it worth $100 when it was previously worth $75. Discovering value can be as privately rewarding as creating it is. The information that the stock is worth more than previously thought is certainly valuable, but it is very unlikely that it is as valuable as it is remunerative. In this way, much of the added value created in the financial sector represents an appropriation of wealth rather than an addition to it.

A firm is most often able to appropriate value it does not create when it holds a strategic asset. It has been many years since the earl of Lauderdale observed the potential addition to profits (Lauderdale 1804, cited in Stigler 1966) and hence, he reasoned, to national wealth, from the creation of a water monopoly. But the profit represents an appropriation, not a creation, of wealth. The added value from plentiful water supplies was always there, and returns arise from the ability to lay claim to it. A competitive advantage is usually a public asset as well as a private one; a strategic asset is often held at the expense of the community.

Public Policy and Business Ethics

The creation of added value at the corporate and the national levels cannot be assumed to be identical, and this raises questions about the ethics of business behavior. When is it right for the corporation to appropriate wealth that it has not itself created?

Two extreme positions can be dismissed more or less immediately.

It is not the job of the corporation to be an arbiter or monitor of social welfare. Even if the company's managers were able to fulfill such obligations sensibly, the experience of state industries given imprecisely defined social objectives has shown that they are generally not well-managed businesses. Simply from the point of view of operational effectiveness, it has been found desirable to aim at narrower, more commercial targets.

It is no more plausible to argue that the company may take any legal action that increases its profits. The supply of artificial limbs to British hospitals by subsidiaries of BTR, which together held around 75 percent of the market, was the subject of an investigation by the Monopolies and Mergers Commission, which established that the company had regularly withheld supplies in order to drive up prices and had supplied misleading information as part of a process of what the company described as "skilful negotiation." Just as there are individual actions that are legal but wrong, so, too, there are corporate actions that are legal but wrong.

Managers often respond to these dilemmas by denying that they exist. Concern for the environment may be in the corporation's long-run interest even if it is damaging to its short-term profits. "Good business is profitable business" is the theme of most of what is written about business ethics. Often this is true. The actions of the limb suppliers ultimately proved commercially foolish as well as morally dubious. The problem with the maxim that honesty is the best policy is not just that it is devoid of ethical content but also that it gives no guidance as to what to do if, as is sometimes the case, honesty is not the best policy. A firm that imposes higher environmental standards on itself than its competitors does put itself at a competitive disadvantage, may derive no long-run benefit that does not accrue equally to them, and can offset the costs only by gains, if any, to its reputation.

Managers often escape this difficulty by persuading themselves that corporate and public interests are identical. The executives of regulated industries routinely argue that increased competition would be damaging to the public interest. Sometimes this is true, but sometimes it is not. No one should doubt that in the main, managers genuinely believe what they say. But what should they do if they know that preserving their monopoly is not in the best interest of the public, even though it is in the best interest of the firm?

To recognize these problems is only to begin to solve them. It is necessary to talk about business ethics in the same way that we do individual ethics. But the manager's position is more difficult because she is responsible not only to herself but also to other stakeholders—shareholders, employees, customers—who have a legitimate concern about the firm's ethical behavior as well as its financial performance. This pulls in many directions. It is more admirable to take a principled stand or to engage in philanthropic behavior with one's own money than with other people's. It is also more difficult to assess what such a stand or behavior would be if one were responsible to a variety of groups with diverse values, expectations, and aspirations.

What are the social obligations of business? The firm has both classical and relational contracts with government and the community. The classical contracts cover matters such as the taxes the company must pay or the prices that a regulated utility may charge. The government makes the rules; the company must observe them; and the state monitors compliance. The firm has absolutely no obligation to pay more tax than is legally required or to keep prices below the level that the regulator allows. If the government, the regulator, or the public does not like the result, then the rules can and should be changed. A new classical contract should be determined.

Other matters cannot be treated in this way. The community is entitled to expect that firms will show concern for the health and safety of its employees, customers, and the public at large. It supports this expectation by means of laws that determine standards and the imposition of civil and criminal penalties on those who fail to meet them. But the reality is that these matters are not handled well by regulations. In most contexts, safety is achieved by attitudes and behavior rather than by close attention to rules.

In these areas—in which social expectations of business behavior must be the subject of interpretation rather than precisely formulated obligations—there is an obvious Prisoner's Dilemma. The short-run commercial interest of every firm is to sail as close to the wind as the law permits. But if many do so, the result necessarily will be a detailed set of regulations for all firms. This is not the best way of ensuring the common objective, and it involves material and probably costly interference with ordinary business behavior. Instead, the best outcome for everyone is for firms to engage in a repeated game and to behave in a responsible manner and for society to respond with a light regulatory rein—to achieve a win–win outcome to this Prisoner's Dilemma.

That is what is properly meant by the social responsibility of business. It is the establishment of standards of behavior in areas in which society has legitimate expectations for business but regarding which these expectations cannot sensibly be precisely defined, quantified, and monitored. Safety is an example; others are the provision of training, the employment of disadvantaged groups, and the determination of transfer prices between divisions of international companies. All these are better handled through relational than classical contracts. Sometimes they can be handled only through relational contracts.

The content of these relational contracts—as with all relational contracts—is context and culture specific. A multinational company cannot establish completely general rules, since being a good citizen means something different in the different jurisdictions in which it operates. That is, the social responsibility of business is not the same in India as in the United States and not the same in Italy as in Britain. And the more extensive and demanding the range of classical contracts is, the less scope there will be for the relational contract. Environments that encourage individualism and tolerate opportunism may take the same view of corporations. Local managers must be sensitive to these nuances within the overall framework of their corporate policy.

An important implication for public policy is that the less often managers are forced to choose between corporate advantage and social concerns, the better it will be for all. Capitalism works best when managers can single-mindedly pursue the interests of their own firm, knowing that by adding value at the corporate level they are also creating wealth for society. That means that environmental policies should ensure that the price of corporate inputs and outputs adequately reflects the costs imposed. It means antitrust policies that make certain that a competitive advantage is achieved only in competitive markets, and it means regulatory policies that clearly define the limits within which unavoidable monopoly power can legitimately be exercised. The United States has, among the Western economies, by far the longest history of antitrust activities and, until recently, had by far the most rigorous record of enforcement. It is by no means coincidental that the United States is also the only Western economy in which there has never been any real public pressure to nationalize the leading private firms and the one in which the power of trade unions has been weakest. Although businesspeople regularly excoriate antitrust and regulatory policies, the more thoughtful among them recognize that without them the prospect that capitalist organizations would survive, or would deserve to survive, would be much weaker.

From the Competitive Advantage of Nations
to the Competitive Advantage of Firms

Firms add value by means of competitive advantages established through innovation, reputation, and architecture and by the management of strategic assets. In an international trading environment, we can look to the competitive advantage of nations within the world economy in the same way as we look to the competitive advantage of firms within their commercial environment.

This analogy holds only loosely. Just as large firms typically consist of many different operating businesses, which can maintain many distinct competitive advantages, so nations encompass many varieties of economic activity. Yet the ways in which value is added and appropriated by countries are sufficiently similar to the ways in which value is added and appropriated by firms, for the comparison to be worth pursuing.

Table 15.1 shows an assessment of added value for some nations of the world. The opportunity cost of factors to countries is less obvious than that for firms. Capital costs are set at 30 percent of GDP, and the cost of labor is calculated so that the added value in Portugal is zero. If competitive advantage is appropriately measured by reference to the performance of the marginal firm in its industry, the competitive advantage of nations is equally measured by reference to the performance of an economy that is marginal in relation to the industrialized world. This figure is not to be taken seriously; instead, it is a demonstration of a concept rather than a sober assessment of national competitive advantage.

One consequence of this benchmark is that for most countries of the world, added value is negative. A majority of the world population lives

Table 15.1. Which Nations Add Value? (U.S.$ billions)

	GDP	Numbers Employed	Labor Cost	Capital Cost	Added Value	Input Output
Switzerland	2,409	3.84	344	724	1,343	0.44
Germany	16,076	29.89	2,677	4,823	8,576	0.47
Norway	1,120	2.14	192	336	592	0.47
France	1,263	24.57	2,202	3,789	6,640	0.47
Japan	31,655	63.84	5,719	9,497	16,439	0.48
Italy	11,555	24.08	2,157	3,467	5,931	0.49
Kuwait	232	0.50	44	70	118	0.49
United States	54,198	123.87	11,098	16,260	26,842	0.50
United Kingdom	10,595	28.27	2,533	3,178	4,884	0.54
Portugal	688	4.99	446	192	0	1.00
Mexico	1,676	28.85	2,585	502	−1,411	1.84
Thailand	811	30.39	2,723	243	−2,156	3.66
Pakistan	394	32.81	2,939	118	2,664	7.77
Nigeria	275	29.97	2,685	82	−2,494	10.08
Bangladesh	182	30.92	2,770	55	−2,642	15.49

Sources: International Financial Statistics; Yearbook of Labour Statistics.

in these countries. This may seem a harsh judgment, but not necessarily an inappropriate one. It is simply an assertion that most world economies are ineffectively using their resources of capital and labor. National economic and social structures are more likely to be persistently value subtracting than corporate ones are, because value-subtracting companies eventually go broke. Although there are some similar forces at work among nations, as the recent experience of Eastern Europe showed, they are much slower and less effective.

The four factors of innovation, reputation, architecture, and strategic assets are instructive in explaining this list, but the balance among them is different. There are national reputations. The reputation for reliability established by many individual Japanese manufacturers may have attached itself to Japanese products as a generic category (and if, as is likely, the factors that make possible the achievement of high product quality for one Japanese manufacturer make the same achievement possible for all, this is a rational attitude for consumers to take). Swiss banks have a reputation for secrecy and security that appears to adhere to Swiss banks collectively rather than individually. American associations are important to the international success of Coke, Marlboro, and McDonald's (Marlboro advertising emphasizes this, and Coke now seeks to play it down). But reputation is principally associated with the individual seller, and the returns to reputation accrue primarily at the level of the individual corporation.

When innovation is specific and appropriable, its value is reaped by the innovator, and the contribution of innovation to the national competitive advantage is broadly equal to the sum of the contributions of individual innovations to the competitive advantage of individual companies. The poor appropriability of much innovation, which works to the detriment of the creation of competitive advantage through innovation at the corporate level, often works to the advantage of the creation of competitive advantage through innovation at the national level. Although scientific knowledge observes no national boundaries, just as it observes no corporate boundaries, the transfer of expertise is always easier between those who work in geographical proximity to one another, meet one another regularly, share the same educational background, and speak the same language. In this way, the individual innovations that form part of the competitive advantage of individual firms in the United States, Germany, and the United Kingdom—countries with strong scientific capabilities and traditions—create a national competitive advantage that adds up to substantially more than the sum of its parts.

Often this creates an innovative *architecture*, and architecture is a competitive advantage that is of even greater importance for the nation than it is for the firm. The benefits of architecture are apparent in the mutually supporting networks of firms that can be observed in locations and industries as different as California's Silicon Valley, the Italian knitwear industry, the City of London's position in financial services, or the *keiretsu* of Japan. Despite their diversity, the similarities among these structures are equally apparent. Each is a network of implicit contracts. Each achieves flexibility of response and the ready exchange of information that the existence of sustained informal relationships makes possible. Each links commercial and social activities in ways that sharply raise the penalties for opportunistic behavior.

If architecture is often a prime source of national competitive advantage, its absence can also be a prime source of national competitive disadvantage. The absence of a structure of trust relationships, the inability to enter effectively binding commitments, and an expectation that those who can behave opportunistically will do so are all recognizable features of the economic organization of poor countries. These nations are in a reiterated Prisoner's Dilemma in which cheat–cheat is the sustained equilibrium, and there are no straightforward mechanisms for moving to a cooperative outcome.

Strategic assets are an important source of national competitive advantage. It is relatively unusual for a corporation to lay exclusive claim to scarce factors—such as a broadcasting license or a natural resource—but it is common for a country to do so. A country like Kuwait derives its international competitive position entirely from this source, and the experience of Kuwait raises questions of the appropriability of national competitive advantages.

Historically, patterns of industrial activity were considerably influenced by access to scarce natural resources. This is why Pittsburgh and Chicago are located where they are: Trading and industrial activities developed around the great natural harbors of the world, such as those at San Francisco and Sydney. According to the textbook analysis of competitive advantage, climatic factors gave England its strength in textile production and Portugal's in vinification. Today, these natural resource industries are much less significant proportions of overall industrial activity, and many of the world's most successful economies are very poorly endowed with natural resources (think of Japan). The scarce factors that influence national competitive advantages today are more often the range and variety of skills to be found in the workforce.

One of Germany's identifiable distinctive capabilities is a labor force with much higher levels of general scientific education and attainment than are achieved in most other countries. Although this forms a central part of the competitive advantage of German companies and explains their strength in industries as different as high-performance automobiles and fitted kitchen manufacture, relatively little of that benefit appears as added value in the accounts of German corporations. The reason is that in each industry and across the German economy as a whole, many German firms are competing for the opportunity to exploit that competitive advantage. Hence the returns to it go to the scarce resource—the German workers themselves—rather than to those who facilitate its exploitation. Because there are several German firms in these industries—Mercedes, BMW, and Audi in automobile manufacture; Poggenpohl and Bulthaup in kitchens—some competitive advantage remains with them, but the wealth created by their activities is mostly in the paychecks of their employees.

An appreciation of the role of architecture and exclusivity helps in understanding the "clustering" phenomenon that is correctly stressed in Porter's (1990) discussion of the competitive advantage of nations. It notes that powerful firms in the same industry are generally found in the same country—whether it is the concentration of auctioneers in the United Kingdom, tile makers in Italy, kitchen manufacturers in Germany, optical firms in Japan, or investment banks in the United States. Porter's discussion overemphasizes, however, the role of technical factors in this phenomenon. A supporting infrastructure certainly sustains these clusters. But their origins lie mostly in architecture or in access to scarce factors. The competitive position of financial service centers in London and New York, for example, is based mainly on its networking, and shared services have developed as a consequence of that. The competitive position of German kitchen manufacturers developed because the national competitive advantage—the ability to recruit highly numerate production-line workers—that is a competitive advantage for one is a competitive advantage for others too. Often, as in Silicon Valley, these two forms of competitive advantage are combined.

Financial Architecture

Architecture is of particular importance in financial services. Those who finance an activity need to monitor both the size and nature of the risks they assume and the honesty and competence of those who manage them. Those who are responsible for the activities have incentives to distort the flow of information, to understate the risk, and to overstate the performance. These issues have been raised at several points in my analysis of relational contracts and of architecture.

One common response is to impose extremely detailed classical contracts, but usually this is not successful. The main consequence of the strict liability that attaches to directors' statements in company prospectuses is that these prospectuses contain little useful information. And classical contracts are binding only to the specifics of the contract, not to their objectives. Relational contracting is usually a better alternative, which is why financial institutions often talk about relationships, even if they are rarely achieved.

In both Britain and the United States, relational contracts work well within the financial sector itself and form the basis of the competitive advantage of those countries in financial services. However, there are few relational contracts between the financial sector and the industrial sector. Banks have traditionally lent principally on the basis of assets rather than their knowledge of the business; equity investors hold small stakes and are positively reluctant to be made "insiders," privy to information not available to the public at large.

Germany, by contrast, has no comparable strengths in its financial sector, but it does have a very different style of relationship between finance and industry, in which both parties have no doubt that they are engaged in a repeated game. It is often suggested that this gives German firms a better system of corporate governance and a greater willingness to undertake and invest in long-term activities. Japan has similar banking relationships and networks of cross-holdings of shares among companies.

It would be naïve to engage in financial transactions on the basis of relational contracts alone. There are many trusting paupers. Nor are all financial services, even successful ones, based on relational contracting. Michael Lewis's description of Salomon Brothers (Lewis 1989) is a caricature of an organization with a strong culture but no architecture. We should note, however, that such a style of operation is associated with activities, such as bond trading, that are concerned with the appropriation of added value but that create virtually none. Real financial architecture may contribute to competitive advantage either, as in the United States, in the financial services sector itself or, as in Germany, in the contribution of the financial sector to economic activity more generally.

Industrial Policy and Corporate Strategy

Successful corporate strategy begins with the identification of a firm's distinctive capabilities. But if wish-driven strategy and copycat strategy are common mistakes of corporations, they are hardly less common mistakes of governments.

Chapter 1 described how each of the principal European powers had sponsored domestic computer manufacturers like ICL in the United Kingdom, Siemens-Nixdorf in Germany, and, most of all, Groupe Bull in France. Wanting to be IBM is not enough to make one be like IBM, and wanting a national champion is not enough to guarantee success. No document epitomizes wish-driven strategy more clearly than the Ryder Report, prepared for the British government in 1975 after the collapse of the only remaining indigenous manufacturer of production cars. Starting from the premise that it was essential that Britain have a major volume car producer, it set out yearly targets for sales, revenues, and investment toward that goal. None of this bore the slightest relationship to reality, in either prospect or retrospect. Willing the objective is not sufficient.

The failures of wish-driven strategy are of two kinds. There is the hopeless aspiration of Groupe Bull. And there is the Pyrrhic victory of Saatchi & Saatchi, which achieved its objective, but at a cost that made it futile. If Leyland illustrates the first, exemplars of the second abound—most of all in France, where magnificent but uneconomic projects can be found in transport, energy, and almost every industry in which the state has played a central role.

A copycat strategy fails to establish a competitive advantage for the firm. It fails partly because it is difficult to know which are the essential and which the peripheral aspects of the success of a firm or group of firms to be emulated. It fails partly because of the efficient-market problem. If everyone can do it, it will cease to offer a competitive advantage, or profit, to anyone. A copycat strategy fails for a nation for the same reasons. It would be foolish not to turn to other countries and hope to learn from their success. But it is fatuous to look to Japan, or another feared competitor, and believe that their achievements can be replicated by adopting some fashionable selection of Japanese practices. Nor is it clear that if Western firms were to achieve Japanese cost and output levels in markets like cars and consumer electronics, in which leadership has already been lost and in which Japan's distinctive capabilities are evidently particularly productive of competitive advantage, that there would be much profit in it for anyone. Learning from the experience of others must be a more sophisticated process.

The lesson for countries, as for firms, is that economic success comes not from doing what others do well but from doing what others cannot do, or cannot do as well. The competitive advantage of nations is equally built around distinctive capabilities, mostly on the exploitation of architecture and strategic assets. Competitive advantage requires the support of complementary assets, and one must concentrate one's efforts in areas in which one has these, not in those in which one does not.

Industrial policy for nations, like competitive strategy for firms, begins from distinctive capabilities.

An industrial policy that reinforces strengths rather than compensates for weaknesses should not be confused with "picking winners"—identifying successful firms, or sectors, and providing them with resources. When firms have competitive advantages themselves, national competitive advantages generally follow. The scope for industrial policy lies in the areas in which that is not the case—in which there are divergences between the competitive strengths of firms and the competitive strengths of countries. Sometimes firms find it difficult to appropriate the competitive advantages they create, or might create—as with precommercial research. Sometimes national competitive advantages exist that firms cannot fully appropriate, or appropriate at all—organizational knowledge or management, or the skills of an educated labor force. It is in areas such as these that industrial policy can help secure competitive advantages for both firms and countries.

The competitive advantage of nations is a subject founded by Smith (1776) but taken up by many subsequent authors: Albert (1991), Olson (1982), and Porter (1990) are recent examples. The fundamental theorems of welfare economics are those of Arrow (1952) and Debreu (1954); a more accessible account of these issues is to be found in the articles by Chipman and Bator, in Townsend (1971). The neo-Austrian school is so named to reflect the contributions of Schumpeter (1934, 1961) and Von Hayek (1944, 1948, 1960). Kirzner (1973, 1989) gives a recent account. On business ethics, Beauchamp and Bowie (1988) is a collection of readings; Barry (1992) and Reidenback and Robin (1989) are assessments of the ethical issues associated with profit maximization. The issues raised here by financial architecture are well discussed in Mayer (1987).

16

Conclusions

It is easy to see why the military analogy continues to exercise such a powerful hold on thinking about corporate strategy. CEOs like to identify with the great field generals of history, alone with their troops, placing divisions here, battalions there, and inspiring their men to heroic feats with a few well-chosen words of encouragement and inspiration.

There is something in the military analogy, of course, but it is as misleading as it is helpful. It is, I believe, directly responsible for two of the most widespread fallacies in the interpretation of business behavior and economic performance. One is the almost universal overestimation of the importance of size and scale. Modern warfare is based on the destruction of opposing forces. Success derives directly from the power to impose such destruction on others and also the capacity to bear it oneself. The United States was the almost inevitable victor in the two world wars this century because of its resources of men and matériel that were essentially limitless relative to those of its opponents. Observe the defeat of Europe's two greatest military machines, those of Hitler and Napoleon, by the vast inhospitable scale of Russia, the worst-governed of European countries.

Business is not like that at all. Success in business derives from adding value of one's own, not diminishing that of one's competitors', and it is based on distinctive capability, not destructive capacity. Distinctive capability becomes harder, not easier, to maintain as size increases. Yet in descriptions of both business and public policy, the equation of scale, power, and effectiveness is often simply assumed, and the generalization from the military to the economic sphere is often assumed to be so obvious as not to require specific elaboration.

But it is wholly false. Although military strength is directly related to the scale of resources that underpins it, economic strength (whatever that means) is not. If economic strength is competitiveness—and it is hard to see what else it could sensibly mean—then the competitiveness of a nation's industry is related to the aggregate size of its resources of labor, capital, and other factors only in the most tenuous and indirect ways. The smallness of Switzerland, Sweden, and Singapore explains why their military forces will never conquer the world. But it is no obstacle to their firms doing precisely that.

The second area in which the military analogy misleads is inviting excessive emphasis on leadership, vision, and determination. Military history abounds with stories of heroism in the face of adversity—Horatio on the bridge, Custer's last stand, the charge of the Light Brigade. It is easy to see why these images are important in a military context. But if General Custer or Lord Raglan had been businessmen, we would not wish to have been their employees or to have bought their shares, and I myself would not have wished to invest much in Horatio either. Fighting against overwhelming odds may sometimes be a necessary military strategy. It is almost never a sensible business strategy.

This perspective relates directly to the rationalist view of strategy, which sees it as something devised for the corporation by its most senior executives. It is commonplace for them to distance themselves physically from the organization to contemplate strategy in weekend retreats. They return refreshed and inspired, to mold the company in light of the strategy they have conceived. Strategy is something that is imposed on the company, and the chief executive is the person who imposes it.

The American business environment, particularly, has developed this personalization of the role of the chief executive, who has come to enjoy the status of the commanding general. His (more often than "her") authority is (for as long as he remains in office) unquestioned. The vision of the organization is his. His primary task is to frame that vision and to inspire his staff and employees with it. If a new chief executive takes the helm, it is possible, indeed often expected, that this will lead to a change in the firm's strategic goals. A business school case in strategy characteristically features a named CEO struggling, frequently alone, to resolve the fundamental issues of his company's strategic direction. The focus on issues of leadership and the management of change in courses and seminars for senior executives follows directly from this view of the world.

The emphasis on merger, acquisition, divestment, and the management of the corporate portfolio in the business environment of English-speaking countries is a closely related phenomenon. These mechanisms are the fastest and most effective ways of engineering changes in strategic direction and accomplishing strategic goals. It is common to encounter senior executives who see the question, "What should our strategy be?" as virtually interchangeable with the question, "What companies should we buy?"

The subject of business strategy as a formal discipline has developed only in the last three decades, principally in the United States. Even those contributions to its literature that originated outside the United

States reflect the U.S. tradition. It is important to note these national origins because they have substantially influenced perspectives on the subject. Business is not done in the same way in all countries, and the strengths and weaknesses of U.S. corporations are not necessarily the same as those of their overseas competitors.

Many of these differences result, in one way or another, from the strongly individualistic nature of U.S. society. This can be seen in contrasting views of the corporation. The U.S. company is a creation of its financial system—a system that emphasizes equity investment and allows hostile takeovers and the free operation of the market for corporate control. Outside the English-speaking world, the corporation is seen in an organic rather than an instrumental way, as an organization with a character of its own and its own internal purposes and dynamism. The identification of the company and its CEO is an aspect of this difference in approach. The notion that GE is an extension of Jack Welch may be seen as a somewhat strained attempt to explain the manifestly collectivist nature of the large corporation in a society that strongly emphasizes that responsibility is individual.

I have also explained why relational contracting is more difficult to achieve in an American business environment than in some others. This can be seen in the much more extensive use of lawyers and the legal process by U.S. firms: Deals are driven; contracts are specified in considerable detail; and the courts exist to enforce them. The price is a loss of the flexibility and capacity to transfer information characterizing relationships that appear looser in form if not in reality.

None of this is to say that the United States has got it wrong or, still less, that the United States would do better to imitate what is done elsewhere. Indeed, it is this same individualism and emphasis on personal responsibility that have helped make the United States the most innovative society the world has seen, and the dominance of world markets by U.S. technology and U.S. brands is a direct consequence.

This broader perspective bears directly, however, on two central themes of this book. One is that competitive advantages are generally based on stability and continuity in relationships, a theme that has been developed in many different ways. It began (in Chapters 1 and 2) with a view of what success in business meant and with the identification of companies that had achieved such success—Disney, BMW, Honda, Microsoft, and Benetton—companies whose names have recurred throughout this book. They are companies with a strong sense of vision and mission, but with a sense of vision and mission that has arisen from within the company and from a recognition of its strengths, not one that has been imposed from outside or created by a corporate communications program. These all are businesses that are clearly focused on that recognition of strengths, and if there is one company on this list that is evidently faltering, it is Benetton, which has drifted from a strong sense of its own identity in the marketplace.

These issues were developed in Chapters 4 and 5, which explained the role of relational contracting and how a network of relational contracts—the firm's architecture—often formed the basis of competitive advantage. Chapter 9 described how competitive advantages are created by the application of distinctive capabilities in particular markets. It follows that added value normally arises at the level of the individual operating business. Chapter 10 reviewed the disappointing record of merger and acquisition activity, and Chapter 11 showed how size and scale rarely form the basis of sustainable competitive advantage and why there are rarely gains from portfolio planning. Chapter 13 reinforced the argument that a firm's performance depends on the creation of added value in operating businesses. Financial engineering contributes nothing to corporate success in the long run.

How should the need for stability and continuity in relationships be reconciled with the equal need for change and flexibility that confronts every organization in business today? If there is a single central lesson from the success of Japan's manufacturing industry, or from Hewlett-Packard, or from many other of the cases developed in this book, it is that the stability of relationships and the capacity to respond to change are mutually supportive, not mutually exclusive, requirements. It is in the context of long-term relationships, and often only in this context, that the development of organizational knowledge, the free exchange of information, and a readiness to respond quickly and flexibly can be sustained.

The second central theme is that corporate success and competitive advantage are built on the distinctive capabilities of the corporation. Such distinctive capabilities are of many kinds. Those of Coca-Cola and Nintendo, Benetton and Marsh & McLellan, Disney and Merck could hardly be more different. They are the product of the corporation's history, have rarely been consciously created, and have never been imposed from the outside. And these differences—the absence of common elements in the distinctive capabilities except at the highest levels of generality—are of critical importance. The search for generic strategies, for recipes for corporate success, is doomed to failure. There can be no such recipes because their value would be destroyed by the very fact of their identification.

Appendix

....

General Electric

If the evolution of business strategy in the West were to be described by reference to the history of a single company, that company would be General Electric (GE). GE has both led and followed every major development in strategic management in the last four decades. This evolution is closely associated with the company's four chief executives during this period, each of whom imposed his own personal sense of strategic direction on the company.

GE emerged from the genius of Thomas Edison, who made electricity a commercial product. By 1900 the company was involved in every aspect of the electrical business. Throughout the first half of the century, GE was responsible for an outstanding range of technical and product innovations, which led to the development of national broadcasting, the peaceful application of nuclear power, and the creation of a market in domestic electrical appliances. Today the company is a widely diversified conglomerate. Its largest business is aircraft engines, but it is also a major bank and financial services firm and is the owner of one of the United States' major television networks, NBC.

In the 1950s and 1960s, GE's philosophy was one of decentralization into individual operating businesses. The departments, the critical unit of this decentralized management, were to be of "a size that a man could get his arms around" (Ralph Cordiner, chief executive 1953–1960). GE established a large management training center at Crotonville, New York, designed to create general managers who would transcend functional specialties, and the principles of general management were enshrined in the company's famous "blue books."

Toward the end of the 1960s, some weaknesses in this system became apparent. In particular, the corporate center's planning functions were poorly related to the operating businesses' activities; the center's capacity to review their plans effectively was very limited; and the attempt by each departmental head to expand the size of his own empire was seen as having led to profitless growth for the corporation as a whole. Following a McKinsey report in 1969, GE created "strategic business units." Each one of a smaller number of operating businesses was to be responsible for its own strategic planning.

The central function was now to be portfolio planning—the allocation of resources among strategic business units. A fresh group of consultants created the "GE screen," a matrix in which businesses were ranked by market share and market growth prospects. It was designed to structure that resource allocation process. GE became one of the first diversified businesses to divest as well as to acquire, although the purchase of new businesses was also a key part of its portfolio-planning approach. In 1976, GE made what was then the largest acquisition by a U.S. company, with the purchase of Utah International, itself a diversified energy and resources business. (Utah was sold eight years later, for about the same price as GE had paid.) With strategic planning at the center of the agenda for each of forty-three business units, the day of the strategic planner and of the strategy consultant had truly arrived.

There still were limitations on the capacity of GE's corporate center to review forty-three strategic business units. Nor was it clear where in the organization major new business opportunities were to be identified. So in 1977 the strategic business units were consolidated into six sectors. The center was to take more responsibility for corporate planning; layers of planning staff were removed; and "arenas" of business development were identified. In acknowledgment of the force of Japanese competition, the international arena was given particular emphasis.

For Jack Welch, who became chief executive in 1981, vision was central to strategy. "Good business leaders create a vision, articulate the vision, passionately own the vision, and relentlessly drive it to completion" (quoted in Tichy and Charan 1989, p. 113). The key elements in Welch's own vision were two: "We will run only businesses that are number one or number two in their global markets. . . . In addition to the strength, resources and reach of a big company . . . we are committed to developing the sensitivity, the leanness, the simplicity and the agility of a small company" (*GE Annual Report* 1988). In pursuit of these objectives, GE rearranged its corporate portfolio. "We started out with 411,000 employees. We acquired an additional 111,150 employees. Through divestitures, we reduced 122,700 employees. We restructured, or downsized to get more efficient, reducing some 123,450 employees. Now we have 276,000. Enormous in and out" (Welch, quoted in HBS 1989). Welch acquired the nickname "Neutron Jack" after the neutron bomb, which destroys people but preserves property.

In 1988, however, Welch felt that the stock market was insufficiently appreciative of the company's performance. "We're not sure why this is the case, but it occurs to us that perhaps the pace and variety of our activity appear unfocused to those who view it from the outside" (*GE Annual Report* 1988). The company began a program of repurchasing its shares, but more important to its strategy was a new Welch initiative, "Work-out at GE."

> Work-out is allowing self-confidence to flourish around our company. As that self-confidence grows, the boundaries are beginning to fall; and as they fall, GE is picking up speed, and with that speed a competitive advantage. Some people are uncomfortable with this soft stuff and press us to quantify it. . . . In a boundaryless company, suppliers aren't outside. They are drawn closer and become trusted partners in the total business process . . . in a boundaryless company, internal functions begin to blur. (*GE Annual Report* 1990)

Behind the florid metaphor and business buzzwords is a recognition of the role of relational contracting in facilitating a flexible response and developing organizational knowledge.

These themes that run through GE's development—the cycles of centralization and decentralization, the shifting role of the corporate center, and the steady move from "hard," quantified concepts of planning to looser, organizationally based ones are exactly paralleled in the literature of business strategy. Has the result been a more successful company?

There are two perspectives on GE's performance. Over a long period, GE's share price tracked the Standard & Poor index extremely closely, but on balance there is evidence of a slight outperformance. As managers of a diversified portfolio of U.S. businesses, GE is ahead of the market, and the executives of GE have beaten the average mutual fund.

There is also a different view, however. Computers and consumer electronics have been among the fastest-growing and most exciting new business opportunities of the last fifty years, and GE, once dominant in U.S. markets for all kinds of electrical equipment, has failed in both of them. Perhaps the company enjoyed no relevant distinctive capabilities, or perhaps despite the unquestioned abilities and sophistication of its managers and management systems, it failed to identify and exploit them fully. "When Japanese managers come to visit us, they don't ask to see our research centers or manufacturing facilities. All they want to know about is our management systems" (anonymous GE executive, quoted in HBS 1981). This Appendix describes the thinking behind the management systems that GE has successively adopted.

The Rationalist School: Assessing the Environment

The sheer volume of information that a company can assemble, about both its environment and itself, is daunting. The first problem that the descriptive phase of strategy formulation must confront is how to organize this mass of data (Houlden 1980). The earliest processes of strategy formulation were closely linked to corporate planning.

These formal planning procedures typically grew out of the budgeting process, which is a key control mechanism in most firms. The budget normally covers revenues and expenditures, cash incomes and outgoings, and the requirements of labor and of materials. The plan extends these projections forward. In the earliest days of planning, this was often done by simple extrapolation. More sophisticated planning procedures were then developed to take account of the firm's expectations of economic growth, the probable development of its markets, and its own established plans and intentions. (Anthony 1965 and Gilmore and Brandenburg 1962 are good expositions of these models of strategy as planning.)

Any well-run firm must have some planning process of this kind. Many important corporate inputs—people, plans, accommodation, finance—cannot be turned on and off as markets evolve but must be projected, determined, and negotiated years ahead. The firm needs estimates of these requirements, as they are essential to management's decisions. (Argenti 1965, 1968, and 1980 explain these procedures.) But planning is not strategy, and those firms that believed that by describing the future—often in considerable detail—they had taken major steps toward making it happen, often found the results of their planning rounds a disappointment. Elaborately quantified corporate plans lay gathering dust on the shelves of managers who went on making the decisions they would have made had the plan never existed. (Increasingly skeptical appraisals are Ansoff 1970, Armstrong 1982, Brown et al. 1969, and Lorange 1979.)

The heyday of such corporate planning in business—the 1960s—was also the time when similar processes were adopted by the governments in many countries. France's planning was widely admired; Britain adopted a national plan for its economy; and every newly independent, less developed country (LDC) saw economic planning as the key to its future development. The results were, in the main, as unsatisfactory for governments as for corporations.

Planning goes beyond forecasting and becomes a basis for strategic choices when it encompasses a variety of possible outcomes. One deliberate approach to this issue is *scenario planning* (Grant and King 1979, McNulty 1977, Wack 1985, Zentner 1982), a widely used technique but one particularly associated with Shell Oil (Beck 1981, de Geus 1988). The company invites its group planners to speculate freely on diverse, internally consistent views of the business's future in the world economy (Figure A.1). For Shell, as for other corporations that adopt similar

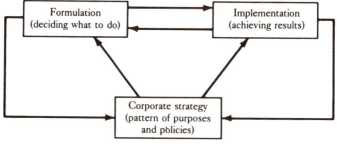

The stages of strategy

Source: Based on Andrews (1971).

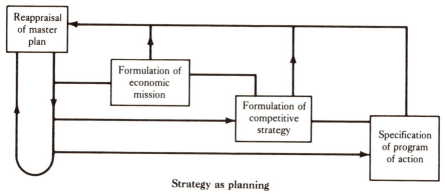

Strategy as planning

Source: Simplified from Gilmore and Brandenburg (1992).

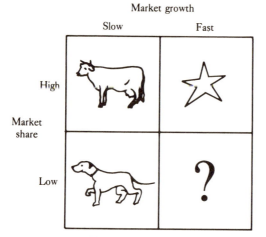

The portfolio-planning matrix

Source: Boston Consulting Group.

Figure A.1. The Evolution of Strategy: Assessing the Environment

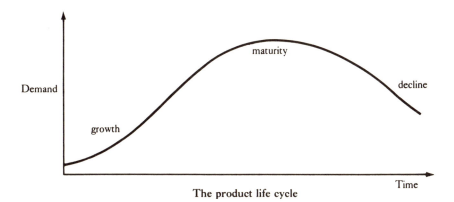

The product life cycle

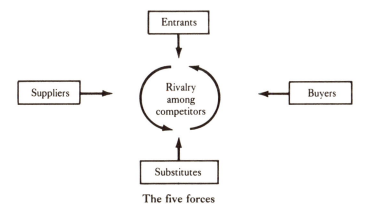

The value chain

Source: Based on Porter (1985).

The five forces

Source: Based on Porter (1985).

approaches—though often in a less formal way—scenarios are a means of organizing its thinking about its environment and of beginning to formulate an agenda of strategic alternatives. What would the company do if the oil price fell to $10 per barrel? How would it react if economic growth were much slower in the 1990s than it had been in earlier decades?

Developing a model of the business environment is a means of both forecasting the business's future and assessing how that future might be influenced by internal or external developments (Lyles 1981). These types of models, which are designed to simulate the functionings of a complete system, may describe an operating business, the firm itself, or even (as with large macroeconomic models) a whole economy. The objective of these models is to describe a more complex set of interactions and feedbacks than can be handled intuitively or with the aid of *analytic models* (which I discuss more fully later). In this way, a simulation model enables the free-ranging speculation of alternative scenarios to be combined with the apparent precision of outcomes associated with the corporate plan. The relationships of the model may be deterministic (as in a financial-planning model, in which many of them are dictated by accounting identities). They may simply be imposed (as in the style of modeling associated with System Dynamics) (Forrester 1961). They may be estimated, statistically or econometrically, from extended time series of data (as in macroeconomic models and their business counterparts).

Such modeling began in the 1960s but has become increasingly widespread as databases and spreadsheets and sophisticated specialized modeling languages, and the universal availability of computers has made it possible for every executive to build his or her own model. But these models are still just ways of assembling data and analyses as a background for strategic decisions. Models cannot be relied on to forecast the future, and even large econometric forecasting models, whose results are widely used even if widely disparaged, are essentially systems of managing information and making judgments rather than true representations of real economies.

The technological determinism of the 1960s—the belief that management was a process that could one day be defined with sufficient precision to be entrusted to a computer—has now sharply diminished. Yet the role that information technology in general and modeling in particular can play in business is still widely misunderstood. The world of business is too complex ever to be adequately described by any model. This observation, trite and obvious as it is, prompts two opposed, but equally mistaken, reactions.

The simpler response is to reject the analytic model altogether. But intuitive responses and judgments are not always right, and whether they are right or wrong they are always the product of some implicit model. Typically, such a model or theory is based on the previous experience of an analogous situation, or series of situations, or some incompletely articulated view of competitive behavior or supplier response. The merit of the model—the explicit process of deductive reasoning—is that it forces this process into the open, spells out the assumptions on which it is based, and identifies those features of reality to which its conclusions may be sensitive. This process may reinforce or reject the initial judgment or, more often, facilitate a better appreciation of what it involves.

An alternative, and more subtle, error is the successive complication of the model in an endeavor to capture a larger fraction of the complex reality. The weakness of this approach is that beyond a certain, quickly reached, point, the additional descriptive value is slight, but the cost in terms of the real objective—a better appreciation of the analytic structure of the relevant relationships—is high. A model is useless that requires many hours to run and that neither forecasts reality in a way that users find credible nor describes a set of relationships that they can readily understand.

Such formal approaches to analyzing the environment proved unattractive to many managers. Some were simply frightened of technical analysis, and others sensed its limitations. Corporate plans seemed to be sterile documents, irrelevant to daily operating decisions; scenarios were the province of distrusted eggheads; and models were the playthings of computer buffs. More qualitative ways of organizing relevant data were needed (Mintzberg 1973, in an early, wide-ranging critique). Many of these techniques were provided by consultants.

The portfolio-planning matrix (Day 1977, Hedley 1977) and the product life cycle (Levitt 1965, Rink and Swan 1979) are examples of these tools. They enable managers to categorize their business as cows, dogs, or stars and to identify phases of growth, maturity, and decline. They also are organizing frameworks that facilitate comparisons of the different businesses in a corporate portfolio or the different products in a business portfolio. Portfolio planning and the product life cycle are means of organizing information about markets and about demand. Other tools are relevant to production and supply. The McKinsey business system, later developed as Porter's value chain (Porter 1985), is a means of describing the successive phases of a production process and analyzing the determinants of costs (cost drivers) in a framework whose objective is support for commercial decision making rather than accounting allocation. Such techniques were used to identify key success factors—points in the production process at which the firm might succeed, or fail, in adding value to its output.

The corporate planners of the 1960s and 1970s were very concerned about such issues as the market and macroeconomic environment, the product portfolio, and the product life cycle. All these emphasize characteristics of the industry or sector and the market. They tend to underplay the role of competitors and competitive behavior in influencing outcomes (Rothschild 1979a, 1979b). Indeed, it is still common to see plans that base output growth on forecasts of the market or to observe industries in which each firm extrapolates its own experience to give overall results that everyone knows are incapable of being realized.

Porter's (1979, 1980) "five forces"—of competition, entry, substitution, suppliers, and customers—offered a more comprehensive checklist of environmental factors (Porter 1981). By the early 1980s, competitor analysis had often replaced, or at least supplemented, environmental analysis. The BCG portfolio matrix, whose dimensions in the 1970s were market growth and market share, was transformed in the 1980s into the strategic environment matrix, which mapped the number of sources of competitive advantage against the size of that advantage.

The Rationalist School: Formulating a Strategy

Having reviewed the business environment and its competitive position, the firm must go on to formulate its strategy. The rationalist school sees the definition of the firm's objectives as the key element in strategy formulation. That view, which owes much to the continuing influence of Drucker on management thinking, is in itself relatively uncontroversial but is the subject of considerable operational difficulty.[1] A firm needs both corporate objectives—what business should we be in?—and business unit objectives—how should the firm position itself relative to its competitors in its chosen markets?

There are two distinct historical phases in the evolution of thought regarding *corporate strategy*. Until the early 1980s, the primary aim of corporate strategy was creating a diversified business portfolio. Such a portfolio might encompass related diversification—motivated by synergy between old and new businesses—and unrelated diversification—supported by portfolio-planning techniques. But by the early 1980s, evi-

---

[1] For the last fifty years, Peter F. Drucker has been one of the most eloquent, and prolific, writers on management issues. A survey of his contributions is Drucker (1977).

dence had accumulated that unrelated diversification added little value (Chapter 10) and that many of the conglomerates created in these earlier decades had succumbed to financial pressures. TRW and Litton Industries were singled out for special praise in Ansoff's readings on business strategy (Ansoff 1969), and ITT was perhaps the most widely admired conglomerate. By 1980, however, Litton was broke, and TRW and ITT were decidedly out of fashion and favor.

Attitudes changed. The trend of the 1980s was to focus on the core business: "stick to the knitting," in the graphic phrase used by Peters and Waterman (1982). Debate on corporate strategy then centered on a view of what this core business was. Is a computer company a manufacturing business or a provider of information management systems? Is a brewer in beer or in leisure? Oil companies have burned their fingers in the resource business, and railroads no longer wish to be seen as transportation companies. Yet the criteria of relatedness have remained poorly defined. Indeed, one influential contribution (Prahalad and Bettis 1986) uses "dominant logic" as its main criterion. Loosely interpreted, a business is related if you think it is.

In formulating business strategy, the "experience curve" popularized by the Boston Consulting Group (BCG 1968, 1972; Yelle 1979) led firms to focus on the critical importance of market share (Figure A.2). This emphasis was reinforced by the observation in the PIMS database of a strong positive correlation between market share and returns (Buzzell, Gale, and Sultan 1975; Buzzell, Heaney, and Schoeffer 1974). PIMS also identified a correlation between relative product quality and return on investment (Buzzell and Gale 1987). With the awakened, or renewed, emphasis on competitive issues, the choice market position was seen as a central element in strategic decision making. Quality, it was perceived, had been an important ingredient in Japan's success. Over time, most markets moved up the quality spectrum. With the aid of phrases such as "quality is free" (Crosby 1979), "total quality management" became a preoccupation of the later 1980s.

Many writers offered taxonomies of generic strategies—checklists from which corporations could choose the objectives most relevant to particular markets. One early list was proposed by Ansoff (1965), who identified market penetration, product development, market development, and diversification as alternative strategic objectives. The Boston Consulting Group's alternatives are invest, hold, harvest, and divest, and Arthur D. Little offers a list of no fewer than twenty-four strategic options (Wright 1974). Porter's (1980) classification of generic strategies proved especially influential. Porter's framework has two dimensions of choice. Firms can pursue either cost leadership—the same product as

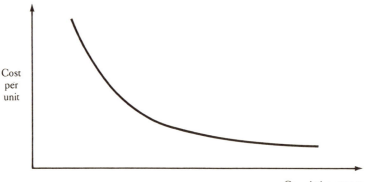

The experience curve

Source: Boston Consulting Group.

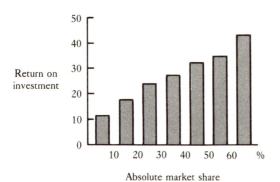

The importance of market share

Source: Buzzell and Gale (1987).

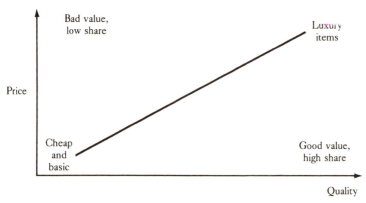

The importance of quality

Source: Davis (1990).

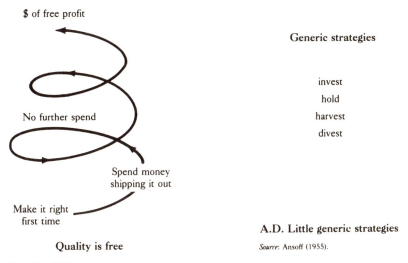

$ of free profit

No further spend

Spend money
shipping it out

Make it right
first time

Quality is free

Source: Price (1990).

Generic strategies

invest
hold
harvest
divest

A.D. Little generic strategies

Source: Ansoff (1955).

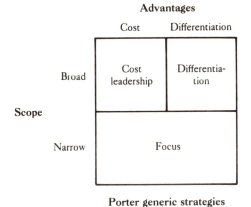

Advantages

Cost   Differentiation

	Cost	Differentiation
Broad	Cost leadership	Differentia-tion
Narrow	Focus	

Scope

Porter generic strategies

Source: Porter (1980).

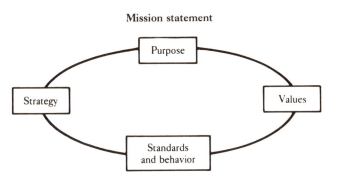

Mission statement

Purpose

Strategy   Values

Standards
and behavior

Formulating the mission

Source: Campbell and Young (1990).

Figure A.2.   Formulating the Strategy

their competitors offer, but at a lower cost—or differentiation. They can range narrowly or broadly, thus generating a range of alternatives encompassing cost leadership, differentiation, and focus. (Galbraith and Schendel 1983, Karmani 1984, Pearce 1983, and White 1986 are surveys of generic strategies.)

The thinking in the 1980s came to support simple, crisp statements of objectives in terms of the corporate vision (Campbell and Yeung 1990) or an assertion of "strategic intent" (Prahalad and Hamel 1985). Today, a debate on the content of the corporate mission is a common starting point for a discussion of strategy. Such a statement can cover objectives in both corporate and business strategy. The mission statement is intended to provide a link between the firm's broad objectives (which may focus exclusively on profit maximization or may profess concern for other stakeholders) and its specific commercial activities.

A different critique of these processes of rationalist strategy formulation—yet one still very much within the rationalist framework—is provided by the shareholder value movement. Like many shifts in thinking about strategy, this is found more or less simultaneously in the thinking of practitioners and the writings of business school academics. American business was stunned in the 1980s by the emergence of a group of corporate raiders. Figures like T. Boone Pickens and the partners of Kohlberg Kravis Roberts, with little in the way of resources of their own but with the aid of the "junk bond" financing pioneered by Michael Milken, could make credible bids for some of the largest corporations in the United States. This threat to incumbent managers led to an anxious reemphasis on "shareholder value." Academics (Jensen 1988, Rappaport 1986) were pressed to explain and justify it, providing both a critique of accounting earnings as a focus of corporate attention and a rationale of the public benefits of an exclusive focus on shareholders' interests.

The most important practical consequence of this activity was to encourage further the breakup of conglomerate firms. The grouping of unrelated businesses tended, it was argued, to conceal the potential strategic value of its individual components to specific purchasers. That message for corporate strategy was clear, but for business strategy, shareholder value had few evident implications. Proponents stressed the need to evaluate investment and acquisitions by reference to their expected cash flows—but this is a theme familiar from every elementary text in corporate finance—and texts on strategy in a shareholder value framework (such as Reiman 1989) do no more than juxtapose Rappaport's critique with Porter's taxonomies of competitive forces and generic strategies.

The threat to established U.S. corporations in the 1980s did not

come only from changes in the capital market. American business attitudes were also transformed by the force of competition from Japan, particularly in automobiles and consumer electronics but also across an increasingly wide range of products. For some writers, this penetration
itself reflected the malign effect of rationalist strategy on U.S. business
(Abernathy et al. 1983). The globalization of markets (Levitt 1983) was a
reiterated theme, and no self-respecting corporation could be without
its global strategy (Prahalad and Hamel 1985). International management
became a subject in its own right (Bartlett and Ghoshal 1986, 1989; Ohmae 1985; Porter 1986).

As the 1990s began, the state of the art in rationalist strategy was
the formulation of a statement of company objectives, often encapsulated
in a "mission statement" and encompassing both corporate strategic objectives—what sort of business we are in—with business strategic objectives—expressed as plans for market share, product quality, and geographic scope. It is not surprising that attention was moving from the
problems of formulating strategy to the issues of implementation.

Copycat Strategy

There is a mechanism for formulating strategy that is apparently simpler
than selecting from a menu of generic strategies in the light of a well-
formulated assessment of the business environment. This is to look at
what other firms do and to copy it, a strategy more felicitously expressed
as *adopting the best practice.*

This strand of strategy has two primary threads. One is the product
of Western concern and admiration for Japan's success in certain manufacturing sectors. Observers are inclined to seize on some particular
characteristic of Japanese practice—just-in-time management of invento-
ries, for example—and advocate its widespread adoption. The current
management preoccupation with quality owes much to this. The other
thread results from the inevitable desire of the number two or number
three firm in an industry to be number one. How better to become number one than to be like number one?

But copycat strategy encounters fundamental problems. The Japanese comparison makes one particularly evident. Many features—some
cosmetic and peripheral, some fundamental—distinguish the functioning of Japanese and European industry. But which are which? And
which superficially cosmetic factors truly support fundamental ones?
Someone aspires to be a great violinist. She goes to a concert and sees a
great violinist in evening dress, holding an expensive violin and drawing

a bow across it. So she dons evening dress, buys an expensive violin, and draws a bow across it. The factors that truly make the great violinist great are not those that are most apparent to the casual observer.

Any attempt at imitation faces this issue, but there is also a second problem peculiar to business strategy. In most fields of human endeavor, one person can do something well without inhibiting the ability of anyone else to do the same thing equally well. I can be a good driver or golfer or singer without any detriment to your ability to drive or play golf or sing. Indeed, these skills are usually mutually enhancing. But successful strategies are—necessarily—peculiar to the firms that adopt them.

The Rationalist School: Implementing Strategy

Chandler's findings directly addressed the implementation of strategy. Structure follows strategy, he argued, and since then, corporation after corporation has rearranged its structure, and rearranged its structure again, in line with changes in its own strategy and in response to changing patterns of strategic thought.

Chandler drew attention to the development of multidivisional forms of organization in response to the increased complexity and diversity of large corporations with multiple activities. Traditionally, firms had decentralized functionally, into accounts departments, marketing groups, and other collections of special skills. The multidivisional firm was decentralized by type of business activity, so that each operating business would have its own accountants and its own marketeers.

But if operating businesses are treated as independent units, what is the corporate center for? There are several answers. One sees strategy as the principal function. The corporate center may act in effect as an internal consulting unit on business-level strategy. Or its primary concern may be corporate strategy. Here the task of the center is to identify and derive synergies from the distinct divisional activities. Wheras Sloan's General Motors sought to perform both functions centrally, more recently, as in General Electric, business-unit strategy was pushed down to a business-unit level. If there are also substantive interactions among these distinct divisions, the company will be driven toward a matrix form of organization (Knight 1976), in which functional groupings coexist with and across divisional boundaries.

The diversification of the 1960s and 1970s led many more companies to pursue multidivisional structures. At General Electric, the degree of central control exercised was sometimes tightened and sometimes relaxed, in ways that often reflected simply a desire for change rather than a revised assessment of the balance of advantages. In the 1980s, the tendency was to decentralize, stripping down the corporate center to minimal levels, even to that of a passive holder of shares in operating businesses (Figure A.3). Traditionally, central functions—like finance, treasury, and planning—were pushed down to lower levels. These moves cast further doubt on the value of the center, and often firms concluded that the corporate function could add no value to some parts of their business. Divestment of peripheral businesses became common.

The implementation of strategy is concerned with not only the structure of a firm's activities but also its style. Burns and Stalker (1966) associated relatively mechanistic, routinized management regimes and well-organized reporting lines with stable strategies and environments, contrasting these with more organic, confused management approaches relevant to more rapid change. These links between strategy and structure have been explored further by many other writers. Mintzberg (1979, 1983) identified five organizational categories—simple structure, machine, bureaucracy, divisionalized form, professional bureaucracy, and adhocracy—effectively adding simple structure (typically the small, owner-managed firm) to Burns and Stalker's classification and subdividing their mechanistic style.

As these typologies were elaborated, there was increasing recognition that structure does not follow only strategy, that structure is itself a determinant of strategy. The essentially interactive nature of this relationship is a theme in Child's work (1974, 1975) and was developed by Miles and Snow (1978), who distinguish prospectors and defenders. The prospector seeks a changing environment; the defender looks to a stable one. From a quite different perspective, the work of Nelson and Winter (1982) reaches analogous conclusions. They envisage the evolution of business as essentially a process of natural selection, in which only those structures well adapted to their environment survive.

According to these perspectives, however, strategic thinking no longer runs unambiguously from environmental assessment through strategy formulation to the process of implementation. If the casual relationship between strategy and structure works in both directions, it may be just as feasible to determine the strategy by defining the structure as it is to choose the structure to match the strategy. This is implicit in the "excellence" identified by Peters and Waterman (1982), who concentrate on the internal attributes of the organization—shared values, "loose-tight" organization—and anticipate that the excellent firm will find environments appropriate to exploiting its excellence. This is a line of think-

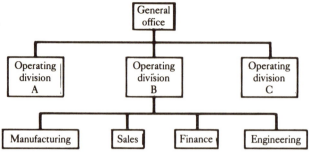

M-form organization

Source: Williamson (1975).

Central influence and control

Source: Based on Goold and Campbell (1987).

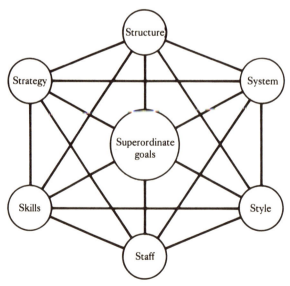

The seven Ss

Source: McKinsey & Co.

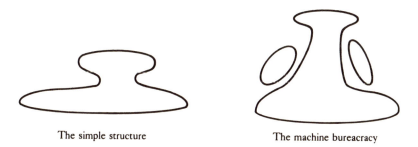

The simple structure   The machine bureacracy

Visualizing organization

Source: Mintzberg (1979).

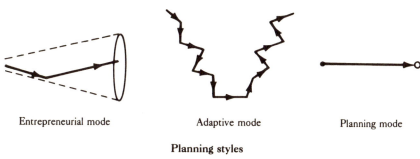

Entrepreneurial mode   Adaptive mode   Planning mode

Planning styles

Source: Mintzberg (1973).

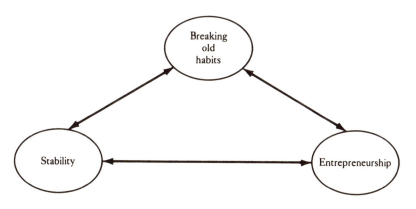

Implementing strategy

Source: Peters and Waterman (1982).

Figure A.3.   Implementing Strategy

ing developed in the burgeoning literature on corporate culture. At this point, the rationalist approach, in which strategy is devised for the organization, gives way to a view of strategy that sees it as derived from the organization.

Critics of Rationalism

Dissatisfaction with the rationalist school is widespread. It centers, in one way or another, on issues of implementation, and there is a growing literature on that topic (Bourgeois and Brodwin 1984, Hamermesh 1986, Hrebiniak and Joyce 1984). The agendas of fashionable consultants and trendier business schools are increasingly filled with related issues—the management of change, the evolution of corporate culture, the coping with a turbulent environment, the institution of programs of total quality management. Rationalism is in retreat, but by no means has been routed, principally because of the absence of equally well-articulated alternative frameworks. The management of change is important, to be sure, but there are logically precedent questions of what change and why.

One expression of this dissatisfaction is the commonly expressed view that "strategy formulation is easy; it is implementation that is difficult." Such a statement reveals much about the weaknesses of the ways in which rationalist strategy has developed. This implied distinction between strategy and implementation rests on a misconception, as a military analogy reveals. Was Napoleon's defeat in Russia a failure of strategy or of implementation? It hardly makes sense to ask the question, because in the hands of a skilled strategist, formulation and implementation are inextricable. But if strategy is nothing more than a vision, a mission statement, an expression of aspiration—and that is often what it is—then it is hardly surprising that it seems easy to formulate strategy but hard to implement it. One might as well say that Saddam Hussein had a fine strategy—defeat the United States Army in a pitched battle and so conquer the oil reserves of the Middle East—but its implementation failed; and this is what he did tell his unsuccessful generals before he murdered them. If the formulation of strategy amounts to little more than a statement of objectives, then all the interesting and important issues of strategy have been redefined as problems of implementation. But this results from a misunderstanding of what strategy is, not from a real characteristic of the business environment.

A related critique is associated with Mintzberg, which stresses the need to consider the strategy process rather than to address the choice of strategy itself:

> One cannot decide reliably what should be done in a system as complicated as a contemporary organisation without a genuine understanding of how that organisation really works. In engineering, no student ever questions having to learn physics; in medicine, having to learn anatomy. Imagine an engineering student's hand shooting up in a physics class. "Listen, prof, it's fine to tell us how the atom does work. But what we want to know is how the atom *should* work." (Quinn, Mintzberg, and James 1988, p. xviii)

The analogy is instructive for both the elements in it that are right and those that are wrong. It is right to emphasize that fundamental knowledge is a prerequisite to practical application. A competent engineer must first learn physics. Imagine the student who shouts, "Stop wasting our time with the theory of the atom; we came here to learn how to make nuclear bombs," and then notes that equivalent statements are made every day by managers and business school students impatient for what they suppose to be practical knowledge. The position is aggravated by the high reputation of many educators who are happy to illustrate the relevance of their material by showing their classes exciting pictures of nuclear explosions, thereby winning their approbation but communicating nothing of any value. Practical knowledge that is not based on a more fundamental analysis is usually knowledge of only the most superficial kind.

Although it contains an element of truth, the preceding analogy is essentially false. The views of the student or the instructor on what the structure of the atom *should* be like are matters of no conceivable interest, since neither of them has any power to influence it. It is realistic, however, to suppose that businesspeople can influence strategy, and it is the prospect that they might do so that is their main reason for studying it. Both the observation of the strategy process and the prescriptive analysis of what that strategy should be are proper questions and legitimate subjects of study, but they are different questions. In just the same way, the issue of how the United States makes its decisions through the mechanisms of the executive, legislative, and judicial branches is different from the issue of what its decisions should be. And although you must understand both if you are to influence policy, it is the second group of questions—what the decisions should be—that are of most general interest. The same is true of strategy.

Emergent Strategy

The study of the strategy process does give further insight into the failings of rationalist strategy. Successful firms often seem to have achieved

their position without going through the processes of analysis, formulation, and implementation that the rationalist school prescribes. Indeed,
the story of Honda's attack on the U.S. cycle market, described in Chapter 1, is often used to illustrate precisely that point.

The notion that successful strategies are often opportunistic and
adaptive, rather than calculated and planned, is a view as old as the
subject of business strategy itself. One of the best expressions of it is
Lindblom's (1959) exposition of "the science of muddling through."
Lindblom wrote from a perspective of public administration, rather than
business administration, and stressed how the political constraints on
policy make a rationalist approach impossible. He argued that the range
of options attainable at any time was necessarily limited, and he contrasted the "branch" method of "successive limited comparison" with
the "root" method of comprehensive optimization.

In his popular volume of readings, Ansoff reprinted Lindblom's
views, but more, it appears, to expose heresy than to commend it.

> Lindblom is wrong when he claims the "root" method to be "impossible."
> . . . The TRW reading shows how one of the world's most dynamic corpo-
> rations goes about a methodical exploration of wide vistas . . . neverthe-
> less, Lindblom's article is instructive, since it describes a widely prevalent
> state of practice in business and government organisations. (Ansoff 1969,
> p. 10)

Twenty years later, this widely prevalent state of practice is still
with us, but the argument is perhaps more open than it was.

Lindblom's perspective was most extensively developed by Simon
(1961) and Cyert and March (1963). They deny that organizations can
sensibly be viewed as entities with personalities and goals like those of
individual people. Rather, firms are better seen as shifting coalitions, in
which conflicting demands and objectives are constantly but imperfectly
reconciled, and all change is necessarily incremental. In this framework,
rationalist strategy—in which senior management chooses and imposes
a pattern of behavior on the firm—denies the reality of organizational dynamics.

The implications of this for strategy were developed by Mintzberg
(1972, 1978), who contrasted *deliberate* and *emergent* strategy. The former is the realization of the rationalist approach, and the latter is the
identification of relatively systematic patterns of behavior in what the
organization actually does. Essentially, the same features distinguish between the adaptive mode of strategic decision making and the planning
mode. In the former, "Clear goals do not exist . . . the strategy-making
process is characterized by the reactive solution to existing prob-

lems . . . the adaptive organization makes its decisions in incremental, serial steps" (Mintzberg 1973, p. 48). By contrast, planning involves "anticipating decision-making . . . a system of decisions . . . a process that is directed toward producing one or more future states" (Ackoff 1970, cited in Mintzberg 1973, p. 49).

As a description of how real organizations operate, this critique is so obviously compelling that at first it is hard to see why the rationalist school of strategy remains influential. But the reasons that it does are clear. Apart from a few disinterested scholars, people study and analyze strategy because they want to know what to do. To observe that organizations are complex, that change is inevitably incremental, and that strategy is necessarily adaptive, however true, helps very little in deciding what to do. Managers wish to learn about a process that they can at least partially control, and whatever its weaknesses, this is what a rationalist strategy appears to offer.

For some, the nihilist conclusion of the critics deals with the matter. Firms do what they do because they are what they are, and the strategy process is one that one can observe and describe but for which it is not possible to prescribe. This seems to be the view taken by Pettigrew in his theoretical argument (Pettigrew 1977) and in his massive history of ICI (Pettigrew 1985). Mintzberg offers at least a partial answer—crafting strategy:

> Imagine someone *planning* strategy. What likely springs to mind is an image of orderly thinking; a senior manager, or a group of them, sitting in an office formulating courses of action that everyone else will implement on schedule. The keynote is reason—rational control, the systematic analysis of competitors and markets, or company strengths and weaknesses. . . . Now imagine someone crafting strategy. A wholly different image likely results, as different from planning as craft is from mechanization. Craft involves traditional skill, dedication, perfection through the mastering of detail. (Mintzberg 1987, p. 66; italics in original)

This metaphor has further implications. The skills of the craftsperson are acquired not from books or lectures but from observing the behavior of established craftspeople. The case-study technique of the business school even finds its parallel in the minor works of the apprentices that preceded the masterpieces of the skilled craftspeople.[2]

At this point, however, the use of metaphor has gotten wholly out

---

[2] The case—in which the student is presented with a quantity of (largely unstructured) information and asked to read a decision in class discussion—is a common teaching technique in business schools. In some institutions—notably Harvard—it is essentially the only method of formal instruction.

of hand. Strategy is necessarily incremental and adaptive, but this does not in any way imply that its evolution cannot be, or should not be, analyzed, managed, and controlled. Neither Lindblom nor Cyert and March had any doubts on that score, and the process of "successive limited comparison" that Lindblom describes is a highly rational process; he underplays his argument, and perhaps misled some readers, by describing it as "muddling through." Indeed, it may be that we are, at least subconsciously, under the grip of a more powerful metaphor—the contrast between grand design and natural selection as accounts of the origin of species. Thus there is an artificial polarization between a view of the world that sees it as potentially wholly receptive to rational control and planning and one in which events fall as they will. Although biological evolution is not one, the world is full of adaptive, incremental processes in which this adaptation is subject to partial but imperfect control—processes ranging from traveling in space to boiling an egg. If we must use analogies, we should look there and learn about guided adaptation and managed incrementalism. In this framework, the false dichotomies between the implementation and the formulation of strategy, between rational analysis and incremental evolution, and between analytic and behaviorial approaches, quickly fall away.

The Content of Business Strategy

The subject of strategy that I have described falls a long way short of an established discipline, characterized by a widely accepted organizing structure and a growing body of empirical knowledge. Indeed, the strongly commercial orientation of the strategy business itself conflicts directly with this objective. The traditions of scholarship demand that authors should explain carefully how their contribution relates to all that has gone before; the dictates of profit suggest that consultants dismiss as bunkum the theories of their rivals and offer their own nostrum as the one true solution.

The best and most familiar example of an organizing framework is SWOT analysis—the definition of the strengths, weaknesses, opportunities, and threats that the business faces. SWOT is simply a list. It conveys no information in itself but is a way of helping us think about the information we already have. For a busy manager, confronted by endless everyday pressures and unused to standing back to think about longer-term issues, it is a particularly useful list, as demonstrated by its continued popularity.

It is easy to generate lists, and the literature of business strategy is full of them, few of which stand the test of time. An organizing framework can never be right or wrong, only helpful or unhelpful. A good organizing framework is minimalist—it is as simple as it is consistent with illuminating the issues under discussion—and it is memorable. That is why alliteration is favored (the seven S's framework of McKinsey or the five forces of Porter). A good list is usually between three and five items long (two is hardly a list, six is too many to remember).

A model is a more sophisticated organizing framework. It goes beyond merely listing items and contains premises and deductions as well. The Prisoner's Dilemma is such a model. It, too, is minimalist—focusing starkly on the problem of cooperation—and all real-life problems are more complex. Because of its deductive structure, this model, and even the simplest models, is more complex than a list. But in a good model, such as the Prisoner's Dilemma, the additional complexity is compensated by the greater insight it conveys. A useful model is a way of learning about processes and interrelationships and so goes beyond the mere structuring of existing knowledge. The suitability of a model, like the value of a list, is determined by the extent of its application, and it is the continued and widespread use of the Prisoner's Dilemma framework across biology, economics, sociology, and psychology after thirty years that indicates that it is, indeed, a good model. Like a useful list, a useful model is also memorable, and memorability is achieved here by the ludicrous but colorful story of the two prisoners in separate cells.

The organizing framework provides the link from judgment through experience to learning. A valid framework is one that concentrates on what skilled managers, at least instinctively, already know. They are constantly alive to the strengths, weaknesses, opportunities, and threats that confront them. They understand that cooperative behavior cannot simply be assumed or exhorted but requires the support of an explicit incentive structure or the expectation of a continued relationship. For them, a successful framework formalizes and extends their existing knowledge. For the less practiced, an effective framework is one that organizes and develops what would otherwise be disjointed experience.

Business strategy also benefits from the accumulation of empirical knowledge. Chandler's hypothesis—that organizational structure follows strategy—falls into this category. As framed by Chandler—reflecting the histories of a limited number of U.S. corporations—it must remain a hypothesis, as it can be validated only by reference to a much wider body of data. As subsequent research has deepened our understanding of the evolution of modern business, however, Chandler's hypothesis has stood up well. There are many other ways of testing arguments. The most extensive body of empirical information about strategic issues is the PIMS database, which reflects the anonymous experience of more than 7,000 business units. Two empirical findings stand out from that research—

the association between profitability and market share and that between quality and return on investment.

The development of frameworks and the accumulation of empirical knowledge go together. There is simply too much information about business available for it to be interpreted without some extensive conceptual structure. So the PIMS observation regarding the association of high profitability with high market share cannot be interpreted without a view of what defines a market, and it is to the credit of the PIMS researchers that they have a clearly specified view on this. The "served market" is what is supplied by the group of firms that the business perceives subjectively as its competitors. The term *market* is used in many other ways by different writers, and its use in this book emphasizes the importance of the consumer perspective and employs the term *strategic group* in a sense similar to that of the PIMS market. Neither this usage nor that of PIMS is right or wrong; the important issue is to understand the difference and be certain which term and which sense are being applied to any particular case.

The valid interpretation of empirical data in a complex world also requires the support of a model and a theory. Certainly it would be wrong to infer from the PIMS findings that an increasing market share is either necessary or sufficient to increase profitability. This issue was discussed at length in Chapter 11, and the conclusion we drew there was that competitive advantage tends to be associated with both high return on investment and high market share—that the relationship is indirect rather than causal. But the same relationship could be interpreted in many other ways. The choice among these interpretations depends on specifying hypotheses and testing them by reference to other observations and more data.

Frameworks, models, and taxonomies can never, in themselves, be prescriptive. We may note that just as people are either fat or thin, we can identify decentralized or matrix organization, and although these are often helpful ways of describing the world, neither observation tells us what any individual or firm should do. If we add the empirical finding that fat people die prematurely or that matrix organization is unsuccessful in particular types of industry, then we have findings that we can apply to practical situations.

These observations about the nature of knowledge are scarcely new. It is more than two centuries since the Scottish philosopher David Hume (1748) spelled them out:

> If we take in our hand any volume . . . let us ask, "Does it contain any abstract reasoning concerning quantity or number?" No. "Does it contain any

experimental reasoning concerning matter of fact or existence?" No. Commit it then to the flames; for it can contain nothing but sophistry and illusion.

It is clear even today that there is much in the literature of business strategy that Hume would have consigned to the flames. Most of all, the view that the construction of lists—the dominant methodology of strategy—is an activity that has empirical content or can form the basis of recommendations for action is one that is widely held and obviously erroneous.

In this book I have tried to avoid making or reproducing statements unless they follow as a result of explicit deduction from stated premises or are verifiable claims about the empirical world. I do not claim to have succeeded, but if the study of business is to develop in any scientific manner, this objective needs to be widely shared.

Contingency and Resource-Based Approaches to Strategy

The analysis presented in this book derives from the contingency theory that is the dominant strand of thought in organizational behavior. Starting from the original work of Burns and Stalker (1966) and Woodward (1965), contingency theory (Grinyer et al. 1986, Steiner 1979) emphasizes that there is no best form of organization and that organizational success rests on matching the organization to its environment. There is a striking congruence here between the sociological tenets of contingency theory and the financial economist's efficient-market perspective, which argues that there can be no universal prescriptions for success, since if there were, their general adoption would reduce their value to everyone. These two approaches taken together lead directly to the conclusion that it is the creation and maintenance of distinctive capabilities that are at the heart of successful strategy.

The successful match of organizational structure and environment is not in itself a source of competitive advantage; rather, it is a necessary, but not sufficient, condition. Banking demands a mechanistic structure—the decentralized processing of millions of daily transactions by means of common procedures simply cannot be managed in any other way. But the sources of competitive advantage in banking are to be found elsewhere, in reputation and in the architecture of lending relationships. Mechanistic structures are, by their very nature, replicable, but certain types of organic structure—those identified here with architecture—are not. Given its origins, contingency theory naturally stresses the organizational contribution to distinctive capabilities.

The contribution of economics to our understanding of distinctive capabilities is both to broaden and to narrow the range. It broadens it by importing factors that are not behaviorial but that nonetheless contribute to competitive advantage, especially the role of strategic assets. It narrows it by focusing on characteristics of the organization that are both appropriable and irreproducible. This latter emphasis, however, is missing in the very wide range of distinctive competencies identified by Snow and Hrebiniak (1980).

The necessary irreproducibility of capabilities that yield a sustainable competitive advantage has been developed by a number of authors. Teece (1986) draws attention to the appropriability problem associated with innovation. Prahalad and Hamel (1990) are concerned with similar issues in the context of organizational knowledge, and Oster (1990) stresses the efficient-market perspective in this context. Lippman and Rumelt (1982) review the issue more generally, and the concept of architecture owes much to their "uncertain imitability" (developed by Barney 1991 and Reed and De Filippi 1990). Copycat strategies fail because, as I suggested earlier, the potential copier cannot easily identify what it is necessary to copy. Grant (1991) draws a number of these themes together.

An emphasis on the creation and maximization of rents as the engine of commercial activity is, of course, hardly a new idea. Elements of it can be found in Ricardo (1819), who came up with the concepts of rents and quasi rents, but by far the most forceful exposition of this perspective remains that of Schumpeter (1934). Yet this work has not been in the mainstream of economic thought. Industrial economics has generally followed the traditions of Alfred Marshall, whose primary unit of analysis was "the representative firm," and in subsequent models of competition, firms differed not at all from one another or did so in essentially trivial ways (see Kay 1991a for an elaboration of these points). It is, indeed, this perspective that justified Ansoff's rejection of microeconomics as a basis for strategy: "Microeconomic theory provides for no differentiation of behavior among firms . . . as a result, the traditional microeconomic theory is neither rich nor extensive enough for our purpose" (Ansoff 1969, p. 13). Although these criticisms are much less valid as applied to microeconomic theory today, the contribution of economics to strategy has remained slight.

Looking to the Future

It is clear that the subject of strategy has suffered from the neglect of its obvious roots in sociology and economics. Too much of what is offered as strategy consists of lists or platitudes. The value of these is not negligible. Lists are aids to structured thought. Platitudes are often platitudes because they are necessary reassertions of important truths. But the claims that can be made for knowledge of this kind are modest indeed.

For centuries, the subject of medicine was mostly nonsense. Doctors applied fashionable nostrums, sometimes bleeding their patients, sometimes starving them. Generally these remedies were useless; sometimes they were fortuitously beneficial; and at other times they were unintendedly harmful. States of health were defined by reference to ascientific categorization, such as the humors or the elements. The prestige of a doctor rested more on the status of his patients and the confidence of his assertions than on the evidence of his cures.

The parallels are obvious, if not exact, and the reasons for the parallels are obvious too. Both medicine and management deal with urgent and pressing problems. The demand for a cure is so pressing that critical faculties are suspended. The quack who promises relief often receives a warmer welcome than does the practitioner who recognizes the limitations of his or her own knowledge, and since it is difficult to measure the effectiveness of treatment, this impression may persist even after it has been completed.

In the last fifty years, the application of scientific method to medical subjects and the development and adoption of knowledge gained in physics, chemistry, and biology have transformed their effectiveness. Medicine remains a practical subject. The experience and judgment of a good doctor are as important as the extent of his or her knowledge and the quality of his or her training. Untrained persons continue to express opinions on medical matters, not all of which are wrong. But few of us would now wish to put ourselves in the hands of doctors who had no such knowledge or training or who professed to despise it.

The subject of management has far to go before it can claim the scientific status achieved by modern medicine. The objective of this book has been to take one or two faltering steps on the road toward that goal.

Glossary

Adaptive strategy   A strategy that responds incrementally to changes in the external environment.

Added value   The difference between the market value of a firm's output and the value that its inputs would have in comparable activities undertaken by other firms.

Appropriability   The ability to realize the benefits of a **Distinctive capability** or **Competitive advantage** for the benefit of the firm itself rather than its customers, suppliers, or competitors.

Arbitrage   Buying a commodity or security in a low-price market to sell unchanged in a higher-price one.

Architecture   A distinctive collection of **Relational contracts.** The benefits of architecture typically rest on the development of organizational knowledge, flexibility in response, and information exchange within or between organizations. A primary **Distinctive capability.**

Asset specificity   Tangible or intangible assets that have value only in the context of a particular business relationship.

Battle of the sexes   A game in which satisfactory outcomes depend on the coordination of the responses.

BCG   The Boston Consulting Group, one of the leading firms of strategic consultants.

BCG matrix   A scheme for categorizing business units by reference to their market share and the expected growth of their markets.

Business strategy   See **Strategy.**

Business system   See **Value chain.**

Capital asset pricing model   A theory of capital markets in which the returns to risk are based on the relationship between individual security risk and overall market volatility.

Chaos, chaotic system   A system of nonlinear differential equations with the property that its evolution may be very sensitive to small changes in initial conditions.

Chicken   A game in which satisfactory outcomes depend on differentiation.

Classical contract   A long-term contact whose terms are fully spelled out in a legal relationship. Compare **Relational contract.**

Commitment   An action that restricts possible or profitable actions subsequently. See **Credible commitment.**

Competitive advantage   The application of a **Distinctive capability** in a particular market in order to achieve lower costs or higher revenues than other firms in that market can.

Competitive strategy   See **Strategy.**

Complementary asset   An asset necessary to the exploration of a **Distinctive capability.**

Concentration   A measure of the dominance of a market by few firms.

Conglomerate   A multidivisional firm in which there are few transactions among divisions.

Consummate cooperation   Cooperative action based on sharing all information.

Contestability   A market that is characterized by free entry and low sunk costs and that is also constantly disciplined by the threat of "hit and run" entry.

Contingency theory   The belief that the best organizational structure is unique to a firm's particular environment.

Contingent contract   A long-term contract in which some provisions are conditional on future unknown events.

Contingent strategy   A strategy distinctive to both the firm and its economic environment.

Contract   A legal agreement for exchange. See **Classical contract** and **Spot contract.**

Cooperation   Actions by two or more firms that maximize the joint product of a relationship rather than the individual takes. See **Perfunctory cooperation** and **Consummate cooperation.**

Cooperative ethic   A systematic pattern of **Consummate cooperation** in an organization.

Coordination   The simultaneous adoption of identical or complementary strategies by independent agents. See **Differentiation.**

Core   Outcomes of negotiation that all parties would prefer to the absence of an agreement.

Core business   The set of markets in which the firm's **Distinctive capability** is likely to yield a **Competitive advantage.**

Corporate control, market for   The process by which capital markets encourage competition for the control of companies.

Corporate strategy   See **Strategy.**

Cost of capital   The return that a firm must earn on incremental investment if the value of existing equity is not to be reduced.

Credible commitment   A promise to engage in a subsequent course of behavior accompanied by actions that increase the profitability of that course or reduce the profitability of others.

Current cost accounting   System of inflation accounting in which the assets' values and depreciation are based on their replacement cost.

Differentiation   The simultaneous adoption of distinct strategies by independent agents.

Differentiation strategy   A strategy of horizontal or vertical differentiation.

Distinctive capability   Those features of a firm's position or organization that cannot readily be reproduced by competitors. They are generally based on **Architecture, Innovation, Reputation,** or the ownership of **Strategic assets.**

Dominant strategy   The action that is best regardless of the action of any other player. Contrast with **Nash equilibrium.**

Dominant strategy equilibrium   The outcome of a game in which all players have dominant strategies.

Earnings per share   After-tax profit divided by the number of shares outstanding.

Economic market   A range of readily substitutable methods of meeting consumer needs.

Economies of scale, scope   See **Scale economies** and **Scope economies.**

Emergent strategy   A strategy that is inferred from patterns of behavior rather than from its conscious adoption.

Engineering method   A means of measuring **Scale economies** by assessing the costs of hypothetical alternative plants.

Entry   The process by which a firm comes to a new market.

EPS   Earnings per share. After-tax profits per unit of equity capital.

Equilibrium (in **Game theory**)   See **Dominant strategy equilibrium** and **Nash equilibrium.**

Equity, equity capital   Capita l provided for the firm by its shareholders. It may be measured by reference to either the value of the company's assets or the market value of its shares.

Excess return   Ex post return to shareholders in excess of the ex ante cost of capital.

Experience curve   The relationship between costs and cumulative output.

Experience good   A commodity whose most important characteristics can be ascertained only after it has been purchased. A long-term expense good is one for which such characteristics emerge only after repeated purchases or a long interval.

Extensive form game (in **Game theory**)   A game in which the players respond to earlier moves by other players.

Externalities   Actions that affect other agents directly (and not through market behavior).

FASB   Federal Accounting Standards Board.

Focal points   Instinctively attractive outcomes of games or negotiations (equal sharing, round numbers, etc).

Focus   Matching the different characteristics of a multiple-attributes commodity in combinations that reflect market demand.

Game theory   The formal study of structures in which the returns to any individual agent depend on both the strategy chosen and the response of other parties.

GE screen   A system of **Portfolio planning.** See also **BCG matrix.**

GNP   Gross national product. The total of incomes accruing to residents of a country.

Gross output   The aggregate value of sales. Compare **Net output.**

Hedging   The deliberate assumption of a risk that offsets a preexisting risk.

Historic cost   Generally accepted accounting principles in which asset values are entered at their historic cost.

Horizontal product differentiation   See **Product differentiation.**

Implicit contract   See **Relational contract.**

Incremental cost   The additional cost of undertaking an activity or producing a unit of output. It differs from average cost when economies of scope or scale are present.

Incumbency   An established presence in a market.

Industry   A group of firms producing technically related products.

Informal contract   See **Relational contract.**

Innovation   New products, processes, or styles of relationship. A primary **Distinctive capability.** Innovation is often used mainly to refer to technological innovations, but here it is used in a much more general sense.

Just in time   See **Kanban.**

Kanban   "Just in time" management. A system (pioneered by Toyota) of managing production processes with minimal inventory.

Keiretsu   A network of Japanese customer/supplier relationships, for example, those around Toyota. Compare **Kigyo shudan.**

Kigyo shudan   A loosely affiliated group of Japanese companies in different industries. The successor to the more tightly organized **Zaibatsu.**

LBO   Leveraged buyout. The highly geared restructuring of a company's capital structure in order to increase the equity stake held by management.

Leverage   The proportion of a company's assets that are financed by debt.

Market   See **Economic market** and **Strategic market.**

Market segmentation   The adoption of price and other strategies to distinguish related markets. See **Price discrimination.**

Matrix organization   A multidivisional organization linking the various functional activities across divisions.

Mission statement   A brief expression of a corporation's objectives.

Model   An algebraic or arithmetic specification of a set of relationships. A model may be a representation of a firm or part of a firm or of the interactions among firms.

Nash equilibrium (in **Game theory**)   An outcome in which each player's strategy is best, given the strategies adopted by the other players.

Natural monopoly   A market in which only one firm can be viable.

Net cash flow   Before-tax profit plus depreciation but minus capital expenditures.

Net output   The aggregate value of sales less the cost of materials (but not labor or capital).

Niche player   A company focusing on a limited market or market segment.

Opportunism   The situation in which one party attempts to gain from **Asset specificity** by driving a harder bargain after the other party has invested in the assets concerned.

Organizational knowledge   Systems, routines, and data in an organization that are only imperfectly understood by any individual member. Their value is therefore partly appropriable by the organization.

Payoff matrix (in **Game theory**)   A description of the returns to each strategy, given the strategies adopted by the other players.

PE ratio   Price–earnings ratio. The share price as a multiple of after-tax **EPS** (earnings per share).

Perfunctory cooperation   The degree of **Cooperation** between two or more parties that can be enforced by agreement.

PIMS   Profit impact of market strategy. An extensive database for the market performance and other characteristics of business units supplied anonymously by 7000 companies.

Portfolio planning   A system of grading business units by reference to market share, market growth, or similar variables. See **BCG matrix** and **GE screen.**

Positioning   In reference to products, the relationship between a firm's products and those of its competitors in commodity space. Positioning is also often used to refer to a firm's overall strategy.

Predation   A pricing strategy whose objective is the elimination of a competitor.

Price discrimination   The sale of the same commodity to different users at different prices.

Prisoner's dilemma   A game with an inferior **Dominant strategy equilibrium.**

Product differentiation   The differences among related products. Product differentiation is "vertical" when based on quality and "horizontal" when reflecting differences in tastes.

Product life cycle   Successive phases of the evolution of the demand for a product.

Relational contract   An exchange relationship between two parties that is not fully articulated. The rules of behavior are implicit, and the enforcement mechanism is the value of the continuing relationship between the parties.

Relationship   An agreement for exchange including both fully specified legal relationships and relational contracts for trust relationships. See **Relational contract.**

Reputation   A name for high-quality characteristics that cannot easily be monitored. It enables contracts to be made or to be made on more favorable terms than would otherwise be possible. A primary **Distinctive capability.**

ROE   Return on equity. Profits as a percentage of the value of shareholders' assets.

ROI   Return on investment. Profits as a percentage of the value of all corporate assets.

ROS   Return on sales. Profits as a percentage of turnover.

Scale economies   Cost reductions attributable to increases in the rate of output.

Scope economies   Cost savings arising when the cost of producing two products together is less than the sum of the costs of producing them separately.

Search good   A product most of whose relevant characteristics consumers can determine before purchasing it. See **Experience good.**

Shareholder value   An approach to business planning that stresses maximizing the value of the shareholders' equity and discounted cash flow methods of investment appraisal.

Sogo shosha   General (largely overseas) trading company within a **Zaibatsu** (before World War II) or a **Kigyo shudan** (today), for example, Mitsui and Co. or C. Itoh.

Spot contract   An immediate bilateral exchange.

Strategic asset   A source of **Competitive advantage** that is based on factors external to the firm rather than from its own **Distinctive capabilities.**

Strategic business unit   The level of a multidivisional organization at which strategy is determined.

Strategic group   Firms that adopt similar strategies and hence see themselves as being in direct competition.

Strategic market   The smallest range of activities across which a firm can viably compete.

Strategy   Corporate strategy is concerned with the firm's choice of markets. Business or competitive strategy is concerned with its relationships with the customers, distributors, suppliers, and competitors in those markets.

Sunk costs   The costs incurred when entering a market that cannot be recouped on exit.

Survivor method   A means of measuring **Scale economies** by reference to changes in the size and distribution of firms and plants over time.

Sustainable   Of a **Distinctive capability** or **Competitive advantage.** Capable of being maintained over time despite entries and competitors' attempts at replication.

SWOT analysis   The discussion of a firm's prospects by reference to its strengths, weaknesses, opportunities, and threats.

Synergy   Added value created by joining two distinct firms.

Value added   As **Net output.** Note that the base for a value-added tax does not include capital expenditures.

Value added   The difference between the value of output and the cost of material inputs. It differs from **Added value** which deducts the cost of all inputs, including those of labor and capital.

Value chain   A breakdown of the production process into segments and functional activities.

Vertical integration   The entry by a firm into the markets served by its suppliers or distributors.

Vertical product differentiation   See **Product differentiation.**

Vertical relationships   The relationships between a firm and its suppliers and distributors.

Winner's curse   A feature of auction behavior: Successful bidders are likely to be those who have overestimated its value.

Wish-driven strategy   Strategy directed toward aspirations that are not unique to the firm's distinctive capabilities.

Yield curve   The relationship between the interest rates on debt and the length of time for which the debt is incurred.

Zaibatsu   Closely knit groups of Japanese companies (e.g., Mitsui, Mitsubishi), dissolved by the Allies after World War II.

Bibliography

Abell, D. F. (1980). *Defining the Business*. Englewood Cliffs, N.J.: Prentice-Hall.

Abell, D. F., and J. S. Hammond (1988). "Cost dynamics: scale and experience effects." In *The Strategy Process*, ed. J. B. Quinn, H. Mintzberg, and R. M. James. Englewood Cliffs, N.J.: Prentice-Hall.

Abernathy, W. J., K. B. Clark, and A. M. Kantrow (1983). *Industrial Renaissance: Producing a Competitive Future for America*. New York: Basic Books.

Abernathy, W. J., and R. H. Hayes (1980, July–August). "Managing our way to economic decline." *Harvard Business Review* 67–77.

Abernathy, W. J., and J. M. Utterback (1978). "Patterns of technological innovation." *Technology Review* 80: 40–47.

Abernathy, W. J., and K. Wayne (1974, September–October). "Limits of the learning curve." *Harvard Business Review* 109–19.

Ackoff, R. L. (1970). *A Concept of Corporate Planning*. New York: Wiley.

Advisory Committee on Science and Technology (1990). *The Enterprise Challenge—Overcoming Barriers to Growth in Small Firms*. London: HMSO.

Agnew, J. H. (1986). *Worlds Apart: The Market and the Theatre in Anglo-American Thought, 1550–1750*. Cambridge: Cambridge University Press.

Akerlof, G. A. (1970, August). "The market for 'lemons': quality, uncertainty and the market mechanism." *Quarterly Journal of Economics* 488–500.

Akerlof, G. A. (1976, November). "The economics of caste and of the rat race and other woeful tales." *Quarterly Journal of Economics* 599–617.

Albert, M. (1991). *Capitalisme contre capitalisme*. Paris: Seuil.

Alberts, W. W. (1989). "The experience curve doctrine reconsidered." *Journal of Marketing* 52: 36–49.

Alchian, A., and H. Demsetz (1972, December). "Production, information costs, and economic organization." *American Economic Review* 777–95.

Allen, F. (1984). "Reputation and product quality." *Rand Journal of Economics* 15: 311–27.

Andrews, K. R. (1980). *The Concept of Corporate Strategy*, rev. ed. Homewood, Ill.: Irwin.

Ansoff, H. I. (1965, September–October). "The firm of the future." *Harvard Business Review* 162–78.

Ansoff, H. I., ed. (1969). *Corporate Strategy*. New York: McGraw-Hill.

Ansoff, H. I. (1970). "Does planning pay?" *Long Range Planning* 3: 2–7.

Anthony, R. N. (1965). "Planning and control systems: a framework for analysis." Division of Research, Harvard Business School.

Aoki, M., B. Gustaffson, and O. E. Williamson (1990). *The Firm as a Nexus of Treaties*. Newbury Park, Calif.: Sage.

Argenti, J. (1965). *Corporate Planning*. London: Allen & Unwin.

Argenti, J. (1968). *Corporate Planning—A Practical Guide*. London: Allen & Unwin.

Argenti, J. (1980). *Practical Corporate Planning*. London: Allen & Unwin.

Armstrong, J. S. (1982). "The value of formal planning for strategic decisions—a review of empirical research" *Strategic Management Journal* 3: 197–211.

Arrow, K. J. (1952). "An extension of the basic theorems of welfare economics." *Proceedings of the Second Berkeley Symposium on Mathematical Statistics and Probability*. Berkeley and Los Angeles: University of California Press.

Arrow, K. J. (1974). *The Limits of Organization*. New York: Norton.

Auerbach, R. (1991). *MBA: Management by Auerbach*. New York: Macmillan.

Axelrod, R. (1984). *The Evolution of Co-operation*. New York: Basic Books.

Bain, J. S. (1956). *Barriers to New Competition*. Cambridge: Cambridge University Press.

Ball, B. C. (1987, July–August). "The mysterious disappearance of retained earnings." *Harvard Business Review* 56–63.

Barney, J. (1991). "Firm resources and sustained competitive advantage." *Journal of Marketing* 17: 99–120.

Barry, N. (1992). *The Morality of Business Enterprise*. Aberdeen: David Hume Institute, Aberdeen University Press.

Bartlett, C. A., and S. Ghoshal (1986, November–December). "Tap your subsidiaries for global reach." *Harvard Business Review* 87–94.

Bartlett, C. A., and S. Ghoshal (1989). *Managing Across Borders: The Transnational Solution*. Boston: Harvard Business School Press.

Baumol, W. J. (1959). *Business Behaviour, Value and Growth*. London: Macmillan.

Baumol, W. J. (1982). "Contestable markets: an uprising in the theory of industry structure." *American Economic Review* 72: 1–15.

Baumol, W. J., J. C. Panzer, and R. D. Willig (1982). *Contestable Markets and the Theory of Industry Structure*. New York: Harcourt Brace Jovanovich.

Beauchamp, T., and N. Bowie, eds. (1988). *Ethical Theory and Business*. Englewood Cliffs, N.J.: Prentice-Hall.

Beck, P. (1981). *Corporate Plans for an Uncertain Future*. London: Shell U.K.

Bishop, M., and J. A. Kay (1988). *Does Privatisation Work? Lessons from the UK.* London: Centre for Business Strategy Report Series, London Business School.

Bishop, M., and J. A. Kay, eds. (1993). *European Mergers and Merger Policy*. Oxford: Oxford University Press.

Blois, K. J. (1990). "Transaction costs and networks." *Strategic Management Journal* 11: 497–99.

Blyth, M. L., E. A. Friskey, and A. Rappaport (1986, winter). "Implementing the shareholder value approach." *Journal of Business Strategy* 48–58.

Bork, R. H. (1978). *The Anti Trust Paradox: A Policy at War with Itself*. New York: Basic Books.

Boston Consulting Group (BCG) (1968). *Perspectives on Experience*. Boston: Boston Consulting Group.

Boston Consulting Group (BCG) (1972). *Perspectives on Experience*. Boston: Boston Consulting Group.

Boston Consulting Group (BCG) (1975). *Strategy Alternatives for the British Motor-cycle Industry*. London: HMSO.

Bourgeois, L. J., and D. R. Brodwin (1984). "Strategic implementation: five approaches to an elusive phenomenon." *Strategic Management Journal* 5: 2412–64.

Bradach, J. L., and R. G. Eccles (1989). "Price authority and trust: from ideal types to plural forms." *Annual Review of Sociology* 97–118.

Brealey, R., and S. Myers (1991). *Principles of Corporate Finance*. New York: McGraw-Hill.

Brown, J. K., et al. (1969). "Long range planning in the USA." *Long Range Planning* 1: 44–51.

Bruck, C. (1989). *The Predator's Ball*. New York: Simon & Schuster.

Burns, T., and G. M. Stalker (1966). *The Management of Innovation*. London: Tavistock.

Burrough, B., and J. Helyar (1990). *Barbarians at the Gate*. London: Jonathan Cape.

Butler, J. E. (1988, January–February). "Theories of technological innovation as useful tools for corporate strategy." *Strategic Management Journal* 15–30.

Buzzell, R. D., and B. T. Gale (1987). *The PIMS Principles—Linking Strategy to Performance*. New York: Free Press.

Buzzell, R. D., B. T. Gale, and R. Sultan (1975, January–February). "Market share—a key to profitability." *Harvard Business Review* 97–106.

Buzzell, R. D., D. F. Heany, and S. Schoeffer (1974, March–April). "Impact of strategic planning on profit performance." *Harvard Business Review* 137–45.

Calori, R., and P. Lawrence (1991). *The Business of Europe: Managing Change*. Newbury Park, Calif.: Sage.

Camerer, C., and A. Vepsalainen (1991). "The economic efficiency of corporate culture." *Strategic Management Journal* 12: 115–26.

Camp, R. C. (1989). *Benchmarking*. Milwaukee: ASQS Quality Press.

Campbell, A., and S. Yeung (1990). *Do You Need a Mission Statement?* London: Economist Publications.

Child, J. (1974, October). "Part I: management and organisational factors associated with company performance." *Journal of Management Studies* 175–89.

Child, J. (1975, February). "Part II: a contingency analysis." *Journal of Management Studies* 12–27.

Child, J. (1984). *Organization: A Guide to Problems and Practice*. New York: Harper & Row.

Christensen, C. R., K. R. Andrews, and J. L. Bower (1978). "Sears Robuck & Co." *Business Policy Text Ad Cases*. Homewood, Ill.: Irwin.

Coase, R. H. (1937). "The nature of the firm." *Economica* 4: 386–405. Reprinted in G. J. Stigler and K. E. Boulding, eds. (1952). *Readings in Price Theory*. Homewood, Ill.: Irwin.

Coase, R. H. (1988). *The Firm, the Market, and the Law*. Chicago: University of Chicago Press.

Coate, M. B. (1983). "Pitfalls of portfolio planning." *Long Range Planning* 16: 47–56.

Commission of the European Communities (1988, March). "The economics of 1992." *European Economy* (whole issue).

Connors, T. D., ed. (1980). *The Non Profit Organization Handbook.* New York: McGraw-Hill.

Cooper, R., R. V. de Jong, R. Forsythe, and T. W. Ross (1989, winter). "Communication in the battle of the sexes game: some experimental results." *Rand Journal of Economics* 568–87.

Copeland, T., T. Kotler, and J. Murrin (1990). *Valuation: Measuring and Managing the Value of Companies.* New York: Wiley/McKinsey.

Cronshaw, M., and J. Kay (1991). "Whatever next?" Mimeo. London: Centre for Business Strategy, London Business School.

Crosby, P. B. (1979). *Quality Is Free: The Art of Making Quality Certain.* New York: McGraw-Hill.

Cubbin, J., and P. Geroski (1987). "The convergence of profits in the long run: inter-firm and inter-industry comparisons." *Journal of Industrial Economics* 35: 427–42.

Curran, J. G. M., and J. H. Goodfellow (1990). "Theoretical and practical issues in the determination of market boundaries." *European Journal of Marketing* 24: 16–28.

Cyert, R., and J. March (1963). *A Behavioral Theory of the Firm.* Englewood Cliffs, N.J.: Prentice-Hall.

Dale, B. G., and J. J. Plunkett, eds. (1990). *Managing Quality.* Hemel Hempstead: Philip Allan.

Dasgupta, P. (1988). "Patents, priority and imitation, or the economics of races and waiting games." *Economic Journal* 98: 66–80.

David, P. A. (1986). "Understanding the economics of QWERTY: the necessity of history." In *Economic History and the Modern Economist,* ed. W. N. Parker. Oxford: Basil Blackwell.

David, P. A., and S. Greenstein (1990). "The economics of compatibility standards: an introduction to recent research." *Economics of Innovation and New Technology* 1: 3–42.

Davies, S., et al. (1991). *The Dynamics of Market Leadership in the UK Manufacturing Industry 1979–1986.* London: Centre for Business Strategy Report Series, London Business School.

Davis, E. (1990). "High quality positioning and the success of reputable products." *Business Strategy Review* 1: 61–75. London: Centre for Business Strategy, London Business School.

Davis, E., S. Flanders, and J. Star (1991). "Who are the world's most successful companies?" *Business Strategy Review* 2: 1–33. London: Centre for Business Strategy, London, Business School.

Davis, E., G. Hanlon, and J. A. Kay (1992). "What internationalisation in services means: the case of accountancy in the UK and Ireland." In *The Growth of Global Business: New Strategies,* ed. J. Clegg, H. Cox, and G. Ietto-Gillies. London: Routledge.

Davis, E., and J. A. Kay (1990). "Assessing corporate performance." *Business Strategy Review* 1: 1–16. London: Centre for Business Strategy, London Business School.

Davis, E., J. A. Kay, and M. Ridge (forthcoming). "Tensions in European integration: central authority, national authority, and market freedom." *Journal of Economic Literature.*

Day, G. S. (1977). "Diagnosing the product portfolio." *Journal of Marketing* 41: 29–38.

Debreu, G. (1954, July). "Valuation equilibrium and pareto optimum." *Proceedings of the National Academy of Sciences* 588–92.

de Geus, A. (1988, March–April). "Planning as learning." *Harvard Business Review* 70–74.

De Lamarter, R. T. (1986). *Big Blue: IBM's Use and Abuse of Power.* New York: Dodd, Mead.

dell'Osso, F. (1990). "Defending a dominant position in a technology led environment." *Business Strategy Review* 1: 77–86, London: Centre for Business Strategy, London Business School.

Demsetz, H. (1973). "Industry structure, market rivalry and public policy." *Journal of Law and Economics* 16: 1–9.

Demsetz, H. (1988). *Ownership, Control and the Firm.* Oxford: Basil Blackwell.

Dixit, A., and B. Nalebuff (1991). *Thinking Strategically: The Competitive Edge in Business, Politics and Everyday Life.* New York: Norton.

Drucker, P. F. (1977). *People and Performance: The Best of Peter Drucker on Management.* London: Heinemann.

Dunning, J. H. (1986). *Japanese Participation in British Industry.* London: Croom Helm.

Eccles, R. G. (1991, January–February). "The performance measurement manifesto." *Harvard Business Review* 131–37.

Edwards, J., J. A. Kay, and C. Mayer (1987). *The Economic Analysis of Accounting Profitability.* Oxford: Clarendon Press.

Eisenhardt, K. (1989). "Agency theory: an assessment and review." *Academy of Management Review* 14: 57–74.

Emerson, M., et al. (1988). *The Economics of 1992: The EC Commission Assessment and the Economic Effects of Completing the Internal Market.* Oxford: Oxford University Press, for the Commission of the European Communities.

Espy, S. N. (1986). *Handbook of Strategic Planning for Non Profit Organizations.* New York: Praeger.

Fallon, I. (1988). *Brothers: The Rise and Rise of Saatchi & Saatchi.* London: Hutchinson.

Fama, E. F. (1970). "Efficient capital markets: a review of theory and empirical work." *Journal of Finance* 25: 383–417.

Fama, E. F. (1980). "Agency problems and the theory of the firm." *American Economic Review* 76: 971–83.

Fama, E. F., and M. C. Jensen (1983). "Agency problems and residual claims." *Journal of Law and Economics* 26: 327–49.

Farrell, J. (1990). "The economics of standardisation: a guide for non-economists." In *An Analysis of the Information Technology Standardisation Process,* ed. J. Berg and H. Shummy. Amsterdam: Elsevier.

Fisher, F. M. (1989). "Games economists play: a non-cooperative view." *Rand Journal of Economics* 20: 113–24.

Fisher, F. M., and J. J. McGowan (1983). "On the misuse of accounting rates of return to infer monopoly profits." *American Economic Review* 73: 82–97.

Forrester, J. (1961). *Industrial Dynamics.* Cambridge, Mass.: MIT Press.

Fortune (1992, December 28). 36.

Fox, A. (1974). *Beyond Contract: Work, Power and Trust Relations*. London: Faber & Faber.

Fudenberg, D., and J. Tirole (1987). "Understanding rent dissipation: on the use of game theory in industrial organization." *American Economic Review* 77: 176–83.

Gabel, L., ed. (1987). "Product standardisation as tool of competitive strategy. Paris: INSEAD Symposium.

Galbraith, C., and D. Schendel (1983). "An empirical analysis of strategy types." *Strategic Management Journal* 4: 153–73.

Gambetta, D., ed. (1990). *Trust: Making and Breaking Cooperative Relations*. Oxford: Basil Blackwell.

GE Annual Report (1988) and (1990).

Geneen, H. (1984). "The strategy of diversification." In *Competitive Strategy Management*, ed. R. Lamb. Englewood Cliffs, N.J.: Prentice-Hall.

Gerlach, M. (1987, fall). "Business alliances and the strategy of the Japanese firm." *California Management Review* 126–42.

Geroski, P. (1993). "Technology and markets." In *Handbook of the Economics of Innovation and Technical Change*, ed. P. Stoneman. Oxford: Basil Blackwell.

Ghemawat, P. (1986, September–October). "Sustainable advantage." *Harvard Business Review* 53–58.

Ghemawat, P. (1991). *Commitment: The Dynamic of Strategy*. New York: Free Press.

Ghemawat, P., and B. Nalebuff (1985). "Exit." *Rand Journal of Economics* 16: 184–94.

Gilmore, F. F., and R. G. Brandenburg (1962, November–December). "Anatomy of corporate planning." *Harvard Business Review* 61–69.

Gilson, R. J., and R. H. Mnookin (1985, January). "Sharing among the human capitalists: an economic inquiry into the corporate law firm and how partners split profits," *Stanford Law Review* 313–97.

Goold, M., and A. Campbell (1987). *Strategies and Styles*. Oxford: Basil Blackwell.

Gordon, D. D. (1988). *Japanese Management in America and Britain*. Brookfield, Vt.: Avesbury.

Granovetter, M. (1985, November). "Economic action and social structure: the problem of embeddedness." *American Journal of Sociology* 481–501.

Grant, J. H., and W. R. King (1979). "Strategy formulation: analytical and normative." In *Strategic Management*, ed. C. W. Hofer and D. E. Schendel. Boston: Little Brown.

Grant, R. M. (1986). "The effects of product standardisation on competition: the case of octane grading of petrol in the UK." *Centre for Business Strategy Working Paper* 11. London: London Business School.

Grant, R. M. (1991). *Contemporary Strategy Analysis*. Oxford: Basil Blackwell.

Griliches, Z., ed. (1984). *R&D, Patents, and Productivity*. Chicago: National Bureau of Economic Research, University of Chicago Press.

Grindley, P. (1990). "Winning standards contests: using product standards in business strategy." *Business Strategy Review* 1: 71–84. London: Centre for Business Strategy, London Business School.

Grinyer, P. H., S. Al-Bazazz, and M. Yasai-Ardekani (1986, January–February).

"Towards a contingency theory of corporate planning: findings in 48 UK companies." *Strategic Management Journal* 3–28.

Grossman, S. (1981). "The information role of warranties and private disclosure about product quality." *Journal of Law and Economics* 24: 461–83.

Grossman, S., and O. Hart (1983, January). "An analysis of the principal-agent problem." *Econometrica* 51: 7–45.

Grossman, S., and O. Hart (1986, August). "The costs and benefits of ownership: a theory of vertical and lateral integration." *Journal of Political Economy* 691–719.

Grover, R. (1991). *The Disney Touch.* Homewood, Ill.: Irwin.

Hamel, G., Y. Doz, and C. K. Prahalad (1989, January–February). "Collaborate with your competitors—and win." *Harvard Business Review* 133.

Hamermesh, R. G. (1986). *Making Strategy Work: How Senior Managers Produce Results.* New York: Wiley.

Hampden-Turner, C. (1990a). *Charting the Corporate Mind: From Dilemma to Strategy.* Oxford: Basil Blackwell.

Hampden-Turner, C. (1990b). *Corporate Culture for Competitive Edge: A User's Guide.* London: Economist Publications.

Hapselagh, P. (1982, January–February). "Portfolio planning: uses and limits." *Harvard Business Review* 58–72.

Harcourt, G. C. (1965). "The accountant in a golden age." *Oxford Economic Papers* 17: 66–80.

Harrigan, K. R. (1983). *Strategies for Vertical Integration.* Lexington, Mass.: Lexington Books.

Harrigan, K. R. (1986). *Managing for Joint Venture Success.* Lexington, Mass.: Lexington Books.

Harrigan, K. R. (1988). "Joint ventures and competitive strategy." *Strategic Management Journal* 9: 141–58.

Harris, C., and J. Vickers (1985). "Patent races and the persistence of monopoly." *Journal of Industrial Economics* 33: 461–81.

Harsanyi, J., and R. Selton (1988). *A General Theory of Equilibrium Selection in Games.* Cambridge, Mass.: MIT Press.

Hart, O. (1988, spring). "Incomplete contracts and the theory of the firm." *Journal of Law, Economics and Organization* 119–40.

Hart, O., and J. Moore (1990). "Property rights and the nature of the firm." *Journal of Political Economy* 98: 1119–58.

Harvard Business School (HBS) (1972). *Prelude Corporation,* Case 373-052.

Harvard Business School (HBS) (1978). *Notes on the Motorcycle Industry—1974,* Case 578-210.

Harvard Business School (HBS) (1981). *General Electric—Strategic Position 1981,* Case 381-174, p. 1.

Harvard Business School (HBS) (1983a). *Honda (A),* Case 9-384-049.

Harvard Business School (HBS) (1983b). *Honda (B),* Case 9-384-050.

Harvard Business School (HBS) (1985). *Caterpillar Tractor Co.,* Case 9-385-276.

Harvard Business School (HBS) (1989). *GE—Preparing for the 1990s,* Case 9-390-091.

Harvard Business School (HBS) (1992). *Prelude Corporation Afterthought,* Case 9-392-125.

Hedley, B. (1977, February). "Strategy and the business portfolio." *Long Range Planning* 9–15.

Heil, O., and T. S. Robertson (1991). "Towards a theory of competitive market signalling." *Strategic Management Journal* 12: 403–18.

Henderson, B. D. (1973). *The Experience Curve Reviewed*. Boston: Boston Consulting Group.

Henwood, F., and H. Thomas, comps. (1984). *Science, Technology and Innovation: A Research Bibliography*. SPRU. Brighton: Wheatsheaf Books.

Hirschman, A. O. (1982). "Rival interpretations of market society: civilising, destructive, or feeble?" *Journal of Economic Literature* 20: 1463–84.

Hitchens, R. E., S. Robinson, and D. P. Wade (1978). "The directional policy matrix." *Long Range Planning* 11: 8–15.

Houlden, B. T. (1980). "Data and effective corporate planning." *Long Range Planning* 13: 106–11.

Hrebaniak, L. G., and W. F. Joyce (1984). *Implementing Strategy*. London: Collier Macmillan.

Hume, D. (1748). *An Enquiry Concerning Human Understanding*.

Jacobsen, R. (1988). "The persistence of abnormal returns." *Strategic Management Journal* 9: 415–30.

Jacobsen, R., and D. A. Aaker (1987). "The strategic role of product quality." *Journal of Marketing* 51: 31–44.

Jarillo, J. C. (1988). "On strategic networks." *Strategic Management Journal* 9: 33–41.

Jarillo, J. C. (1990). "Comments on transactions costs and networks." *Strategic Management Journal* 11: 497–99.

Jensen, M. C. (1984, November–December). "Takeovers—folklore and science." *Harvard Business Review* 109.

Jensen, M. C. (1986, summer). "The takeover controversy: analysis and evidence." *Midland Corporate Finance Journal* 6–32.

Jensen, M. C. (1988). "Takeovers: their causes and consequences." *Journal of Economic Perspectives* 2: 21–48.

Jensen, M. C. (1989, September–October). "Eclipse of the public corporation." *Harvard Business Review* 61–74.

Jensen, M. C., and W. H. Meckling (1976). "Theory of the firm, managerial behaviour, agency costs and ownership structure." *Journal of Financial Economics* 3: 305–60.

Jensen, M. C., and R. Ruback (1983). "The market for corporate control." *Journal of Financial Economics* 11: 5–50.

Jevons, J. A. (1871). *The Theory of Political Economy*. London: Augustus M. Kelley.

Johanson, J., and L. G. Mattson (1987). "Interorganisational relations in industrial systems: a network approach compared with the transactions-cost approach." *International Studies in Management and Organisation* 17: 34–48.

Johnston, R., and P. R. Lawrence (1988, July–August). "Beyond vertical integration—the rise of the value-adding partnership." *Harvard Business Review* 94–104.

Jones, J. P. (1986). *What's in a Name? Advertising and the Concept of Brands*. Lexington, Mass.: Lexington Books.

Jordan, A. G., and J. J. Richardson (1987). *Government and Pressure Groups in Britain.* Oxford: Clarendon Press.

Karmani, A. (1984). "Generic competitive strategies—an analytical approach." *Strategic Management Journal* 5: 367–80.

Kay, J. A. (1990). "Identifying the strategic market." *Business Strategy Review* 1: 2–24. London: Centre for Business Strategy, London Business School.

Kay, J. A. (1991a). "Economics and business." *Economic Journal* (special issue) 57–63.

Kay, J. A. (1991b). "The economics of mutuality." In *Demutualization of Financial Institutions—Annals of Public and Cooperative Economics,* ed. D. Heald (special issue) 62: 309–18. Brussels: De Boeck University.

Kay, J. A. (1993). *Foundations of Corporate Success.* Oxford: Oxford University Press.

Kay, J. A., and C. P. Mayer (1986). "On the application of accounting rates of return." *Economic Journal* 96: 199–207.

Kay, J. A., C. P. Mayer, and D. J. Thompson, eds. (1986). *Privatisation and Regulation: The UK Experience.* Oxford: Clarendon Press.

Kay, J. A., and P. Willman (1991). "Managing technological innovation: architecture, trust and organisational relationships in the firm." *Centre for Business Strategy Working Paper* 102, London Business School.

Kihlstrom, R. E., and M. H. Riordan (1984). "Advertising as a signal." *Journal of Political Economy* 92: 427–50.

Kirzner, I. M. (1973). *Competition and Entrepreneurship.* Chicago: University of Chicago Press.

Kirzner, I. M. (1989). *Discovery, Capitalism and Distributive Justice.* Oxford: Basil Blackwell.

Klein, B. (1983). "Contracting costs and residual claims." *Journal of Law and Economics* 26: 367–74.

Klein, B., and K. Leffler (1981). "The role of market forces in assuring contractual performance." *Journal of Political Economy* 89: 615–41.

Knight, K. (1976, May). "Matrix organisation—a review." *Journal of Management Studies,* 111–30.

Kono, T. (1990). "Corporate culture and long range planning." *Long Range Planning* 23: 9–19.

Kreps, D., and R. Wilson (1982). "Reputation and imperfect information." *Journal of Economic Theory* 27: 253–79.

Lamb, R., ed. (1984). *Competitive Strategy Management.* Englewood Cliffs, N.J.: Prentice-Hall.

Landes, D. (1969). *The Unbound Prometheus.* Cambridge: Cambridge University Press.

Landes, W. M., and R. A. Posner (1981). "Market power in antitrust cases." *Harvard Law Review* 94: 937.

Law Society (1991). *Maintenance and Capital Provision on Divorce.* London: Law Society.

Levin, R. C., W. M. Cohen, and D. C. Mowery (1985). "R & D, appropriability and market structure: new evidence on some Schumpeterian hypotheses." *American Economic Review* 75: 20–24.

Levitt, T. (1965, November–December). "Exploit the product life cycle." *Harvard Business Review* 81–94.

Levitt, T. (1983, May–June). "The globalization of markets." *Harvard Business Review* 92–102.

Levitt, T. (1986). *The Marketing Imagination.* New York: Free Press.

Lewis, M. (1989). *Liars Poker: Two Cities, True Greed.* London: Hodder & Stoughton.

Lieberman, M. B., and D. B. Montgomery (1988). "First mover advantages." *Strategic Management Journal* 9 (special issue): 41–58.

Lindblom, L. E. (1959, spring). "The science of muddling through." *Public Administration Review* 79–88.

Lippman, S. A., and R. P. Rumelt (1982). "Uncertain imitability: an analysis of interfirm differences in efficiency under competition." *Bell Journal of Economics* 23: 418–38.

Lloyd, T. (1990). *The Nice Company.* London: Bloomsbury.

Lorange, P. (1979). "Formal planning systems: their role in strategy formulation and implementation." In *Strategic Management,* ed. D. E. Schendel and C. W. Hofer. Boston: Little Brown.

Lorenz, E. (1991). "Neither friends nor strangers: informal networks of subcontracting in French industry." In *Markets, Hierarchies & Networks: The Coordination of Social Life,* ed. G. Thompson et al., Open University. London: Sage.

Lorenzoni, G. (1979). *Una politica innovativa nelle piccole e medie imprese: L'analisi del cambiamento nel sistema industriale pratese.* Milan: Etas libri.

Luce, D. R., and H. Raiffa (1957). *Games and Decisions: Introduction and Critical Survey.* New York: Wiley.

Lutz, N. A. (1989). "Warranties as signals under consumer moral hazard." *Rand Journal of Economics* 20: 239–55.

Lyles, M. A. (1981). "Formulating strategic problems: empirical analysis and model development." *Strategic Management Journal* 2: 61–75.

MacAulay, S. (1963). "Non-contractual relations in business: a preliminary study." *American Sociological Review* 28: 55–67.

Macneil, I. R. (1974). "The many futures of contract." *Southern California Law Review* 47: 691–738.

Macneil, I. R. (1978). "Contracts: adjustment of long term economic relations under classical, neoclassical and relational contract law." *Northwestern University Law Review* 72: 854–905.

Macneil, I. R. (1980). *The New Social Contact: An Inquiry into Modern Contractual Relations.* New Haven, Conn.: Yale University Press.

Manne, H. G. (1965). "Mergers and the market for corporate control." *Journal of Political Economy* 73: 110–20.

Marris, R. (1966). *The Economic Theory of Managerial Capitalism.* New York: Macmillan.

Marschak, J., and R. Radner (1972). *Economic Theory of Teams.* New Haven, Conn.: Yale University Press.

Marshall, A. (1890). *Principles of Economics,* 8th ed. New York: Macmillan.

Mathias, P., and J. A. Davis, eds. (1991). *Innovation and Technology in Europe.* Oxford: Basil Blackwell.

Mayer, C. (1987). *The Real Value of Company Accounts.* Leeds: University of Leeds Press.

McCann, J. E. (1991). "Design principles for an innovating company." *Academy of Management Executive* 5: 76–93.

McNulty, C. A. R. (1977, April). "Scenario development for corporate planning." *Futures* 128–38.

Meeks, G. (1977). *Disappointing Marriage: A Study of the Gains from Merger.* Cambridge: Cambridge University Press.

Mercer, D. (1987). *IBM: How the World's Most Successful Corporation Is Managed.* London: Kogan Page.

Miles, R. E., and C. C. Snow (1978). *Organizational Strategy, Structure and Process.* New York: McGraw-Hill.

Miles, R. E., and C. C. Snow (1986). "Network organizations: new concepts for new forms." *California Management Review* 28: 62–73.

Milgrom, P. R., and J. Roberts (1986). "Price and advertising signals of product quality." *Journal of Political Economy* 96: 796–821.

Milgrom, P. R., and J. Roberts (1992). *The Economics of Organisation and Management.* Englewood Cliffs, N.J.: Prentice-Hall.

Mintzberg, H. (1972). "Research on strategy making." *Academy of Management Proceedings* 90–94.

Mintzberg, H. (1973). "Strategy making in three modes." *California Management Review* 16: 44–53.

Mintzberg, H. (1978). "Patterns in strategy formation." *Management Science* 934–48.

Mintzberg, H. (1979). *The Structuring of Organizations: A Synthesis of the Research.* Englewood Cliffs, N.J.: Prentice-Hall.

Mintzberg, H. (1983). *Power in and Around Organizations.* Englewood Cliffs, N.J.: Prentice-Hall.

Mintzberg, H. (1987, July–August). "Crafting strategy." *Harvard Business Review* 66–75.

Mönnich, M. (1989). *BMW eine deutsche geshichte.* Vienna: Zsolnay.

Mönnich, H. (1991). *The BMW Story—A Company in Its Time.* London: Sidgwick and Jackson.

Monteverde, K., and D. J. Teece (1982). "Supplier switching costs and vertical integration in the US auto industry." *Bell Journal of Economics* 13: 206–13.

Morgan, G. (1986). *Images of Organization.* Beverly Hills, Calif.: Sage.

Mueller, D. C., ed. (1980). *The Determinants and Effects of Merger: An International Comparison.* Cambridge, Mass.: Oelschlager, Gunn and Hain.

Mueller, D. C., ed. (1986). *Profits in the Long Run.* Cambridge: Cambridge University Press.

Nash, J. F. (1950). "The bargaining problem." *Econometrica* 18: 155–62.

Nash, J. F. (1953). "Two-person co-operative games." *Econometrica* 21: 128–40.

Nelson, P. (1970). "Information and consumer behaviour." *Journal of Political Economy* 78: 311–29.

Nelson, P. (1974). "Advertising as information." *Journal of Political Economy* 81: 729–54.

Nelson, P. (1975). "The economic consequences of advertising." *Journal of Business* 48: 213–45.

Nelson, R. R., and S. C. Winter (1982). *An Evolutionary Theory of Economic Change.* Cambridge, Mass.: Harvard University Press.

Netter, J. M. (1988). "The market for corporate control." *Journal of Economic Perspectives* 2: 49–68.

Nicolaides, P., and C. Baden Fuller (1987). "Price discrimination and product differentiation in the European domestic appliance market." London: Centre for Business Strategy, London Business School. (Paper for Cescom Conference, Milan, July 1987.)

Norburn, D., and R. Schoenberg (1990). "Acquisitions and joint ventures—similar arrows in the strategic quiver." *Business Strategy Review* 1: 75–90. London: Centre for Business Strategy, London Business School.

Odagiri, H. (1991). *Growth Through Competition: Competition Through Growth.* Oxford: Clarendon Press.

Odagiri, H., and H. Yamawaki (1990). "The persistence of profits: international comparison." In *The Dynamics of Company Profits,* ed. D. C. Mueller. Cambridge: Cambridge University Press.

OECD (annual). "Competition policy in OECD countries." *Annual Report of the OECD Committee on Competition Law and Policy.*

Ohmae, K. (1985). *Triad Power: The Coming Shape of Global Competition.* New York: Free Press.

Ohmae, K. (1989, March–April). "The global logic of strategic alliances." *Harvard Business Review* 143–54.

Olson, J. (1982). *The Rise and Decline of Nations: Economic Growth Stagflation and Social Rigidities.* New Haven, Conn.: Yale University Press.

Olson, M. (1965). *The Logic of Collective Action.* Cambridge, Mass.: Harvard University Press.

O'Reilly, C. (1989). "Corporations, culture and commitment: motivation and social control in organizations." *California Management Review* 31: 9–25.

Oster, S. (1990). *Modern Competitive Analysis.* New York: Oxford University Press.

Ouchi, W. G. (1981). *Theory Z: How American Business Can Meet the Japanese Challenge.* Reading, Mass.: Addison-Wesley.

Pascale, R. T. (1984). "Perspectives on strategy: the real story behind Honda's success." *California Management Review* 26: 47–72.

Pearce, J. A., II (1983). "Selecting among alternative grand strategies." *California Management Review* 14: 23–31.

Perrow, C. (1986). *Complex Organisations: A Critical Essay.* Glenview, Ill.: Scott, Foresman.

Peters, T. J., and R. H. Waterman (1982). *In Search of Excellence.* New York: Harper & Row.

Pettigrew, A. M. (1977). "Strategy formulation as a political process." *International Studies of Management and Organisation* 7: 78–87.

Pettigrew, A. M. (1985). *The Awakening Giant: Continuity and Change in Imperial Chemical Industries.* Oxford: Basil Blackwell.

Pfeffer, J., and P. Nowak (1976). "Joint ventures and interorganizational interdependence." *American Science Quarterly* 21: 398–418.

Piore, S., and C. Sabel (1984). *The Second Industrial Divide.* New York: Basic Books.

Porter, M. E. (1979, March–April). "How competitive forces shape strategy." *Harvard Business Review* 137–45.

Porter, M. E. (1980). *Competitive Strategy: Techniques for Analyzing Industries and Competitors*. New York: Free Press.

Porter, M. E. (1981). "The contributions of industrial organisation to strategic management." *Academy of Management Review* 4: 609–20.

Porter, M. E. (1985). *Competitive Advantage: Creating and Sustaining Superior Performance*. New York: Free Press.

Porter, M. E., ed. (1986). *Competition in Global Industries*. Boston: Harvard Business School Press.

Porter, M. E. (1990). *The Competitive Advantage of Nations*. New York: Macmillan.

Posner, R. A. (1975). "The social costs of monopoly and regulation." *Journal of Political Economy* 83: 807–27.

Potts, M., and P. Behr (1987). "General Electric: charting a fast new course for a once stodgy corporate giant." In *The Leading Edge: CEOs Who Turned Their Companies Around*, ed. M. Potts and P. Behr. New York: McGraw-Hill.

Prahalad, C. K., and R. A. Bettis (1986). "The dominant logic: a new linkage between diversity and performance." *Strategic Management Journal* 7: 485–502.

Prahalad, C. K., and G. Hamel (1985, May–June). "Strategic intent." *Harvard Business Review* 63–76.

Prahalad, C. K., and G. Hamel (1990, May–June). "The core competence of the corporation." *Harvard Business Review* 79–91.

Pratt, J. W., and R. J. Zeckhauser (1985). *Principals and Agents: The Structure of Business*. Boston: Harvard Business School Press.

Pratten, C. (1988). "A survey of the economics of scale." In *Research on the Cost of Non-Europe*, vol. 2. Brussels: Commission of the European Communities.

Price, F. (1990). *Right Every Time*. London: Gower.

Quinn, J. B., H. Mintzberg, and R. M. James (1988). *The Strategy Process*. Englewood Cliffs, N.J.: Prentice-Hall.

Radner, R. (1985). "The internal economy of large firms." *Economic Journal Supplement* 96: 1–22.

Rappaport, A. (1986). *Creating Shareholder Value: The New Standard for Business Performance*. New York: Free Press.

Rappaport, A. (1990, January–February). "The staying power of the public corporation." *Harvard Business Review* 96–104.

Rasmusen, E. (1989). *Games and Information: An Introduction to Game Theory*. Oxford: Basil Blackwell.

Ravenscraft, D. J., and F. M. Scherer (1987). *Mergers, Sell-offs and Economic Efficiency*. Washington, D.C.: Brookings Institution.

Reed, R., and R. J. De Filippi (1990, January). "Causal ambiguity, barriers to imitation and sustainable competitive advantage." *Academy of Management Review* 88–102.

Reidenback, R., and D. P. Robin (1989). *Ethics and Profits*. Englewood Cliffs, N.J.: Prentice-Hall.

Reiman, B. C. (1989). "Creating value to keep the raiders at bay." *Long Range Planning* 22: 18–27.

Reve, T. (1990). "The firm as a nexus of internal and external contracts." In *The

Firm as a Nexus of Treaties, ed. M. Aoki, B. Gustaffson, and O. E. Williamson. Newbury Park, Calif.: Sage.

Reynolds, B. (1989). *The 100 Best Companies to Work for in the UK.* London: Fontana/Collins.

Ricardo, D. (1819). *The Principles of Political Economy and Taxation.*

Richardson, G. B. (1972). "The organization of industry." *Economic Journal* 82: 883–96.

Rink, D. R., and J. E. Swan (1979, September). "Product life cycle research: a literature review." *Journal of Business Research* 219–42.

Rodgers, F. G. (1986). *The IBM Way.* New York: Harper & Row.

Rogerson, W. (1983). "Reputation and product quality." *Bell Journal of Economics* 14: 508–16.

Rothschild, W. E. (1979a, July). "Competitor analysis." *Management Review* 37–39.

Rothschild, W. E. (1979b, autumn). "Competitor analysis—the missing link in strategy." *McKinsey Quarterly* 42–53.

Rumelt, R. P. (1991, March). "How much does industry matter?" *Strategic Management Journal* 167–86.

Salop, S. (1979). "Strategic entry deterrence." *American Economic Review* 69: 335–38.

Schapiro, C. (1982). "Consumer information, product quality and seller reputation." *Bell Journal of Economics* 13: 20–35.

Scheffman, D. T., and P. T. Spiller (1987). "Geographic market definition under the US Department of Justice Merger Guidelines." *Journal of Law and Economics* 30: 123–48.

Scherer, F. M., and D. Ross (1990). *Industrial Market Structure and Economic Performance,* 3rd ed. Boston: Houghton Mifflin.

Schleifer, A., and L. H. Summers (1988). "Breach of trust in hostile takeovers." In *Corporate Takeovers: Causes and Consequences,* ed. A. J. Auerbach. Chicago: National Bureau of Economic Research.

Schmalensee, R. (1978). "A model of advertising and product quality." *Journal of Political Economy* 86: 485–503.

Schmalensee, R. (1981). "Economics of scale and barriers to entry." *Journal of Public Economics* 89: 1228–38.

Schumpeter, J. A. (1934). *The Theory of Economic Development.* Cambridge, Mass.: Harvard University Press.

Schumpeter, J. A. (1943). *Capitalism, Socialism and Democracy.* London: Unwin.

Schumpeter, J. A. (1961). *The Theory of Economic Development.* Oxford: Oxford University Press.

Sharkey, W. W. (1982). *The Theory of Natural Monopoly.* Cambridge: Cambridge University Press.

Sharpe, W. F. (1964, September). "Capital asset prices: a theory of market equilibria under conditions of risk." *Journal of Finance* 425–42.

Shaw, W. (1990). "An empirical analysis of organisational strategies by entrepreneurial high technology firms." *Strategic Management Journal* 11: 129–40.

Shepherd, W. (1984). "Contestability vs. competition." *American Economic Review* 74: 572–87.

Silva, M., and B. Sjogren (1990). *Europe 1992 and the New World Power Game.* New York: Wiley.

Simon, H. A. (1960). "The corporation: will it be managed by machines?" In *Management and Corporations,* ed. M. Anschen and G. L. Back. New York: McGraw-Hill.

Simon, H. A. (1961). *Administrative Behaviour,* 2nd ed. London: Macmillan.

Simon, H. A. (1964, June). "On the concept of the organizational goal." *American Science Quarterly* 1–22.

Smith, A. (1776). *An Inquiry into the Nature and Causes of the Wealth of Nations.* Reprinted London: G. Bell & Sons, 1925.

Snow, C. C., and L. G. Hrebiniak (1980). "Strategy, distinctive competence, and organizational performance." *American Science Quarterly* 25: 317–36.

Sobel, R. (1981). *IBM: Colossus in Transition.* New York: Times Books.

Spence, M. (1973, August). "Job market signalling." *Quarterly Journal of Economics* 355–74.

Spence, M. (1977, autumn). "Entry, capacity, investment and oligopolistic pricing." *Bell Journal of Economics* 534–44.

Springer, C., and C. W. Hofer (1978). "General Electric's evolving management system." In ed. C. W. Hofer, E. A. Murray Jr., R. Charan, and R. A. Pitts (1980). *Strategic Management: A Casebook in Business Policy and Planning.* St. Paul: West Publishing.

Steer, P. S., and J. Cable (1978). "Internal organization and profit: an empirical analysis of large UK companies." *Journal of Industrial Economics* 27: 13–30.

Steiner, G. (1979). "Contingent themes of strategy and strategic management." In *Strategic Management,* ed. D. E. Schendel and C. W. Hofer. Boston: Little Brown.

Stewart, G. B. (1991). *The Quest for Value: A Guide for Senior Managers.* New York: HarperCollins.

Stigler, G. J. (1966). *The Theory of Price,* 3rd ed. New York: Macmillan.

Stigler, G. J., and R. A. Sherwin (1985). "The extent of the market." *Journal of Law and Economics* 28: 555–86.

Stoneman, P. (1983). *The Economic Analysis of Technological Change.* Cambridge: Cambridge University Press.

Sutton, J. (1991). *Sunk Costs and Market Structure.* Cambridge, Mass.: MIT Press.

Taylor, J. (1987). *Storming the Magic Kingdom.* New York: Ballatine Books.

Teece, D. J. (1986). "Profiting from technological innovation: implications for integration, collaboration, licensing and public policy." *Research Policy* 15: 285–305.

Teece, D. J. (1987). *The Competitive Challenge: Strategies for Industrial Innovation and Renewal.* Cambridge, Mass.: Mosi Balinger.

Thompson, D., and S. Meadowcroft (1987). "Partial integration: a loophole in competition law." *Fiscal Studies* 8: 24–47.

Thompson, G., et al., eds. (1991). *Markets, Hierarchies & Networks: The Coordination of Social Life.* Open University. London: Sage.

Thorelli, H. B. (1986). "Networks: between markets and hierarchies." *Strategic Management Journal* 1: 37–52.

Tichy, N. (1989). "GE's Crotonville: a staging ground for corporate revolution." *Academy of Management Executive* 3: 99–106.

Tichy, N., and R. Charan (1989, September–October). "Speed, simplicity and self-confidence: an interview with Jack Welch." *Harvard Business Review* 112–20.

Tirole, J. (1988). *Theory of Industrial Organization*. Cambridge, Mass.: MIT Press.

Townsend, H., ed. (1971). *Price Theory*. Harmondsworth: Penguin Books.

van Fleet, D. D. (1984). "Organizational differences in critical leader behaviors: industrial and military." In *Military Leadership: In Pursuit of Excellence*, ed. R. L. Taylor and W. E. Rosenbach. Boulder, Colo.: Westview Press.

Vickers, J. (1985). "Strategic competition among the few—some recent developments in the economics of industry." *Oxford Review of Economic Policy* 1: 39–52.

Vickers, J., and G. Yarrow (1988). *Privatization—An Economic Analysis*. Cambridge, Mass.: MIT Press.

Von Hayek, F. A. (1944). *The Road to Serfdom*. Chicago: University of Chicago Press.

Von Hayek, F. A. (1948). *Individualism and Economic Order*. London: Routledge & Kegan Paul.

Von Hayek, F. A. (1960). *The Constitution of Liberty*. Chicago: University of Chicago Press.

von Neumann, J., and O. Morgernstern (1944). *Theory of Games and Economic Behavior*. Princeton, N.J.: Princeton University Press.

Von Weizsacker, C. C. (1980). *Barriers to Entry: A Theoretical Treatment*. New York: Springer-Verlag.

Wack, P. (1985, November–December). "Scenarios, shooting the rapids." *Harvard Business Review* 139–50.

Weber, M. (1925). *The Theory of Social and Economic Organization*. New York: Free Press.

Weigelt, K., and C. Camerer (1988). "Reputation and corporate strategy: a review of recent theory and applications." *Strategic Management Journal* 9: 443–54.

Wernerfelt, B. (1988). "Umbrella Branding as a signal of new product quality: an example of signalling by posting a bond." *Rand Journal of Economics* 19: 458–66.

White, R. E. (1986). "Generic business strategies, organisational content and performance: an empirical investigation." *Strategic Management Journal* 7: 217–31.

Whittington, G. (1983). *Inflation Accounting: An Introduction to the Debate*. Cambridge: Cambridge University Press.

Williamson, O. E. (1975). *Markets and Hierarchies: Analysis and Antitrust Implications*. New York: Free Press.

Williamson, O. E. (1983). "Hostages—using credible commitments to support exchange." *American Economic Review* 73: 519–40.

Williamson, O. E. (1985). *The Economic Institutions of Capitalism: Firms, Markets and Relational Contracting*. New York: Free Press.

Williamson, O. E. (1986). *Economic Organisation*. Brighton: Wheatsheaf Books.

Williamson, O. E. (1987). *Antitrust Economics: Mergers, Contracting and Strategic Behaviour*. Oxford: Basil Blackwell.

Williamson, O. E., and S. G. Winter (1991). *The Nature of the Firm*. Oxford: Oxford University Press.

Willman, P. (1986). *Technological Change, Collective Bargaining and Industrial Efficiency*. Oxford: Clarendon Press.

Woodward, J. (1965). *Industrial Organisation: Theory and Practice*. Oxford: Oxford University Press.

Woodward, J. (1982). *Science in Industry: Science of Industry*. Aberdeen: Aberdeen University Press.

Wright, M., B. Chiplin, and S. Thompson (1993). "The market for corporate control: divestments and buy-outs." In *European Mergers and Merger Policy*, ed. M. Bishop and J. A. Kay. Oxford: Oxford University Press.

Wright, R. V. C. (1974). *A System for Managing Diversity*. Cambridge, Mass.: A. D. Little.

Yao, D. A. (1988). "Beyond the reach of the invisible hand: impediments to economic activity, market failures and profitability." *Strategic Management Journal* 9 (special issue): 59–70.

Yelle, L. E. (1979). "The learning curve: historical review and comprehensive survey." *Decision Sciences* 10: 302–28.

Zentner, R. D. (1982). "Scenarios, past present and future." *Long Range Planning* 15: 12–20.

Zucker, L. G. (1986). "Production of trust: istitutional sources of economic structure, 1840–1920." *Research in Organisational Behaviour* 8: 53–111.

Company Index

Abbott Labs, 22, 61
Airbus, 99
Akai, 64
Allegis Corporation, 127
Allstate Insurance, 20
American Airlines, 126, 133
American Tobacco, 143
Amex, 102
Apple, 96, 104, 156–57
Astra, 61
Atari, 96
AT&T, 117, 118–19, 161, 126
Avis, 82, 94

Bain, 71
Banco Bilbaō Vizcaya, 194
Banco Santander, 194
Bank One, 100
Bankcorp, 216–25
Barclays, 194
Beatrice Foods, 143
Benetton, 131–32, 244, 245
Berec, 130
Bloomingdale's, 191
Blue Cross of New York, 177, 178
BMW, 3, 4–6, 244
    after World War II, 5
    competitive advantage of, 95
    market position of, 134–35
    sportswear, 91
    sustaining market share and, 169
Boeing, 99, 112, 114, 164
Boston Consulting Group (BCG)
    assessment of quality of business, 170
    experience curve of, 112, 255
    portfolio matrix of, 254
    study on Japan's penetration of Western
        markets, 6, 7
Bowmar, 96
Bowring, 145

Braniff, 161
British Gas, 195–98
British Leyland, 165–66
BTR, 232
Budweiser, 133
Butterworths, 93

Canon, 132
Caterpillar, 13, 64, 71
Celtics, 16–17, 66–69
Citibank, 138
CNN (Cable News Network), 172
Coca-Cola Corporation, 22, 23, 61, 183–84,
        236
    advertising and, 89, 90
    Diet Coke, 101
    distinctive capabilities of, 245
    quality of, vs. Pepsi, 133
    in strategic group, 126
Columbia Pictures, 145
Conrad Hotels, 92
Consco, 25
Continental Airlines, 183
Cravath, Swaine and Moore, 70, 176
Cunard Line, 126

Daiichi Kangyo, 77
Daimler-Benz, 16
De Havilland, 96
DEC, 96
Design and Manufacture, 75
Disney Corporation, 3, 4, 22, 244
    appropriation of added value and, 177,
        178
    distinctive capabilities of, 245
    sustainability of advantage and, 157–58
    Walt Disney's vision and, 13
Distco, 36
Drexel Burnham Lambert, 73, 176
Duracell, 130

Eastern Airlines, 161
Electricité de France (EDF), 178–79, 181, 188
Electrolux, 157
Elsevier, 23
EMI, 96
Eurotunnel, 114–15, 207–9
Eveready, 130
Exxon, 16, 181

Fiat, 139
Finserco, 215–25
Ford, 64, 73, 137

General Electric (GE), 13, 16, 96, 244, 246–73
General Motors (GM), 106–7, 151, 168, 260
Glaxo, 96, 152
Great Northern Corporation, 3, 8, 10
Groupe Bull, 3, 9, 10, 240

Hanson, 130, 131
Harrods, 111
Harvard University, 177–78, 188
Hennessy, 23
Hertz, 82, 94, 127
Hewlett-Packard, 63–64, 66, 72, 73, 105, 230
Hilton Hotel Corporation, 92
Hoffmann-La Roche, 152
Honda, 3, 6–7, 64, 244
    Civic, 132, 137
    NSX, 158
    product positioning and, 132
    size and competitive advantage and, 165–66
    sustainability of advantage and, 158

IBM, 3, 11–12, 70, 73, 96, 111
    antitrust cases against, 118–19
    corporate success and, 15
    personal computer market and, 3, 11–12, 104
    size, success, and, 165
    sustainability of advantage and, 156–57
ICL, 9, 240
Indesit, 157
ITT, 255

JVC, 102, 104, 112

Kellogg, 22
Kmart, 12–13, 20–21, 191
Kohlberg Kravis Roberts, 258
Kresge, 20

Lakers, 16, 66
Lexis, 137
Litton Industries, 255
Liz Claiborne, 23, 61, 131, 142
Lloyds of London, 75, 194
Lockheed, 112
Lotus, 100, 111
LVMH, 23

Marks & Spencer, 74, 135
Marlboro, 236
Marsh & McLellan, 23, 61, 144, 145, 245
MasterCard, 102
Matsushita, 158–59
McDonald's, 134, 183, 236
McDonnell Douglas, 112
MCI, 117
McKinsey, 71
Mercedes, 134–35, 172
Merck, 22, 23, 61, 95, 191, 203, 245
Microsoft, 3, 11–12, 61, 111, 244
    added-value statement of, 17–18, 21
    Apple and, in standards battle, 104
    appropriation of added value and, 177, 178
    CEO of, 13
    competitive advange of, 95
    sustainability of advantage and, 156, 157
Midland, 194
Miller brewery, 144
Mitsui group, 77
Moët et Chandon, 23
Motel 6, 134, 135

Nabisco, 146–47, 148
National Semiconductor, 96
National Westminster, 194
NEC, 77, 132
New York Times, 132, 133
Next Group, 172
Nike, 22–23, 61
Nintendo, 23, 96, 245
Nissan, 193
Nissan UK, 184
Nixdorf, 9, 240

Olivetti, 9

Peat Marwick, 82
PeopleExpress, 161
Pepsi-Cola, 126, 133
Philip Morris, 16, 22, 61, 131
    appropriation of added value and, 179–80
    government and, 181

mergers in strategy of, 142
  Miller brewery acquisition by, 144
Philips, 19, 152
Popular Energy, 217, 219, 223–24
Prelude Corporation, 8, 10
Price Waterhouse, 82
Procter & Gamble, 63–64, 66, 72, 73, 230
PSA, 193, 199
Pschitt, 127

R. J. Reynolds, 146
Reuters, 23, 61
Roper, 75
Rover, 165

Saatchi & Saatchi, 3, 9–10, 240
Salomon Brothers, 101, 239
Sears, 19–20, 75, 191, 192, 199
Shell Oil, 16, 249
Siemens, 9, 16
Siemens-Nixdorf, 240
Singapore Airlines, 126
Skadden, Arps, Slate, Meagher and Flom,
  17, 70
SmithKline, 96
Société générale, 76
Sonico, 216–23
Sony, 101
  architecture, innovation, and, 105, 107
  Betamax, 102, 104, 112
  collaboration with Philips, 152
  high-definition TV and, 145
  mid-market positioning of, 133

Southwest Airlines, 126
Sprint, 117
Standard Oil, 143
Statoil, 179, 181, 188

Ted Bates, 10
Texas Instruments, 96
3M, 132
Touchstone Pictures, 4
Toyota, 77, 92, 151, 164, 168, 193
TRW, 255
TWA, 160, 183

United Airlines, 19, 21, 127, 179
United Brands, 75, 76
Universal Airlines, 216–24

Vasotec, 22
Visa, 102

Wal-Mart, 16, 20–21, 134, 191
Wang, 96
Washington Post, 132, 133
Whirlpool, 75
William H. Mercer, 144
Woolworth, 134
Wrigley, 22, 61

Xerox, 96, 97, 139, 158

Zanussi, 157

General Index

Accounting
  current-cost, 196–97, 199–200
  historic-cost, 195, 196, 197, 198–200
Accounting firms, reputation and, 94
Added value, 15–24
  appropriability of, 174–77. *See also*
    Appropriability
  business relationships and, 25
  cash flow and, 203
  competitive advantage and, 192–95. *See*
    also Competitive advantage
  concept of, 16–17
  core markets and, 140
  corporate performance measures and,
    204–7
  distinctive capabilities and, 60
  efficient-market hypothesis and, 60
  European and U.S. corporations and, 21–
    24
  European banking industry and, 192–
    95
  Eurotunnel and, 208–9
  historic-cost accounts and, 198–99
  measurement of capital costs and, 195
  measuring risk and, 200–202
  mergers and, 144–45, 148, 149
  national wealth creation and, 229–31
  negotiating share and, 183–88
  organizational knowledge and, 69
  portfolio planning and, 254–55
  reputation and, 60, 81
  strategic audit and, 222–24
  successful companies and, vi
  U.S. retailers and, 19–21
Added-value statements, 17–18
  appropriation in, 177–81
  of auto producers, 193
"Adopting the best practice." *See* Copycat
    strategy
Advertising agencies
  Saatchi & Saatchi, 3, 9–10
  Ted Bates, 10

Advertising and branding
  Coca-Cola and, 89, 90
  commitment and, 89
  conveying information about products
    by, 84–86, 89
  expenditures of, as sunk costs, 116
  purpose of, 82
  to support a brand, 91
Aircraft industry
  Boeing's market position in, 112, 114
  world market and, 138, 139
Airline industry
  adding value in, 223, 224
  deregulation of, 161
    mergers and, 145
  focused airlines in, 137
  identifying distinctive capabilities in,
    216
  matching markets to distinctive
    capabilities in, 218–19
  scale advantage in, 168
  scope economies in, 139
  sustaining and appropriating competitive
    advantage in, 222
  United Airlines, 19
  TWA acquisition and, 160
Antitrust policies, 118–20
  mergers and, 150
  social responsibilities of business and,
    234
Antonini, Joseph, 12–13
Appropriability, 174–89
  of added value, 174–77
    on national level, 229–31, 234–38
    by shareholders, 181
  definition of, 174
  influences on, 181–83
  innovation and, 100, 106
  shareholders and, 188–89
  strategic audit and, 219–22
Architecture, 63–80
  appropriating returns from, 181, 182

Architecture (*continued*)
  Celtics and, 67
  competitive advantage and, 65–66, 79,
    271–72
    in national economies, 236–37, 238–
      39
  corporate culture and, differences, 73
  external (networks), 63, 68–69, 74–76,
    237
  individuality and, 79
  internal, 63, 68, 72–74
  in Japan, 76–78
  market position and, 134
  matching, to market, 131
  organizational knowledge and, 67, 69–71
  of Procter & Gamble/ Hewlett-Packard,
    63–64, 66, 72–73
  relational contracts and, 66, 71
  social context of, 78–79
  Sony's, 105
  as source of national added value, 229–
    30
  sources of, 71–72
  sustaining advantage of, 159–60
  that supports innovation, 105–6
Asset specificity, long-term contracts and,
  50
Authority. *See also* Hierarchy
  standards battles and, 104
Automobile industry
  BMW, 3, 4–6
  competitive advantage of, 193
  deregulation and, 117
  GM, 106–7
  Japanese and, 64, 88
  marginal firms in, 192–93
  reputation and, 82
  scale advantage in, 168
  sustaining sunk costs advantage in, 161
  world market and, 138, 139

Banking industry
  adding value in, 223
  Citibank's efforts in Europe, 138
  competitive advantage in, 106
    sustaining and appropriating, 219–20
  European, added value in, 192–95
  identifying distinctive capabilities in,
    215–16
  industrial concentration in, 164
  matching markets to distinctive
    capabilities in, 218
  regulation in, 117
  sources of competitive advantage in, 271
  sustaining architecture advantage in, 159

"transactions" vs. "relationship"
  banking, 159
Battle of the Sexes, 36–37, 43
  standards battles and, 102
"Big Six" international accounting firms,
  144–45
Binding agreements, 29
Botnar, Octav, 184
Branch networks, as strategic asset, 215–16
Brand extension, 91
Branding. *See* Advertising and branding
Broiler chicken market, 112, 114
Business, defining, 126
Business ethics, public interest and, 231–
  34
Business models, developing, at GE, 252–
  53
Business relationships. *See* Classical
  contracts; Contracts and
  relationships; Cooperation;
  Coordination; Relational contracts

Campeau, Robert, 143–44
Capital asset-pricing model, cost of risk
  and, 201
Capital costs, measurement of, 195–98
Capital investment
  shareholders and, 200
  sunk costs and, 115–16
Cash flow
  added value and, 203
  Eurotunnel and, 207
  evolution of, 204, 205
  as measure of capital costs, 195
  as measure of corporate performance,
    191
Celebrity endorsements, to spread a
  reputation, 91
CEOs
  perception of, in U.S. vs. Europe and
    Japan, 13
  problems of coordination and, 37–38
  role of, in corporate success, 243
  U.S., high profile of, 12–13
  vision of, success and, 13–14
Chandler, Alfred, 143
Chandler's hypothesis, 269
Channel Tunnel, 114–15, 207–9
Chicken games, 41–43
  commitment and, 112
  innovation and, 97–99
  natural monopolies and, 111–12
  reputation and, 99
Cigarette advertising, 89
Classic novels, market for, 131

Classical contracts, 46, 48–51
  enforcement of, 152
  in financial services sector, 238–39
  information exchange in, 54
  marriage as, 51
  opportunism and, 56
  social obligations of business and, 233
"Clear performance," 26
"Clustering" phenomenon, national
        competitive advantage and, 238
Commercial relationships. See Classical
        contracts; Contracts and
        relationships; Relational contracts;
        Spot contracts
Commitment, 38–41
  Battle of the Sexes and, 37
  Chicken games and, 112
  credible, 40
  enforcing, 39
  inability to make, 40
  to innovation, 99
  minority shareholdings and, 154
  paying endorsement fees and, 91
  product advertisement and, 89
  reputation and, 87, 88
  voluntary, 40
Common Market, 119
Common-objective venture, 152, 154
"Common-value" property, 187
Competitive advantage, 190–210
  added value and, 192–95. See also
        Added value
  corporate performance and, 190–91
  cost of risk and, 200–202
  deregulation and, 117
  distinctive capabilities and, 59–61
    architecture, 65–66, 72, 73, 79
    innovation, 60, 96–97, 100, 101–2,
      105, 106–7
    reputation, 93, 94–95
    strategic assets, 60, 109–10
  equivalence of financial measures of
        performance and, 204–7
  in financial services industry, 106
  historic vs. current cost, 198–200
  marginal firms and, 192
  matching, to geographic markets, 138–39
  matching capabilities to markets for,
        123–24. See also Markets
  measurement of capital costs and, 195–
        98
  Microsoft's, 18
  national economies and, 234–38
  organizational knowledge and, 70
  preserving, through mergers, 145

profitability and, 161–64
scale/scope economies and, 139
shareholder value and cash flows, 202–3
size and, 164–68
of supplier networks, 75–76, 237
sustaining, 158–60. See also
      Sustainability
  and appropriating, in strategic audit,
      219–22
Computer industry. See also Personal
      computer industry
  IBM and Microsoft, 11–12
  preannouncement of innovative products
      and, 99
Consultants
  management, 71
  organizational knowledge and, 70
Consumer durables, 83, 91
Consumer electronics industry
  Betamax vs. VHS, 102, 104
  Japanese and, 64, 88
  Sony and, 105
  Sony Walkman and, 101
Consumers
  advertising and, 89
  defining a market and, 128
  learning about products' characteristics
      by, 84–86, 89
  product quality and, 83–84
Consummate cooperation, 28, 29, 68
Contestable industries, discount retailing
      as, 192, 199
Contestable markets
  in discount retailing industry, 192, 199
  theory of, 120
Contingency theory, of organizational
      behavior, 271
Contingent contracts, 48
Contracts and relationships, 25–26, 46–58.
      See also Cooperation; Coordination
  classical, 46, 48–51. See also Classical
      contracts
  contingent, 48
  franchise, 56
  marriage, 51–53
  relational, 29, 46, 48, 51–54. See also
      Relational contracts
  spot, 46–51, 53
Cooperation, 27–45
  Celtics and, 67–68
  commitment and, 38–41
  consummate, 68
  developing ethic of, 67–68
  encouraging collective vs. individualistic
      behavior, 72

Cooperation (continued)
  joint venture and, 27–29, 32
  long-term relationships and, 51
  perfunctory vs. consummate, 28, 29
  Prisoner's Dilemma and, 29–34
Coordination, 27–45
  Battle of the Sexes and, 36
  Battle of the Sexes games and, 102
  game theory and, 35–38
  long-term relationships and, 51
  seniority systems and, 38
Copycat strategy, 259–60
  in national economies, 239, 240
Core business, 125, 126, 127
Corporate behavior, ethical, public interest
      and, 231–34
Corporate center, purpose of, 260–61
Corporate culture, 63–64, 73
Corporate diversification, mergers and,
      146
Corporate interests, public interest and,
      232
Corporate performance, financial measures
      of, 190–91, 204–7
Corporate plan and planning, 213–14
  strategy formulation at GE and, 248–49
Corporate raiders, 258
Corporate strategy. See also Strategy(ies)
  as formal discipline, 243–44
Corporate success. See also Added value;
      Competitive advantage; Distinctive
      capabilities
  CEO's vision and, 13–14
  criteria for, vi, 15–16
  examples of, 4–7
  identifying distinctive capabilities and,
      14, 24
  overestimation of size/scale and, 242–43
  role of CEO in, 243
Corporations
  contrasting views of, 244
  "hollow," 22, 23
  social responsibility of, 231–34
  U.S., successful, 21–22
Craftsmen and guilds, 81
Credible commitments, 40
Credit card industry, standards in, 102
Criminal's Revenge, 33
  Nash equilibria in, 35
  Prisoner's Dilemma and, differences, 36
Current market value, 197
Current-cost accounts and accounting,
      196–97, 199–200
  historic-cost accounts vs., 205

De Benedetti, Carlo, 76
Deliberate strategy, 266–67
Deregulation
  of airline industry, 161
    mergers and, 145
  competitive advantage and, 117
Diamonds, world market in, 138
Differentiation, 27, 41–43
  horizontal vs. vertical, 133
  random behavior and, 43
Discount retailing industry, as contestable
      industry, 192, 199
Disney, Walt, 13
Distinctive capabilities, 59–61
  appropriating returns from, 181–82
  architecture and, 63–80. See also
      Architecture
  competitive advantage and, 271–72
  corporate success and, 14, 24
  geographic markets and, 138
  of IBM, 11
  identifying, 123–24
    in strategy formation, 215–17
  innovation and, 96–108. See also
      Innovation
  matching market position to, 134–36
  matching of, to markets, 123–24, 217–19.
      See also Markets
  mergers and, 144
  national competitive advantage and,
      236–39
  organizational knowledge and, 67, 69–71
  reputation, 81–95. See also Reputation
  successful U.S. firms and, 21–22
  sustaining, 156–73. See also
      Sustainability
  in up- or mid-market positions, 136
Diversification, mergers and, 146
Divestiture, 143
Domestic appliance industry
  European Union and, 157
  in Germany, 238
  scale economies in, 139
Dominant strategy
  equilibrium, 35
  in Prisoner's Dilemma, 33
Down-market products, 134

Earnings per share. See also Shareholder/
      stockholders: returns to
  as measure of corporate performance,
      191
Economies of scale/scope. See Scale
      economies; Scope economies

Efficient-market hypothesis, 59–60
Eisner, Michael, 4, 13
Electronic payment systems (EFTPOS), 104
Emergent strategy, 266–67
Empirical knowledge, content of business strategy and, 269–70
Employment contracts, 53, 72
  preventing opportunistic behavior and, 72
Employment system, in Japan, 77
Enabling technologies, 132
Endorsement, developing reputation by, 91
England. See United Kingdom
Enterprise unionism, in Japan, 77
Environment, assessing of, at GE, 248–54
Environmental factors
  appropriation of added value and, 230
  national competitive advantage and, 237
Environmental policies, corporate activity and, 234
Equilibrium(a)
  associated with Prisoner's Dilemma, 86
  types of, 34–35
Europe. See also France; Germany; United Kingdom
  banking industry in, added value in, 192–95
  Citibank's efforts in, 138
  industrial concentration in, 163–64
  minority shareholdings in, 154
European Union (EU), 119
  commodities prices in, 129
  domestic appliance industry in, 157
  mergers and, 148, 151
  single market in, 129
Excess return, 198, 202
Experience curve, 112–16, 255
  incumbency and, 112
Experience goods, 83–84, 89, 93
Explicit contracts, 48. See also Classical contracts
Externalities
  appropriation of added value and, 230
  assessing of, at GE, 248–54
  national competitive advantage and, 237

Fashion industry
  characteristics of markets in, 131–32
  external networks in, 74–75
  relational contracts in, 54, 55
Federal Trade Commission (FTC), mergers and, 150
Financial services industry
  adding value in, 223

competitive advantage and, 106
  of national economies, 238–39
  sources of, 271
  sustaining and appropriating, 219–20
Finserco and Bankcorp, 215–16
  matching markets to distinctive capabilities in, 217–18
  regulation in, 117
Financial services market, sustaining innovation advantage in, 158
Focused products, 137–38
Food industry, diversification in, 146–48
France
  banking industry in, 193–94
  cost of risk in, 202
  Groupe Bull, 3, 9
  sustaining profitability in, 162, 163
  wish-driven strategy and, 240
Franchise contracts, 56
Free-market system, 228

Game theory, 27, 43–44
  Battle of the Sexes, 36–37, 43
  Chicken games, 41–43
  commitment in, 38–41
  Criminal's Revenge, 33, 35, 36
  differentiation in, 41–43
  innovation game, 97–99
  joint-venture games, 152–54
  maintaining reputation in, 92–93
  Nash equilibrium(a), 34
  natural monopolies in, 111–12
  payoff matrix in, 29, 34
  Prisoner's Dilemma, 28, 43. See also Prisoner's Dilemma
  product-quality game, 86–88
  relational contracts in, 54, 55
  repeated games, 31, 32, 154, 160, 186
  social responsibilities of business in, 233
  splitting a pie in, 185–86
  standards games, 102–4
Gates, Bill, 13
Gaziano, Joseph S., 8
"GE screen," 247
Germany
  banking industry in, 193–94
  CEOs in, 13
  cost of risk in, 202
  financial architecture in, 239
  hostile takeovers in, 151
  labor force of, national competitive advantage and, 237–38
  sustaining profitability in, 162, 163
  wish-driven strategy and, 240

Glass-Steagall Act, 117
Global markets, 128–29, 138, 139, 259
Government. *See also* Regulation
  appropriation of added value and, 178–79, 180–81
Great Britain. *See* United Kingdom

Halsbury's Laws of England, reputation of, 93
Hart-Scott-Rodino Act, 150
Herfindahl index, 150
Hierarchy, Battle of the Sexes and, 37, 38, 104
High-definition TV, 102, 145
Historic-cost accounts and accounting, 195, 196, 197, 198–200
  current-cost accounts vs., 205
  from cash flow to, 204
"Holding back," as dominant strategy, 28
"Hollow" corporation, 22, 23
Horizontal differentiation, 133
Hostages, taking of, 56
Hostile takeovers, 143
  in Japan, 151
  of Nabisco, 146–48
  in Western economies, 151

Icahn, Carl, 160
Imitability, of architecture, competitive advantage and, 72
Implicit contracts, 25, 29, 48, 51. *See also* Relational contracts
Incomplete contracts. *See* Implicit contracts; Relational contracts
Incumbency
  commitment and, 112
  experience curve and, 112
  as strategic asset, 109, 112, 114
Individualistic behavior, internal architecture and, 72–73, 79
Industrial concentration, 163
Industry
  defining, 126, 139–40
  internationalization of, reputation and, 138
Information
  conveying, about products, 84–86, 89
  problems of, appropriation of added value and, 231
Information exchange
  in Japanese business networks, 78
  joint venture and, 30, 154
  in relational vs. classical contracts, 54
Innovation, 96–108
  appropriability of, 106, 176, 182

architecture that supports, 105–6
  competitive advantage and, 60, 96–97, 100, 101–2, 105, 106–7
  in national economies, 236
  firm-specific, 99–100
  identifying markets for, 132
  market position and, 134
  Microsoft and, 95
  process of, 97–100
  protecting and exploiting, 100–102
  Sony and, 101
  as source of national added value, 230
  standards of, 102–4
  sustaining advantage of, 158–59
Insurance companies, 69, 73
International car rental firms, reputation and, 94
Internationalization, of industry. *See also* Global markets
  reputation and, 138
Investment
  in business relationships, 49–50
  of capital, sunk costs and, 115–16
  long-term contracts and, 56
  return on, product quality and, 255
Italy, small-firm networking in, 64–65, 75

Japan
  architecture-based competitive advantage in, 230
  CEOs in, 13
  cost of risk in, 202
  financial architecture in, 239
  hostile takeovers in, 151
  industrial concentration in, 163–64
  minority shareholdings in, 154
  penetration of Western markets by, BCG study, 6, 7
  shareholders in, 189
  sustaining profitability in, 162
Japanese firms
  architecture of, 76–78
  distinctive capabilities of, 64
  entry into automobile and consumer electronics markets, by, 88
  lifetime employment in, 77
  reputation of, for reliability, 236
  size of, success and, 16
  sogō shōsha (trading companies), 76
  up-market positioning and, 135
Joint ventures, 27–29, 151–54
  commitment in, 38
  common-objective, 152, 154
  cooperation in, 32
  in game theory, 152–54

implicit contracts in, 29
mutually beneficial exchange in, 153–54
sharing information in, 30
Just-in-time inventory management, 77

Keiretsu (supplier group), 77, 237
Kigyō shūdan (company network), 77
Kuwait, 237

Labor contracts, 72
"Law of one price," 129
Law reference books, reputation and, 93
Leadership. *See also* CEOs
corporate success and, 243
"Lemons" problem, 95
Leveraged buyouts, 147
Licensing, as strategic asset, 116–18
Limited-liability corporation, 200
Local markets, natural monopolies in, 110–11
Long-term contracts, 46, 48–51
asset specificity and, 50
investment and, 56
opportunism and, 49

Management, sustaining advantage through architecture and, 159–60
Management consultants, 71
Marginal economies, 235
Marginal firms, 192
added value and, 192
competitive advantage and, 199
cost of risk capital and, 201
Market dominance, antitrust policies and, 118–20
"Market for corporate control," 155
Market growth, 170
Market value(s)
as criterion for corporate success, 16
current, 197
significance of, 203
Markets, 125–41. *See also* Mergers and acquisitions
boundaries of, 128–30
core, 140
defining, 126–27
European, 129
free-market system, 228
geographic, matching competitive advantage to, 138–39
historical definition of, 128
local, natural monopolies in, 110–11
matching, to distinctive capabilities, 123–24, 125–26, 130–32, 217–19

matching position to distinctive capabilities, 134–36
multidomestic vs. global, 128–29
product positioning in, 132–34, 136–38
mid-market, 132–33
scope of industry and, 139–40
share of, sustaining, 169
strategic, defining, 140
strategic group and, 140
sustaining position in, 171–72
Marriage contracts, 51–53
Marshall, Alfred, 272
Mergers and acquisitions, 142–55
adding value through, 144–45
financial issues of, 146–48
performance evaluation of, 148–50
public policy and, 150–51
TWA and, 160
in U.S. history, 143
Metalworking industry, in Lumezzane valley, 64–65, 75
Microeconomic theory, strategy and, 272
Mid-market positioning, 132–33, 136
Milken, Michael, 176
Minority shareholding, 154
Mission statement, 10, 258
"Modern equivalent asset," 196
Monopolies
mergers and, 150
natural
as strategic assets, 109, 110–12
sustaining advantage of, 160–61
Morgan, J. P., 75
Morgan, Lee, 13
Morita, Akio, 13
Motorcycle industry
British, 7
U.S., Honda and, 6–7
"Muddling through, science of," 266, 268
Multidivisional organizations, 260–61
Multidomestic market, 128
Mutually beneficial–exchange venture, 153–54

Nash equilibrium(a), 34, 45
in Battle of the Sexes game, 36
in Chicken games, 42
Criminal's Revenge and, 35
National economies, 227–41
added value and wealth creation in, 229–31
competitive advantage and, 234–38
industrial policy and, 241
public interest and business ethics in, 231–34

National economies (continued)
  wish-driven and copycat strategies in, 239–40
Natural monopolies, 109, 110–12, 160–61
Negotiating share, of added value, 183–88
Neo-Austrian school, 228, 229
Net output, 18
Networks, 74–76, 237
  geographical proximity and, 78
  in Japan, 77–78
  scope economies and, 139
  small-firm, 64–65, 75, 76
  as strategic asset, 215–16
Newspaper industry
  appropriation of added value and, 183
  markets in, 136–37
"Nexus of treaties," 58
Not-for-profit organizations, added value and, 174–75, 177–78

Oil companies, redefining business of, 127
"One-set-ism," 78
Operating profit, 18
Opportunism
  classical contracts and, 56
  long-term contracts and, 49
  relational contracts and, 55–56, 72
  reputation and, 57, 72
  in U.S. vs. other countries, 57
Organizational knowledge, 69–71
  added value and, 69
  Celtics and, 67
  negative effects of, 73–74
  sustaining advantage through, 159
Organizational structures. See also Architecture
  types of, implementing strategy and, 261
Organizing frameworks, 268–69
Oxford English Dictionary, 130–31

Pascale, Richard, 6
Patents and copyright, innovation and, 100
Payoff matrix, in game theory, 29, 34
Payoff structure
  in Chicken game, 42
  Prisoner's Dilemma and, 28–29, 33
  product-quality game and, 87
Personal computer industry. See also Computer industry
  natural monopolies in, 111
  Xerox and, 96, 97
Personal computer market
  IBM vs. Microsoft in, 12
  standards battle in, 104
Pharmaceuticals, patents and, 101

Pickens, T. Boone, 258
PIMS database, 169, 170, 255, 269–70
"Poison pill" defenses, 150–51
Porter, Michael, 132
Porter's value chain, 253
Portfolio planning
  added value and, 254–55
  at GE, 247
  matrix, 253–54
Post-it notes, 132
Principal–agent problems, 58
Prisoner's Dilemma, 28–29, 43
  commitment and, 38–39, 40
  cooperation and, 29–34, 67
  Criminal's Revenge and, differences, 36
  inability to make credible promises and, 40
  joint ventures and, 154
  maintaining reputation and, 92–93
  as organizing framework, 269
  product-quality game and, 86–88
  relational strategy for, 55
  repeated trials in, 31
  social responsibilities of business in, 233
  TWA acquisition and, 160
Product availability, 84
  advertising and, 89
Product features, 84–85
  advertising and, 89
Product life cycle, 253, 254
Product portfolio, 254
Product positioning, 132–34
  down-market, 134
  mid-market, 132–33
  sustaining, 171–72
Product/process innovations, 60. See also Innovation
Product quality, 85
  celebrity endorsements and, 91
  consumers and, 83–84
  definition of, 133
  perceived, 133
  quality of firm strategy vs., 134
  reputation and, 81–82
  return on investment and, 255
  search and experience goods, 83–84, 89, 93
Product-quality game, 86–88
Product reliability, 83
Products, focused vs. unfocused, 137–38
Profitability
  as measure of corporate performance, 191
  sustaining, 161–64
Public funding, of innovation, 100

Public interest, business ethics and, 231–34
Public policies. See Antitrust policies
Publicly owned companies, appropriation of added value and, 178–79

Quality. See also Product quality
  definition of, 133
  perceived, 133
Quandt, Herbert, 5, 13
QWERTY typewriter keyboard, 108

Railroad companies, reputation and, 93
Randomizing behavior, game of Chicken and, 43
Rate of return, as criterion for success, 16
Rationalist school
  assessing the environment by, 248–54
  criticism of, 264–68
  formulating strategy by, 254–59
  implementing strategy by, 260–64
  strategy implementation and, 264
Regulation
  strategic advantage by, 116–18
  strategic assets and, 109
Relational contracts, 29, 46, 48, 51–54. See also Architecture
  advantages of, 54
  architecture and, 66, 71
  disadvantages of, 54–55
  employment contract as, 53
  enforcement of, 152
  in financial services sector, 238
  at GE, 248
  long-term relationships and, 51
  marriage as, 51
  opportunism and, 55–56, 72
  short-term gains and, 56–57
  social context of, 78–79
  social obligations of, 233, 234
  in U.S. business environment, 244
Rent, 24. See also Added value
Repeated games, 31
  cooperation and, 32
  joint ventures and, 154
  negotiating share of added value and, 186
  reputation and, 87, 92–93
  TWA acquisition and, 160
Reputation, 81–95
  added value and, 60, 81
  appropriating returns from, 181–82
  automobile industry and, 82
  building of, 88–89, 91
  in Chicken games, 99

competitive advantage and, 93, 94–95
  in national economies, 236
  in game theory, 86–88
  international, 138
  international accounting firms and, 94
  international car rental firms and, 94
  maintaining, 91–93
  market position and, 135
  mergers and, 144–45
  milking or devaluing, 92
  opportunism and, 57, 72
  product quality and, 81–82
  profitability and, 93–95
  search and experience goods, 83–84, 93
  of Sony, 105
  as source of national added value, 229
  spreading, 91–92
  in strategy formation, 215–16
  sustaining advantage through, 160
  "value-for-money," 135
  value in the market and, 130–31
Restaurants, focused, 137–38
Retailers, U.S., added value and, 19–21
Revenues, as criterion for corporate success, 16
Reverse engineering, innovation and, 101
Risk capital, 200–201
Rome Treaty, 119
Ryder Report, 240

Scale, overestimation of, corporate performance and, 242
Scale economies, 115, 138–39, 140
  mergers and, 145
  sunk costs vs., 115
  sustaining advantage in, 164–68
Scenario planning, 249
Schumpeter, Joseph, view of competitive markets, 228, 229
Scope economies, 138, 139, 140
  mergers and, 145
Search goods, 83–84, 93
"Second-price" rule, 187
Secrecy, protecting innovation by, 101
Seniority system
  in Japan, 77
  problems of coordination and, 38
"Served market," 270
Shareholder value, 202, 258
  Eurotunnel and, 208–9
Shareholders/stakeholders
  added value and, 174, 181, 188–89
  cost of risk and, 200–201
  returns to, 197–98
Sherman Antitrust Act, 118, 143

Shipping companies, reputation and, 93
Short-term gains, relational contracts and,
    56–57
Silicon Valley, 75, 237, 238
Size, overestimation of, corporate
    performance and, 242
Sloan, Alfred, 143
Small-firm networking, in Lumezzane
    valley, 64–65, 75
Smith, Adam, 227–28
Smith, Roger, 106
Social relationships, relational contracts
    based on, 78–79
Social welfare, business ethics and, 231–34
Software, innovative, protection of, 100
Spain, banking industry in, 194–95
Splitting-a-pie game, 185–86
Spot contracts, 25–26, 46–48, 160
    commodities and, 50
    employment contracts as, 53
    scope of, 50
    weakness of, 48–51
Standards, 102–4
    compatibility, natural monopolies and,
        111
State-owned companies, appropriation of
    added value and, 178–79
Strategic alliances, 151–52
Strategic assets, 109–21
    antitrust policies and, 118–20
    appropriating returns from, 182, 183
    appropriation of added value and, 231
    competitive advantage and, 60, 109–10
    creating, 124
    licensing and regulation as, 116–18
    mergers and, 145
    Microsoft's operating system as, 12
    national competitive advantage and, 237
    natural monopolies as, 109, 110–12
    sunk costs and, 112–16
    sustaining, 160–61
Strategic audit, 211, 213–26
    adding value, 222–24
    assessing strategy, 213–15
    formulating strategy at GE, 248–59
    identifying distinctive capabilities, 215–
        17
    matching markets to distinctive
        capabilities, 217–19
    sustaining and appropriating competitive
        advantage, 219–22
Strategic business units, at GE, 246–47
Strategic environment matrix, 254
Strategic group, 140, 270
    defining, 126–27

Strategic market, defining, 140
Strategy(ies)
    contingency and resource-based
        approaches, 271–72
    copycat, 240, 259–60
    deliberate vs. emergent, 266–67
    dominant
        "holding back" as, 28
        in Prisoner's Dilemma, 33
    as formal discipline, 243–44
    global, 259
    implementing of, 260–64
    Japanese entry, 135
    mergers and, 142
    microeconomic theory and, 272
    mixed, 42–43
    organizing frameworks for, 268–69
    quality of firm's, vs. product quality,
        134
    wish-driven, 8, 10, 239–40
Strategy weekends, 213–14
Sunk costs, 154
    capital investment and, 115–16
    economies of scale vs., 115
    experience curve and, 112–16
    sustaining advantage of, 161
Supermarkets
    appropriation of added value and, 182–
        83
    brand value and, 187–88
    markets for, 136–37
Supernormal profit, 24. See also Added
    value
Supplier networks, 74–76
    competitive advantage of, 75–76, 237
    in Japan, 77–78, 237
Sustainability, 156–73
    attractive markets and market positions,
        169–70
    competitive advantage and, 158–60
    of market share, 169
    of profits, 161–64
    scale economies and, 164–68
    of strategic assets, 160–61
    strategic audit and, 219–22
Swiss banks, reputation of, 236
SWOT analysis, 268–69

Taxation, appropriation of added value
    and, 179, 180
Team spirit and cooperation, 66–69
Technical knowledge, 69
Technologies, enabling, 132
Technology development. See Innovation
Telecommunications industry

deregulation and, 117
natural monopolies in, 111
scale advantage in, 168
Television, focused channels, 137
Tennis clubs, added value and, 174–75
Tobacco industry, diversification in, 146–48
"Total quality management," 255
Totalitarianism, economic performance and, 228
Trading companies, in Japan, 76
Transaction-cost economics, 44
Transport industry. *See also* Airline industry
sunk costs and, 115
Travel market, 127
Trump, Donald, 143
Trust relationships, 51. *See also* Relational contracts
national competitive advantage and, 237

Unfocused products, 137
Unionism, in Japan vs. West, 77
United Kingdom
banking industry in, 194
cost of risk in, 201–2
Eveready in, 130
financial architecture in, 239
financial services institutions in, competitive advantage and, 145
hostile takeovers in, 151
investigations of BTR, 232
Monopolies Commission, 119
motorcycle industry, Honda's success and, 7
sustaining profitability in, 162, 163
wish-driven strategy and, 240
United States
corporate strategy as formal discipline in, 243–44
cost of risk in, 201–2
financial architecture in, 239

industrial concentration in, 163–64
relational contracting in, 244
sustaining profitability in, 162–63
view of the corporation in, 244
Universities, added value and, 174–75
Up-market positioning, 135–36
Utilities
adding value in, 223–24
French, appropriation of added value and, 178–79
identifying distinctive capabilities of, 217
licensing and, 116
as natural monopolies, 110
sunk costs and, 115
sustaining strategic assets in, 161

Value-added. *See* Added value
Vertical differentiation, 133
Voluntary commitment, 40
Von Hayek, F. A., 228

Wall Street Journal, 111
Warranties, 87, 88
Wealth creation, added value and, 229–31
Welch, Jack, 13
vision of, 247
"Work-out at GE" initiative, 248
Welfare economics, 228, 229
public interest and business ethics in, 231–34
Whipple, W. D., 8
Williamson, Oliver, 44
"Winner's curse," 187
Wish-driven strategy, 8, 10
in national economies, 239–40
"Working to rule," 53
"Work-out at GE" initiative, 248
World markets, 128–29, 138, 139, 259

Zaibatsu (company network), 76, 77

ties to distributors, customers, etc. He ranges through industries from airlines to retail clothing, pointing out the the reasons for successes and failures. Kay also draws on game theory to underscore the importance of stable, long-term relationships.

Other writers have hit upon some of these points, the *Financial Times* noted: "But none has explored them as thoroughly as Kay, who succeeds in marrying an authoritative grasp of economic, legal, and sociological theory with an impressively detailed knowledge of contemporary business practice." This volume transforms Kay's theoretical and practical knowledge into a powerful tool for today's American business manager.

John Kay is Professor of Economics at the London Business School, where he has served as Director of the Center for Business Strategy.